The Letters and Other Writings of Gustavus Vassa (Olaudah Equiano, the African)

Documenting Abolition of the Slave Trade

The Letters and Other Writings of Gustavus Vassa (Olaudah Equiano, the African)

DOCUMENTING ABOLITION OF THE SLAVE TRADE

Karlee Anne Sapoznik, Editor

Foreword by Paul E. Lovejoy

Markus Wiener Publishers
Princeton

For information, write to: Markus Wiener Publishers
231 Nassau Street
Princeton, NJ 08542
www.markuswiener.com

Library of Congress Cataloging-in-Publication Data

Equiano, Olaudah, b. 1745.
  The letters and other writings of Gustavus Vassa (Olaudah Equiano, the
African) : documenting abolition of the slave trade / Karlee Anne Sapoznik,
editor ; foreword by Paul E. Lovejoy.
  p. cm.
  Includes bibliographical references and index.
  ISBN 978-1-55876-557-3 (hardcover : alk. paper)
  ISBN 978-1-55876-558-0 (pbk. : alk. paper)
1. Equiano, Olaudah, b. 1745—Correspondence. 2. Equiano, Olaudah,
b. 1745—Travel. 3. Slavery—West Indies, British—Early works to 1800.
4. Antislavery movements—Great Britain—Early works to 1800. 5. Slave
trade—Africa—History—Early works to 1800. 6. Slave trade—America—
History—Early works to 1800. I. Sapoznik, Karlee Anne. II. Lovejoy, Paul E.
III. Title.
  HT869.E6A4 2013
  306.362--dc23
                                2012036256

Markus Wiener Publishers books are printed in the United States of America
on acid-free paper and meet the guidelines for permanence and durability
of the Committee on Production Guidelines for Book Longevity of the
Council on Library Resources.

Contents

Illustrations

Foreword

PAUL E. LOVEJOY

This publication of the collected letters and papers of Gustavus Vassa, better known as Olaudah Equiano, is an important contribution to the study of the movement that resulted in the abolition in 1807 of the British slave trade. Vassa was a key figure in mobilizing public opinion against slavery, because he could speak to his personal experience of being enslaved in Africa, crossing the Atlantic, and living in slavery under the ownership of a British naval officer and then a merchant in the Caribbean. His autobiography, *The Interesting Narrative of the life of Olaudah Equiano, or Gustavus Vassa, the African*, was a personal testimony of slavery in the Anglophone world and has often been considered the first of the classic "slave narratives." Its publication in 1789 propelled Vassa into prominence among the literate public in Britain, despite the fact that he acquired fluency in English only in his teenage years while he was enslaved. As his birth name, Olaudah Equiano, demonstrates, his prominence was based on his African origins and his ability to master a language and culture that were imposed on him through slavery.

Vassa is usually referred to as Equiano, which is the name chosen by those who have compiled his biography and by virtually all literary scholars and historians when referring to the man.[1] The use of his birth name rather than the name he used himself is a curious reflection of how individuals and events are remembered. The question is examined in Karlee Anne Sapoznik's introduction. As Sapoznik's thorough collection of correspondence and documents demonstrates clearly, the man always referred to himself as Vassa; he only rarely used the name Equiano, and never alone. It remains to explain why he is popularly known as Equiano, when this was clearly not his intention.

Vassa participated in the reform movements that were sweeping across Britain in the 1780s and early 1790s, most especially the struggle to secure rights for slaves and former slaves, and then to end the slave trade and slavery. The movement to abolish the slave trade was a strategic choice; the real campaign was against slavery itself. As Christopher Brown has argued, the abolition movement developed in the specific historical context following Britain's loss of its North American colonies.[2] The literate and religious elites of England, Scotland, Ireland, and Wales inevitably had to explain to themselves why their vision of empire had been shaken. Many people were willing to question slavery as a feature of empire, and, in particular, what was clearly most shocking—the horrors of the notorious "Middle Passage," which Vassa had experienced as a child. Vassa was essential to the abolition campaign because of his eloquence; his handsome physique, which commanded attention; his education aboard British naval ships and in London; and his personal experience. Moreover, Vassa was not associated only with the abolition movement. During the heady days influenced by revolutionary France, he was one of the earliest members of the London Corresponding Society, which advocated Parliamentary reform. Hence, he was publicly involved in reforms beyond the abolition of the slave trade and, implicitly and sometimes explicitly, the ending of slavery. As Sapoznik observes, Vassa was arguably the most influential African or person of African descent in London in the late 1780s and 1790s, when the black community numbered perhaps as many as 20,000 people, giving London one of the largest "African" populations of any city in the world. After being officially appointed "Commissioner of the Black Poor" in London in 1787 in connection with the first Sierra Leone project, he became—with the publication of his autobiography eighteen months later, in early 1789—the foremost outspoken advocate of the abolition movement.

The ongoing interest in Vassa and in his autobiography has established Vassa's place in literary history. Vassa provided an inspiring voice for those who had suffered the humiliation and violence of slavery—a voice that ensured his importance as a major spokesman in the British abolition movement and eloquent representative of those who had been enslaved. His vivid and personal account ignited the imaginations of those in his own time who tried to comprehend the evils of slavery, just as his autobiography continues to have meaning today for students and the literate public who want to understand the horrors of slavery and the movement to abolish what is now regarded as a crime against humanity. His autobiography is widely read in English literature, Black Studies, and African history courses, and it remains in print in several popular editions. Vassa's story is written in the rich prose of eighteenth-century literature, by someone who did not know any English until he was eleven. This interest in "Equiano's World" has resulted in the establishment of a website of that name (http://harriet.tubman1.yorku.ca/equianosworld) at the Harriet Tubman Institute for Research on the Global Migrations of African Peoples, York University, Canada. The website was funded through a grant from the Social Sciences and Humanities Research Council of Canada and was part of the endeavors of the Canada Research Chair in African Diaspora History.

This edition of Vassa's letters, relevant papers, and documents brings together in a single collection all the known public and private correspondence of and other documentation on this remarkable man. The correspondence and papers in this volume embrace most of the leading abolitionists, intellectuals, and political figures of the late eighteenth century, many of whom also subscribed to one of the editions of *The Interesting Narrative*. Sapoznik has assembled the correspondence, documents, and other writings of Vassa from previously published materials in specialized journals and in the various editions of *The Interesting Narrative*—most extensively in the edition of *The Interesting Narrative* edited by

Vincent Carretta.[3] These materials not only provide the basis for a scholarly analysis of Vassa's life but also are essential for understanding the development of the abolition movement.

This project builds on the earlier scholarship of many individuals, although it should be noted that considerable historical work remains to be undertaken, including research on the following: Vassa's commercial activities and observations in the Caribbean in the 1760s; his involvement in the Mosquito Shore venture of Dr. Charles Irving in 1776; Vassa's fascination with the Muslim world of the Ottoman Empire; the relationship of Vassa to the black poor of London in the 1780s; his friendship with radical leader Thomas Hardy, who founded the London Corresponding Society in 1792 and was tried for treason in 1794; his marriage to Susannah Cullen, a white woman; and his life with her and their children.

The correspondence and other materials presented in this volume help to elucidate Vassa's involvement in the radical politics of London in the early 1790s and the context in which his autobiography was received. Sapoznik establishes the context that is so important to our understanding of the significance of "Equiano's World" and the role that Gustavus Vassa played during the abolition movement. Vassa's autobiography does not always clearly establish context, and sometimes his own misunderstandings cloud an appreciation of his own evolution as an intellectual and political activist. Vassa's rendition of the notorious "Middle Passage," for instance, has to be understood in context. (Sapoznik includes Vassa's account of the Middle Passage in Appendix 3.) Similarly, Vassa's exploration of different religions is worthy of reflection, while his role in the abolition movement has spawned an important scholarly literature. Vassa's slavery overlapped with the Seven Years' War (1756–1763), prompting the desire to understand where he was and when, and the impact that his risky adventures must have had on him. His role in the first Sierra Leone colonization scheme (1787–1788) and his importance in the abolition movement also are clearly revealed in the collection that Sapoznik has assembled.

Vassa traveled extensively, first as a slave and then as a free man. He came from the interior of the Bight of Biafra, in the heart of Igboland in present-day Nigeria, and was taken to the coast, probably leaving Africa in 1754 via the slave port of Bonny. By his own account, he crossed the Atlantic to Barbados and then to Virginia, where he was bought by British naval captain Michael Henry Pascal and taken to England in early 1755. Captain Pascal was his master until the end of the Seven Years' War in 1763. Vassa's subsequent travels and details of the places he went and people he met are outlined on the "Equiano's World" website. The maps that are in this volume and on the website depict Vassa's extensive travels in the Caribbean, the Mediterranean, and the Arctic. This volume also includes maps that identify the places where Vassa went in Great Britain and the places with which he was associated in London.

Vassa met many influential individuals during his life, some while he was a slave and others after he had earned his emancipation. He was on the same ship as General James Wolfe, who led British troops in the conquest of Canada, after the siege of Louisbourg (1756). He was on the same Arctic expedition of Sir Constantine Phipps (1772) with the future Lord Nelson, and they toiled together to break through the ice that imprisoned the expedition near Spitzbergen. Because of his association with Dr. Charles Irving, including on the Arctic expedition, Vassa met other important individuals, such as Sir Joseph Banks, president of the Royal Society, who later would introduce Vassa to the German ethnographer and founder of modern anthropology, Johann Friedrich Blumenbach, who reviewed Vassa's autobiography in Berlin. Irving's partner was the industrialist Alexander Blair, who subscribed to the first edition of *The Interesting Narrative*. Vassa knew all the leading abolitionists (William Wilberforce, Thomas Clarkson, Granville Sharp, George Ramsay, etc.), which accounts for some of the correspondence included in this volume. He lived with radical Thomas Hardy, founder of the London Corresponding Society and charged with treason in 1794 during the repression that accompanied war with revolutionary France.

Vassa was well known to other individuals of import, including Queen Charlotte, to whom Vassa dedicated his autobiography. It is clear from the correspondence following Hardy's arrest in 1794 that other, unnamed individuals in high office, probably Prime Minister William Pitt himself, followed Vassa's movements. Other significant individuals figure prominently in his life, although he had little or no contact with them. The Sapoznik collection helps to establish who he knew, who knew him, and where he was at different times. We also are better able to assess his public persona, his political ambitions in the Sierra Leone project, and then his role in the abolition movement. The collection provides information on how he navigated the world of Sharp, Clarkson, Wilberforce, Hardy, Banks, and other associates. The lists of his subscribers, which are published in each edition of his autobiography, reflect a wide range of individuals across Britain, Scotland, and Ireland. The correspondence clearly has to be seen in the context of who his subscribers were and other information we have, but it plainly establishes Vassa's prominence at the time. To assist in analysis and interpretation, Sapoznik has compiled a detailed Chronology (Appendix 2) that encompasses most of the people, places, and events that relate to Vassa's life.

There remains the issue of the mysterious letters of the 1770s under Vassa's name. How to interpret these letters is still a problem, as recognized by Carretta.[4] The letter that Vassa wrote to Granville Sharp in 1780 reveals a level of sophistication and a command of the English language that warrants close comparison with the letters to the editors that were written under Vassa's name in 1777 and 1778. The use of the name as a pseudonym is certainly possible, but why "Gustavus Vassa" was used is unclear. Who was Vassa associating with at the time? After returning from the Caribbean in early 1777, he worked as a barber in Haymarket until he was employed by Mathias MacNamara, the former governor of the

British province of Senegambia—who had been recalled to London in the summer of 1777—before the first letter was published. MacNamara was known for his criticisms of the British government pertaining to the way the North American revolt was being handled. By early 1779, Vassa was living at MacNamara's house as his barber. At the time, MacNamara wrote a letter of reference (included in this volume) to the Bishop of London on behalf of Vassa's efforts to be appointed as a missionary to Africa.

In 1754, when Captain Pascal named his new slave boy Gustavus Vassa, he was drawing on knowledge of the Swedish liberator King Gustavus Vasa I—knowledge derived from the play of the same name, which was censored under the restrictions imposed on theatre by Prime Minister Walpole. The name became better known to the educated, British public when Gustav Vasa III ascended to the Swedish throne in 1771, ruling until his death on 29 March 1792. In the context of the rebellion in North America, which the several mysterious letters address, there may have been renewed interest in the story of the liberating king fighting tyranny. However, whether anyone commented to Vassa on the significance of his namesake is not known, and whether the name was otherwise used as a pseudonym is also not known.

The study of Gustavus Vassa's life has considerable merit in the teaching of subjects encompassing slavery, abolition, and social justice. As one of the leading literary and political figures of African descent in the era of the abolition movement, Vassa serves as a role model for young people who encounter discrimination and racial stereotyping. As this comprehensive volume makes clear, the available documentation enables a fuller understanding of Vassa's life than does the autobiographical *Interesting Narrative* alone. These materials are essential to any biographical interpretation and indeed to contextualizing the literary achievements of *The Interesting Narrative*. Hence, specialists in history, literary criticism, and cultural studies will all welcome this volume.

Paul E. Lovejoy

Notes

1. See especially Vincent Carretta, *Equiano, the African: Biography of a Self-Made Man* (Athens: University of Georgia Press, 2005); and James Walvin, *An African's Life: The Life and Times of Olaudah Equiano, 1745-1797* (Washington, D.C.: Cassell, 1998).
2. Christopher Leslie Brown, *Moral Capital: Foundations of British Abolitionism* (Chapel Hill: University of North Carolina Press, 2006).
3. Vincent Carretta, ed., *The Interesting Narrative and Other Writings* (London and New York: Penguin Books, 1995; 2d ed., 2003).
4. Vincent Carretta, "Possible Gustavus Vassa/Olaudah Equiano Attributions," in Robert J. Griffin, ed., *The Faces of Anonymity: Anonymous and Pseudonymous Publication from the Sixteenth to the Twentieth Century* (New York: Palgrave Macmillan, 2003), 103-139.

Acknowledgments

First and foremost, my sincere thanks to Paul E. Lovejoy FRSC CRC, Director of the Harriet Tubman Institute and Distinguished Research Professor in the Department of History, York University, Toronto. His inspiring work ethic, teaching, and intellectual mentorship have been instrumental. This book would not have been possible without his dedication to his graduate students, advice, encouragement, and generous feedback, both in person and over email.

I would also like to thank the following individuals for their insightful feedback and suggestions during the various stages of this project: Douglas Peers, who co-supervised my Master's thesis; Neil Marshall, who shared his exciting finding of the 6 May 1780 letter from Vassa to Granville Sharp; John Bugg, whose concept of "The Other Interesting Narrative" was a source of inspiration when I began this project in 2008; Arthur Torrington, Secretary of The Equiano Society in London, who generously shared documents and his expert advice; Michel Verrette of l'Université de Saint-Boniface; the York University Graduate History Department; and my wonderful colleagues and mentors in the Harriet Tubman Institute, including Annie Bunting, Carlos Algandona, Jeffrey Gunn, Karolyn Smardz Frost, Katrina Keefer, Michele Johnson, Shiemara Hogarth, Shoshawnah Lautenschlager, Vanessa Oliveira, Ugochi Umeugo, and Yacine Daddi Addoun, University of Kansas. I have also benefited greatly from the feedback of James Walvin, University of York, and Suzanne Schwarz, University of Worcester, and from the meticulous research of Mark Duffill, who has been working on a project focusing on various aspects of Vassa's life and contacts.

While working on this project, I was blessed to receive scholarships from the Ontario Graduate Scholarship Program and the Social Sciences and Humanities Research Council of Canada. I am grateful for the valuable feedback I received from colleagues and audience members at conferences at Carleton University, York University, and the University of Alberta.

I would like to thank Markus Wiener Publishers, especially Janet Stern and Markus Wiener, for believing in this project, and providing me with wonderful guidance and support. My sincere thanks also go to Sue Sampson, Senior Archivist, Cambridgeshire Archives; Joseph Keith and Melissa Atkinson, Religious Society of Friends in Britain; Christine Reynolds, Assistant Keeper of Muniments, The Library, Westminster Abbey; Valerie Harris, Special Collections Department at the University of Illinois at Chicago; and Amelia Walker, Senior Library Assistant of the Wellcome Library for permission to reproduce illustrations in this collection.

This book would not have come to fruition without the encouragement and support of many loved ones and friends. My thanks to Joseph, Sharon, Kaylee, and Joshua. The rest of you know who you are, and you have my deepest gratitude.

Last and most important, I dedicate this book to the Alliance Against Modern Slavery. Through his tireless efforts, Gustavus Vassa—Olaudah Equiano, the African—provided a face, name, and voice for millions of enslaved Africans and their descendants. His *Interesting Narrative*, letters, and other writings are an invaluable resource for scholars, students, the general public, and abolitionists around the world. They continue to remind us why slavery and the slave trade must end.

Note on Names:
Gustavus Vassa and/or
Olaudah Equiano

This collection refers to the author of *The Interesting Narrative of the Life of Olaudah Equiano; or, Gustavus Vassa, the African* (London, 1789) as Gustavus Vassa. This approach follows the review of Paul Lovejoy, who has asked: "Olaudah Equiano or Gustavus Vassa–What's in a Name?" Lovejoy considers the literary, historical, and biographical reasons why the man is most commonly known as Olaudah Equiano rather than by the name that he actually used during his life, which was Gustavus Vassa. As Lovejoy concludes, the use of Olaudah Equiano "has more to do with the politics of representation and political correctness of a later generation of scholarship, not with the intention of the man."[1]

As the letters and other writings that are assembled in this collection reveal, "the man" was known in his own day as "Gustavus Vassa," and sometimes as "the African," but rarely as "Equiano." Indeed, when Vassa published his autobiography in 1789, he was known to his public by this name, which he was given in 1754, when he became the slave of Captain Michael Henry Pascal. Pascal named him after Gustav I of Sweden, later known as Gustavus Vasa (d. 29 September 1560), who is remembered in Swedish nationalist tradition as the king revered for liberating his people from Danish tyranny and "slavery."

As Vincent Carretta explains, "to choose to use the name Equiano rather than Vassa … is to go against the author's own practice."[2] Vassa's public and private letters and correspondence confirm that he "*rarely* used the name 'Equiano.'" He adopted the name only in the last decade of his life, when he had become a public, and published, figure. To his friends, his wife, in his will, in his daughters' name, in the letters to the press, to and from friends and in the great majority of other references we know of, Equiano used the name 'Gustavus Vassa.'"[3] Vassa is the name he signed on his marriage certificate in 1792, the name used to record and announce his marriage to Susannah Cullen (1762–1796) in the London press, and the name given to his two daughters.

Vassa used the name "Equiano" only in solicitations and advertisements for his autobiography and in personal letters and correspondence from November 1788 onwards. However, in all of the advertisements of his *Narrative*, readers never see the name "Olaudah Equiano" on its own. In each example, the expression "or, Gustavus Vassa, the African" immediately follows "Olaudah Equiano." Furthermore, apart from a letter to William Dickson on 25 April 1789, and one to Parliament in March 1789, he never signed "Olaudah Equiano" in his correspondence after the publication of *The Interesting Narrative*. Similarly, when people wrote to him, he was addressed as Gustavus Vassa, not Olaudah Equiano. For instance, in March 1791, Susannah Atkinson addressed her musings "To Gustavus Vassa." One year later, Rev. Dr. J. Baker similarly writes "Mr. Gustavus Vassa."[4] William Langworthy, in his letter of introduction to William Hughes, refers to Vassa as Olaudah Equiano, but immediately clarifies this indicator with "Gustavus Vassa" in parentheses.[5]

A note, written after Vassa's death in 1797, on the verso of a letter from Vassa to Granville Sharp, dated 6 May 1780, confirms that he was rarely addressed by the name of "Equiano." Indeed, he "fell into fits" if "Olaudah Equiano," the name he was given at birth, was pronounced.[6] This note cites J. Phillips of Middle Hill, Cornwall, as the source of information. As Lovejoy explains, J. Phillips's father, James Phillips, knew Vassa and was the Quaker printer who published many of the major abolitionist works of the 1780s, including Thomas Clarkson's Cambridge thesis, "An essay on the slavery and commerce of the human species, particularly the African, translated from a Latin Dissertation," in 1785.[7] The note is also interesting because Phillips considered that Vassa's birth name, Olaudah Equiano, was his "real" name, even though he chose to use the name by which he was legally known.

Note on Editorial Method

Whenever possible, I have retained the original typography, capitalization, spelling, spacing, indentation, and punctuation of the documents included in this collection. Spaces are closed around all dashes with the exception of those rendered "—" in transcriptions of primary sources I was unable to see firsthand. The square brackets in the documents signal changes rendered to the documents, including those made by other transcribers of primary source versions. These bracket insertions help ensure a clearer, more fluid rendition of the documents. In the majority of cases, they reflect spelling corrections, punctuation, name additions, or the indication of a signature.

Introduction

Gustavus Vassa (c. 1742-1797), alias Olaudah Equiano, "the African," was so influential in shaping public opinion on "the problem of slavery" that Folarin Shyllon has described him as "the vanguard of the Abolitionist movement in England."[1] Vassa was the most famous member of a small Black community that had developed in Britain by the end of the eighteenth century at the height of the transatlantic slave trade. Thanks to the success of *The Interesting Narrative of the Life of Olaudah Equiano, or Gustavus Vassa, the African. Written by Himself* (1789), Vassa was probably the most well-known person of African descent in the Atlantic world at the time of his death in London on 31 March 1797. His death was marked by *The Gentleman's Magazine* in their "Obituary of Remarkable Persons," which listed the passing of "Mr Gustavus Vassa, the African . . . well known to the publick by the interesting narrative of his life."[2] Over the past two centuries, and especially in the past forty years, Vassa and his *Interesting Narrative* have attracted a great deal of scholarly and public attention.

Historians, literary critics, and the general public have come to recognize Gustavus Vassa as one of the most accomplished English-speaking writers of his age, and arguably one of the most accomplished authors of African descent.[3] Today there are countless academic courses that make use of his *Narrative*, and several Vassa biographies have prompted a number of debates that are premised on his text. A special edition of *Historically Speaking* (2006) even addressed the question "Does Equiano Still Matter?"[4] On the whole, Vassa has the status, at one and the same time, of an African writer, the reputed founder of the slave narrative, an abolitionist, a leading spokesman for the Afro-British community, a key figure in late-eighteenth-century activism for democratic reform, and the most quoted survivor of the Middle Passage.

Several questions led to the research that eventually gave birth to this collection of his letters and other writings. First, in the work that had been done on Vassa, it was not always apparent to what extent scholars had made use of his published and unpublished works other than the *Narrative*—a clear lacuna in historical scholarship. Vassa's letters and other works remained scattered, making a collection of these documents an obvious project to undertake. Second, in doing so in collaboration with colleagues in 2008, we became aware that some documents had been privileged, while other enlightening findings had not. The latter include Vassa's letter to Granville Sharp of 6 May 1780.

John Bugg has cleverly coined the phrase "The Other Interesting Narrative" in his article on Vassa's book tour, which is one subject, among several others, where newly discovered material suggests that more of Vassa's writings exist. Consequently, there is more to understanding Vassa than has often been recognized. The entire *known* canon of Vassa's writings and written interactions is essential to understanding what we can learn of this important historical figure.

Altogether, this collection includes 125 documents and 25 accompanying illustrations, which shed additional light on aspects of Vassa's life and significance beyond what he said and included in his *Interesting Narrative*. Chapter I contains 8 documents categorized under "Legal Records"; Chapter II contains 34 documents categorized under "Correspondence"; Chapter III has 57 documents categorized under "Newspapers"; Chapter IV includes 14 documents categorized under "Possible Attributions"; and Chapter V contains 12 documents of interest categorized under "Miscellaneous."[5] These documents cover Vassa's life from the mid-1760s until his death in the late 1790s, as well as references to him in the nineteenth century. In order to capture the ways in which these materials have been utilized by scholars, I have examined as many primary materials and as much of the secondary literature as possible, all of which are listed in the bibliography.[6]

At the end of the collection, there are four appendixes. Appendix 1 contains four maps, which chart Vassa's travels. Appendix 2 is a chronology of his life. Appendix 3 is an excerpt from Vassa's description of the Middle Passage, which was at the core of what he said on his speaking tours, and central to the campaign to abolish the slave trade. Appendix 4 comprises a list of places and a list of individuals and groups associated with Vassa, both of which provide leads for further research.

Most of Vassa's correspondence, letters to editors, and other documents date to the period 1780 to 1794. With the exception of an anti-war essay penned under the pseudonym "Othello," which may have been written by Vassa, nothing of his hand, apart from two subscriptions and his will, has been discovered from June 1794 until his death in 1797. His letters were written in the context of the American Revolution, the French Revolution, the successful slave revolt in Saint Domingue, and the warfare that broke out between France and England after 1793. Despite Vassa's involvement in the abolition movement, the London Society for Effecting the Abolition of the Slave Trade (SEAST) was dissolved by the mid-1790s, and it was not until 1807, ten years after Vassa's death, that abolition was achieved. Vassa was associated with radical Irish thinkers and Scottish intellectuals, as well as the London Corresponding Society, the "Jacobin city" of Norwich, and American Quakers in Philadelphia. Because of his association with revolutionary principles being espoused in France and in Tom Paine's *Rights of Man*, among other places, Vassa seems to have been at some risk in Britain when reaction to the French Revolution began to solidify.[7] Apart from a November 1794 subscription to Carl Bernhard Wadstrom's *An Essay on Colonization particularly applied to the West Coast of Africa*; a subscription to a fund "for defraying the Expence of Defendants in the late Trials for HIGH TREASON," which appeared in the *Morning Post and Fashion-*

able World of 19 May 1795; and his will of 28 May 1796, he does not appear to have been especially active. Probably safety concerns, along with the success of his bookselling tours and his greater familial responsibilities, explain his public silence.

In 1977, Shyllon published twenty-seven pages of Vassa documentation—what he entitled "Letters of a Black Abolitionist"—in a first appendix, and "Letters of Sons of Africa" in a second appendix.[8] Like Paul Edwards's edition in 1967 and Shyllon's book in 1977, Vincent Carretta's 1995 edition of *The Interesting Narrative* (revised in 2003) includes a collection of letters and other documents written by, or pertaining to, Vassa. Carretta, writing twenty-eight years after Edwards and eighteen after Shyllon, published some material that was undiscovered in 1967 and in the 1970s. All in all, Carretta included fourteen letters and entries published in the ninth edition of Vassa's autobiography, forty letters and other Vassa writings, Vassa's Will and Codicil, and comprehensive lists of Vassa's subscribers—these being his English subscribers, including those in Hull, Bristol, Norwich, Lynn, and Wisbech, and his subcribers in Ireland and in Scotland. Writing in 1977, however, when Shyllon located, transcribed, and contextualized twenty-four letters relating to Vassa, he was well aware that his collection of documents was incomplete: "I have no doubt that I have missed some of Equiano's letters in the volumes I have examined."[9] This holds true today as researchers seek to find more of Vassa's writings. The present collection lays the basis for further, deeper research on Vassa's letters and other works besides his *Interesting Narrative*.

After almost a generation of considerable scholarly activity, the interest in Vassa shows every sign of continuing. Indeed, he is more popular today than ever. Pictures of him festoon book covers, his face is used on posters to promote exhibitions, and he has his own postcard and postage stamp. Whenever slavery or Black writers are mentioned, Vassa is often close to the center of attention, and The Equiano Society, founded in London in 1996, is dedicated to honoring his legacy. Assuredly, as the documents concerning this important eighteenth-century figure are explored, we will continue to refine our knowledge of his life, and of this revolutionary period of history.

CHAPTER

I

Legal Records

This chapter includes eight legal documents. The Muster List of August 1755 (document 1) reveals that Vassa lived aboard the *HMS Roebuck*, the naval ship on which his master, Michael Henry Pascal, an Officer in the Royal Navy, worked as First Lieutenant. Pascal's cousins, the Guerin sisters, sent Vassa to school and urged Pascal to have him baptized.[1] The Baptismal Record (document 2) of 9 February 1759 reveals that he was baptized "Gustavus Vassa" at St. Margaret's Church in Westminster, London.

Vassa was officially a free man on 11 July 1766, when Robert King wrote and signed his Certificate of Emancipation (document 3). On 17 May 1773 (document 4), he was hired aboard the *HMS Racehorse* as Dr. Charles Irving's assistant on the Arctic expedition of Constantine John Phipps (later Lord Mulgrave).[2] Nineteen years later, on 7 April 1792, Vassa married Susannah Cullen of Soham, Cambridgeshire, at St Andrew's Church, Soham (document 5).[3]

Susannah and Gustavus Vassa had two daughters, Anna Maria (born 16 October 1793; died 21 July 1797) and Joanna (born 11 April 1795; died 10 March 1857). Susannah died on 20 February 1796, less than a year after Joanna's birth.[4] Vassa wrote his will and last testament a month after Susannah's death (document 6) and died just over a year after her, on 31 March 1797 in London.

Anna died three months after her father (document 7), leaving Joanna the sole survivor of the family. On her 21st birthday, Joanna inherited her father's estate of £950.[5] Joanna married Rev. Henry Bromley, and on 10 March 1857 she died at the age of 61 (document 8).

1. *HMS Roebuck* Muster Book, 6 August 1755

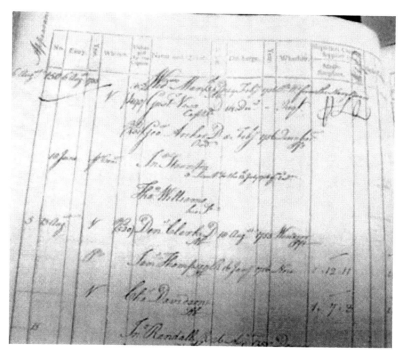

Vassa appears on line two as a "Volunteer," and "Gust. Vassa Capt. St." is listed as one of eight servants permitted to Matthew Whitwell, the captain of the *HMS Roebuck*. National Archives, Kew, England: ADM 36/6472.

2. Baptismal Register, St. Margaret's Church, London, 7–11 February 1759

Vassa's baptism is recorded on line eight of this image as "9. Gustavus Vassa a Black born in Carolina. 12 years old." Copyright: Dean and Chapter of Westminster.

3. Certificate of Emancipation, 11 July 1766[6]

Montserrat. –To all men unto whom these presents shall come: I Robert King, of the parish of St. Anthony, in the said island, merchant, send greeting: Know ye, that I the aforesaid Robert King, for, and in consideration of the sum of seventy pounds current money of the said island, to me in hand paid, and to the intent that a negro man slave, named Gustavus Vasa, shall and may become free, have manumitted, emancipated, enfranchised, and set free, and by these presents do manumit, emancipate, enfranchise, and set free, the aforesaid negro man-slave, named Gustavus Vasa, for ever; hereby giving, granting, and releasing unto him, the said Gustavus Vasa, all right, title, dominion, sovereignty, and property, which, as lord and master over the aforesaid Gustavus Vasa, I have had, or which I now have, or by any means whatsoever I may or can hereafter possibly have over him the aforesaid Negro, for ever. In witness whereof, I the abovesaid Robert King, have unto these presents set my hand and seal, this tenth day of July, in the year of our Lord one thousand seven hundred and sixty-six.

ROBERT KING

Signed, sealed, and delivered in the presence of Terry Legay.

Montserrat,
Registered the within manumission, at full length, this eleventh day of July, 1766, in liber D. TERRY LEGAY, Register.

4. *HMS Racehorse* Muster Book, 17 May 1773

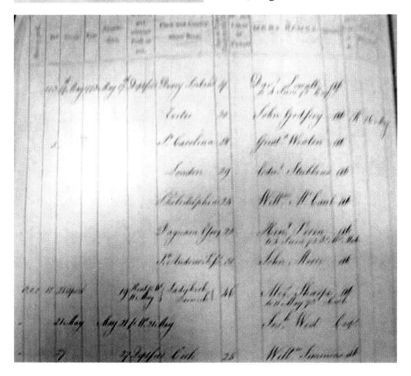

Vassa's birthplace is listed below in the *HMS Racehorse* Muster Book as "South Carolina," and his name is recorded at entry number three as "Gustavus Weston." National Archives, Kew, England: ADM 36/7490.

7 August 1773, "View of the Racehorse and Carcass" in Constantine John Phipps, *A Voyage towards the North Pole, Undertaken by His Majesty's Command* (London: J. Nourse), 1774.

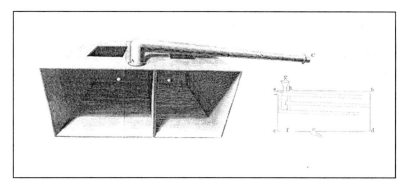

While on the *Racehorse*, Vassa worked as the assistant of Dr. Charles Irving, who was celebrated for his successful experiments making seawater fresh. "Dr. Charles Irving's Apparatus for Distillation of Seawater" in Constantine John Phipps, *A Voyage towards the North Pole, Undertaken by His Majesty's Command* (London: J. Nourse), 1774.

5. Marriage Certificate, 7 April 1792

The marriage certificate of Gustavus Vassa and Susannah Cullen. Cambridgeshire Archives: P142/1/11.

Watercolor of St. Andrew's Church, where Vassa and Susannah Cullen were married on 7 April 1792.

6. The Will and Codicil of Gustavus Vassa, 28 May 1796[7]

In the Name of God Amen. I Gustavus Vassa of Addle Street Aldermanbury in the City of London Gentleman being sound in mind and Body and in perfect health and firm in my belief of a future State in the death and Corruption of the Body and hopeful in the rise of the Soul depending in the Mercy of God my Creator for forgiveness of my Sins Give Devise and Bequeath unto my Friends John Audley and Edward Ind both of Cambridge Esquires All my real and personal Estate of what Nature Kind or sort soever either in possession reversion remainder or expectancy and which Estate and property I have dearly earned by the Sweat of my Brow in some of the most remote and adverse Corners of the whole world to solace those I leave behind me. To Hold to them the said John Audley and Edward Ind their Executors Administrators and Assigns In Trust that they the said John Audley and Edward Ind shall and do receive and take the produce and profits arising from my Estate both real and personal and apply the same or a sufficient part thereof towards the Board Maintenance and Education of my two infant Daughters Ann Maria and Johanna Vassa until they shall respectively attain their respective Ages of Twenty one years. Then Upon this further Trust that from and after their Attaining their said Age of Twenty one years equally to be divided between them Share and Share alike but if either of them shall happen to die then I give and bequeath the Share of her so dying to the Survivor of them but in Case of the decease of both my Children before they arrive at their said Age of Twenty one years then and in that Case I give devise and bequeath the whole of my Estate and Effects hereinbefore given one Moiety thereof to the Treasurer and Directors of the Sierra Leona Company for the Use and Benefit of the School established by the said Company at Sierra Leona and the other Moiety thereof to the Treasurer and Directors of the Society instituted at the Spa Fields Chapel on the twenty second day of September one thousand seven hundred and ninety five for sending Missionaries to preach the Gospel in Foreign parts. I Do hereby Give and Bequeath unto the said John Audley and Edward Ind the

Sum of Ten Pounds each. And I do hereby nominate constitute and appoint the said John Audley and Edward Ind Executors of this my last Will and Testament hereby revoking and making void all and every other Will and Wills at any time heretofore by me made and do declare this to be my last will and Testament. In Witness whereof I have hereunto set my hand and Seal this twenty eighth day of May in the year of our Lord one thousand seven hundred and ninety six.

[Signed] Gustavus Vassa

Signed Sealed Published and declared by the above named Gustavus Vassa as and for his last Will and Testament in the Presence of us who at his request and in his Presence have subscribed our Names as Witnesses thereto. Elizabeth Melliora Cooss No.9 Adam Street. J. Gillham No.9 Adam Street Adelphi. George Streetin, Clerk to Mr. Gillham.

National Archives, Kew, England: 10/3372.

THE SCHEDULE or Inventory of the principal part of my Estate and Effects which I am possessed of at the Time of making this my Will

Two Acres of Copyhold Pasture Ground with the Appurtenances thereunto belonging situate lying and being in Sutton and Mepal in the Isle of Ely and County of Cambridge which devolves to me [and] my heirs or assigns after the decease of Mrs. Ann Cullen of Fordham in Cambridgeshire by the last Will and Testament of my late Wife Susanna Vassa[.] And I have Mrs. Cullen's Bond for one Quarter of her Worth[:] One Annuity of James Parkinson Esquire of the Leverian Museum Blackfriars road in the County of Surrey of the yearly value of Twenty six pounds thirteen Shillings and Eight pence;

One other Annuity of Francis Folkes and Frances his wife of Pleasant passage near Mother Red Caps Hampstead Road in the County of Middlesex of the yearly value of Fifty Eight pounds two Shillings and Eight pence;

One other Annuity of Mrs Ann Leybourn of Westwell in the County of Oxford of the yearly value of One hundred pounds all payable quarterly[.]

Three hundred pounds secured to me by an Assignment of the Lease of Plaisterers Hall situate in Addle Street No. 25 in the City of London[.]

Sundry Household Goods and Furniture wearing Apparel and printed Books at present on the Premises at Plaisterers Hall[;]

The Sum of Three hundred pounds at present undisposed of and such other Property as I may in future accumulate.

I do hereby desire my Executors to insure the Lives on which the several Annuities are granted at the Assurance Office in Bridge Street Blackfriars[.]

The Deeds of which Estate are lodged in the possession of James Gillham Attorney No.9 Adam Street Adelphi or with Messrs. Down[,] Thornton and Compy Bankers Bartholomew Lane in the City of London.

[Signed] Gustavus Vassa

   Witnesses[:] Eliz[abe]th Melliora Cooss. Js. Gillham. George Streetin Cl[er]k to Mr. Gillham.

---

7. Anna Maria Vassa Epitaph – b. 1793 d. 1797

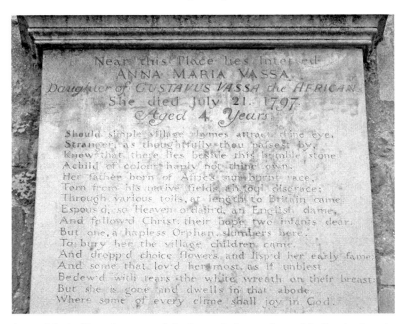

Anna Maria Vassa's memorial plaque is located outside St. Andrew's Church, Chesterton, Cambridge. It reads:

Near this Place Lies Interred Anna Maria Vassa
Daughter of Gustavus Vassa, the African
She Died July 21 1797
Aged 4 Years

Should simple village rhymes attract thine eye,
Stranger, as thoughtfully thou passest by,
Know that there lies beside this humble stone
A child of colour haply not thine own.
Her father born of Afric's sun–burnt race,
Torn from his native field, ah foul disgrace:
Through various toils, at length to Britain came
Espoused, so Heaven ordain'd, an English dame,
And follow'd Christ; their hope two infants dear.
But one, a hapless orphan, slumbers here.
To bury her the village children came.
And dropp'd choice flowers, and lisp'd her early fame:
And some that lov'd her most, as if unblest,
Bedew'd with tears the white wreath on their breast:
But she is gone and dwells in that abode,
Where some of every clime shall joy in God.[8]

8. Joanna Vassa – b. 1795 d. 1857

On 21 March 1857, Joanna Vassa's death was reported in *The Ipswich Journal* as follows:

"DIED. 10th inst., at Benyon–terrace, Beckingham–road, London, in her 62nd year, Joanna, wife of the Rev. Henry Bromley, daughter of Gustavus Vasa, the African, and ward of the late John Audley, Esq.: some years since a well known and highly-respected resident in Cambridge."[9]

Joanna Vassa's gravestone at Abney Park Cemetery shortly after its re-discovery in 2005, awaiting restoration. Joanna and her husband, Reverend Henry Bromley, ran a Congregational Chapel at Clavering near Saffron Walden in Essex, before moving to London in 1845. She died on 10 March 1857 at the age of 61, and was buried at Abney Park Cemetery in Stoke Newington on 16 March 1857. Her husband Henry survived her for 20 years and was eventually buried alongside her on 12 February 1878. It's not yet known whether they had any children. The inscription on her gravestone reads "Memory of Joanna beloved wife of Henry Bromley, daughter of Gustavus Vassa, the African. Born April 11, 1795 and died March 1857.

CHAPTER

II

Correspondence

This chapter comprises four sections, each featuring Vassa's correspondence. Section 1 contains fifteen letters written by Vassa. Section 2 includes two letters he wrote in collaboration with other Africans. Section 3 contains three letters written to Vassa. Finally, Section 4 contains fourteen character references, letters of introduction, and letters of recommendation.

SECTION 1
Vassa

This section contains letters that Vassa sent to other Africans, employers (document 1), Members of Parliament and the Treasury (documents 3 and 8), religious officials (documents 9 and 15), leading reformers (document 10), and Queen Charlotte (document 5). He forgave a debt owed to him by Ann Berry (document 7) and wrote letters to fellow abolitionists (documents 2, 6, and 13), to subscribers of his *Interesting Narrative*, and to individuals he met during his book tours (documents 12 and 14). His letter to Lord Hawkesbury (document 4) was printed with the evidence of the 1789 Parliamentary Report on the Slave Trade.[1] After Vassa faced accusations in the press surrounding his place of birth, Vassa wrote a letter to his readers in a note that was included in 1794 on the first page of the 9th edition of his *Interesting Narrative* (document 11).[2]

This section also includes correspondence with Thomas Hardy (document 10), the founder of the London Corresponding Society. In February 1792, Vassa wrote a letter to a group of abolitionist clergy at Nottingham, announcing his marriage (document 9). His letter to Mr. or Mrs. Liversege (document 14) locates Vassa in Colchester in June 1794, and possibly under political surveillance during Prime Minister William Pitt's persecution of democratic reformers.[3]

Together, these documents provide insights into the diversity of Vassa's individual correspondence, the people he knew, and the wide audience he reached.

1. Letter to the Right Reverend Father in God, Robert Lowth, Lord Bishop of London, March 1779[4]

The MEMORIAL OF GUSTAVUS VASSA
SHEWETH,

THAT your memorialist is a native of Africa, and has a knowledge of the manners and customs of the inhabitants of that country.

That your memorialist has resided in different parts of Europe for twenty–two years last past, and embraced the Christian faith in the year 1759.

That your memorialist is desirous of returning to Africa as a missionary, if encouraged by your Lordship, in hopes of being able to prevail upon his countrymen to become Christians; and your memorialist is the more induced to undertake the same, from the success that has attended the like undertakings when encouraged by the Portuguese through their different settlements on the coast of Africa, and also by the Dutch: both governments encouraging the blacks, who, by their education are qualified to undertake the same, and are found more proper than European clergymen, unacquainted with the language and customs of the country.

Your memorialist's only motive for soliciting the office of a missionary is, that he may be a means, under God, of reforming his countrymen and persuading them to embrace the Christian religion. Therefore your memorialist humbly prays your Lordship's encouragement and support in the undertaking.

GUSTAVUS VASSA.

At Mr. Guthrie's, taylor,
No. 17, Hedge–lane.

2. Letter to Granville Sharp Esq.r, In Old Jewry Chepside, 6 May 1780[5]

Sierra Leone Collection, box 4, supplement 1, folder 1. University of Illinois at Chicago Library, Special Collections.

(continues on next page)

my present master is a mile man, But a fornicator, & how soon I may be Removed from his Service I knows not as I am not much in favour with the fornicatress who has the Ruleing of him & the whole house.

Most Worthy & Benevolent Sir. &c.

I Conclude in Praying & in wishing you & all yours Every Blessings of the Old & new Testment, may you all shine in Glory here after. Aman.

I am with Respect & Gratitude &c.&c. yours humble Serv.t

Gustavus Vassa, at Mr Delamain wine merchant N.o 67. Berners Street oxford Road — Saturday May the 6th —oo.—

Most Worthy and Benevolent and Truly Favoured Sir,–

Thus with my inmost, & utmost Respect, Gratitude, & Thanks to you for all your kindnesses: Sir. Not having time before to Read the three Last good Books you was so kind to Give me till with in this week, I first have Read the just Limitation of Slavery, & the Law of Passive Obedience with Very Great Satisfaction: I Now have Read the Law of Retribution which I think is Quite Ravishing, for which I Do Request the pray hearing God to hear my prayers & Infinitely Reward you & all yours: for all your Labours, pains, and Love to the poor, and Very much Afflected Brethren of mine: may the Good Lord Reward you aboundently for these four pages in the Law of Retribution, which I thinks is Exceedingly Striking. Viz. all the 149th page and all of the 151st & page 320th, & Lastly the four Last Lines But two in page 331st.–if God spares me I shall

Read the next week the Law of Liberty: & if god spares me to Visit you again I will be Glad to Beg of you: the Tract of the Law of Nature & principles of Action in man. Thanks to the Lord I have good Deal time to Read in this place I am now in. my present master is a mile *[sic]* man, But a fornicator. & how soon I may be Removed from his service I knows not as I am not much in favour with the fornicatress who has the Ruleing of him & the whole house.

Most Worthy & Benevolent Sir. &c. I Conclude in Praying & in wishing you & all yours every Blessings of the Old & New Testment *[sic]*, may you all shine in Glory here after. Aman.

I am with Respect & Gratitude &c. &c.
yours hum.ble serv.t

Gustavus Vassa, at Mr
Delamain wine merchant
N.o 67. Berners Street oxford
Road–Saturday May the 6,th–00.

---

3. Petition to the Right Honourable the Lords Commissioners of His Majesty's Treasury, 12 May 1787[6]

The Memorial and Petition of Gustavus Vassa, Black Man, late Commissary to the Black Poor, going to Africa.
HUMBLY SHEWETH,
    That your Lordships' Memorialist was by the Honourable the Commissioners of His Majesty's Navy on the 4th December last appointed to the above Employment by Warrant from that Board, That He, accordingly proceeded to the execution of his Duty on board of the *Vernon* being one of the Ships appointed to proceed

to Africa with the above Poor. That your Memorialist to his great grief and Astonishment received a Letter of Dismission from the Honble. Commissioners of the Navy by your Lordships' Orders. That conscious of having acted with the most perfect Fidelity and the greatest Assiduity in discharging the Trust reposed to him he is altogether at a loss to conceive the Reasons your Lordships' having altered the favourable opinions you were pleased to entertain him. Sensible that your Lordships would not proceed to so severe a measure without some apparent good Cause, he therefore has every reason to believe that his Conduct has been grossly misrepresented to your Lordships and he is the more confirmed in this Opinion because by opposing measures of others concerned in the same Expedition which tended to defeat your Lordships' humane intentions and to put the Government to a very considerable additional expence he created a number of Enemies whose misrepresentations he has too much reason to believe laid the foundation of his Dismission.

Unsupported by Friends and unaided by the advantages of a liberal Education he can only hope for Redress from the Justice of his Cause. In addition to the mortification of being removed from his Employment and the advantage he might reasonably have expected to have derived therefrom he has the misfortune to have sunk a considerable part of his little property in fitting himself out and in other expences arising out of his Situation an account of which he herewith annexes. Your Memorialist will not trouble your Lordships with a Vindication of any part of his Conduct because he knows not what crimes he is accused, he however earnestly wishes that you will be pleased to direct an Enquiry into his behaviour during the time he acted in the Public Service and if it shall be found that his Dismission arose from false Representations he is confident that your Lordships' Justice he will find redress.

Your Petitioner therefore humbly prays that your Lordships will take his Case into Consideration and that you will be pleased to order Payment of the above referred to Account Amounting to

£32.4.0 and also the Wages intended me.

Which most humbly
Submitted
GUSTAVUS VASSA.

P.S. This Account the Navy Board do not think themselves authorized to allow without the order of the Lords of the Treasury.[7]

London 12th May 1784.
A List of sundy Expences of Gustavus Vasa the late Commissary
for the Black Poor going to Africa, not allowed by the Navy Board.

13 Febry. 1787
4 Aprl.
28

	£	s.	D.
To paid for a Flag for the Settlement in Africa	5.	5.	0.
To his Expences from London to Plymouth	2.	16.	0.
To Dr. From Plymouth with his Baggage	4.	6.	0.
To withdrawing the Insurance on £400	2.	0.	0.
To a Letter of Attorney and Policy	1.	4.	6
To Discount on Goods	13.	7.	6.
To Dr. On Provisions	3.	5.	0.
	£32.	4.	0.

4. Letter to The Right Honourable Lord Hawkesbury, 13 March 1788[8]

My Lord,   London, 13th March, 1788.

   As the illicit Traffic of Slavery is to be taken into consideration
of the British Legislature, I have taken the Liberty of sending you

the following Sentiments, which have met the Approbation of many intelligent and commercial Gentlemen.

Sir,

A SYSTEM of commerce once established in Africa, the Demand for Manufactories will most rapidly augment, as the native Inhabitants will sensibly adopt our Fashions, Manner, Customs, &c. &c.

In proportion to the Civilization, so will be the Consumption of British Manufactures.

The Wear and Tear of a Continent, nearly twice as large as Europe, and rich in Vegetable and Mineral Productions, is much easier conceived than calculated. A Case in point. It costs the Aborigines of Britain little or nothing in Clothing, &c. The Difference between our Forefathers and us, in point of Consumption, is literally infinite. The Reason is most obvious. It will be equally immense in Africa. The same Cause, viz. Civilization, will ever produce the same Effect. There are no Book or outstanding Debts, if I may be allowed the Expression. The Word Credit is not to be found in the African Dictionary; it is standing upon safe Ground.

A commercial Intercourse with Africa opens an inexhaustible Source of wealth to the manufacturing Interest of Great Britain; and to all which the Slave Trade is a physical Obstruction.

If I am not misinformed, the manufacturing Interest is equal, if not superior to the landed Interest as to Value, for Reasons which will soon appear. The Abolition of the diabolical Slavery will give a most rapid and permanent Extension to Manufactures, which is totally and diametrically opposite to what some interested People assert.

The Manufactories of this Country must and will in the nature and Reason of Things have a full and constant Employ by supplying the African Markets. The Population, Bowels, and Surface of Africa abound in valuable and useful Returns; the hidden treasuries of Countries will be brought to Light and into Circulation.

Industry, Enterprise, and Mining will have their full Scope, proportionably as they civilize. In a Word, it lays open to endless Field of Commerce to the British Manufacturer and Merchant Adventurer.

The manufacturing Interest and the general Interest of the Enterprise are synonymous; the Abolition of Slavery would be in reality an universal Good, and for which a partial Ill must be supported.

Tortures, Murder, and every other imaginable Barbarity are practised by the West India Planters upon the Slaves with Impunity. I hope the Slave Trade will be abolished: I pray it may be an Event at hand. The great Body of Manufacturers, uniting in the Cause, will considerably facilitate and expedite it; and, as I have already stated, it is most substantially their Interest and Advantage, and as such the Nation at large. In a short Space of Time One Sentiment alone will prevail, from Motives of Interest as well as Justice and Humanity.

Europe contains One hundred and Twenty Millions of Inhabitants; Query, How many Millions doth Africa contain? Supposing the Africans, collectively and individually, to expend Five Pounds a Head in Raiment and Furniture yearly, when civilized, &c.–an Immensity beyond the Reach of Imagination: This I conceive to be a Theory founded upon Facts; and therefore an infallible one. If Blacks were permitted to remain in their own Country they would double themselves every Fifteen Years: In Proportion to such Increase would be the Demand for Manufactures. Cotton and Indigo grow spontaneously in some Parts of Africa: A Consideration this of no small Consequence to the manufacturing Towns of Great Britain.

The Chamber of Manufactories of Great Britain, held in London will be strenuous in the Cause. It opens a most immense, glorious, and happy Prospect.

The Cloathing, &c. of a Continent Ten thousand Miles in Circumference, and immensely rich in Productions of every Denom-

ination, would make an interesting Return indeed for our Manufactures, a free Trade being established.

I have, my Lord, the Honour to subscribe myself,

Your Lordships very humble and devoted Servant,
GUSTAVUS VASSA,
the late Commissary for the African Settlement.
No. 53, Baldwin's Gardens, Holborn.

5. Letter to the QUEEN's most Excellent Majesty [Queen Charlotte], 21 March 1788[9]

MADAM,

Your Majesty's well known benevolence and humanity embold-
ens me to approach your royal presence, trusting that the obscurity
of my situation will not prevent your Majesty from attending to
the sufferings for which I plead.

Yet I do not solicit your royal pity for my own distress; my sufferings, although numerous, are in a measure forgotten. I supplicate
your Majesty's compassion for millions of my African countrymen,
who groan under the lash of tyranny in the West Indies.

The oppression and cruelty exercised to the unhappy negroes
there, have at length reached the British legislature, and they are
now deliberating on its redress; even several persons of property
in slaves in the West Indies, have petitioned parliament against its
continuance, sensible that it is as impolitic as it is unjust—and what
is inhuman must ever be unwise.

Your Majesty's reign has been hitherto distinguished by private
acts of benevolence and bounty; surely the more extended the misery is, the greater claim it has to your Majesty's compassion, and
the greater must be your Majesty's pleasure in administering to its
relief.

I presume, therefore, gracious Queen, to implore your interposition with your royal consort, in favour of the wretched Africans; that, by your Majesty's benevolent influence, a period may now be put to their misery; and that they may be raised from the condition of brutes, to which they are at present degraded, to the rights and situation of freemen, and admitted to partake of the blessings of your Majesty's happy government; so shall your Majesty enjoy the heartfelt pleasure of procuring happiness to millions, and be rewarded in the grateful prayers of themselves, and of their posterity.

And may the all–bountiful Creator shower on your Majesty, and the Royal Family, every blessing that this world can afford, and every fulness of joy which divine revelation has promised us in the next.

I am your Majesty's most dutiful and devoted servant to command,

GUSTAVUS VASSA,

The Oppressed Ethiopean.

No. 53, Baldwin's Gardens.

---

6. Letter to Josiah Wedgwood Written on the Printed Solicitation for Subscriptions to *The Interesting Narrative*, November 1788[10]

Worthy Sir &c. this is my Dutiful Respect to you I Pray you to Pardon this freedom I have taken in beging [*sic*] your favour, or the apperence [*sic*] of your Name amongst others of my Worthy friends.–& you will much oblige your Huml. Servt. To Command.

Gustavus Vassa

The African

7. Letter to Ann Berry, 6 March 1789[11]

Mr. Gustavus Vassa to Ann Berry} Release
Middlesex April Session 1789

Know all Men by these presents That I Gustavus Vassa of Union Street in the Parish of St. James's in the County of Middlesex Gentleman have Remised Released and for ever quit claymed and by these presents do Remise Release and for Ever quit clayme unto Ann Wife of Arthur Berry late of the Parish of St. James's within the Liberty of Westminster in the County of Middlesex Victualler her Heirs Executors and Administrators all and all manner of Action and Actions Cause and Causes of Action Suits Bills Bonds Writings Obligatory Debts Dues Duties Accompts Sum and Sums of Money Judgements Executions Extents Quarrells Controversies Trespasses Damages and Demands whatsoever both in Law and Equity or otherwise howsoever which against the said Ann Berry I ever had and which my Heirs Executors or Administrators shall or may hereafter claim challenge or demand for or by reason or means of any Matter Cause or Thing whatsoever from the beginning of the World until the day of the date of these presents In Witness whereof I have hereunto set my Hand and Seal the Sixth Day of March in the Twenty Ninth Year of the Reign of our Sovereign Lord George the Third by the Grace of God of Great Britain France and Ireland_____King Defender of the Faith and in the Year of our Lord One Thousand Seven Hundred and Eighty Nine

Sealed and Delivered being first duly Stamped In the presence of Ja^s
Hunt}
[signed] Gustavus Vassa

[over]
James Hunt of Liquor Pond Street in the Parish of Saint Andrews

Holborn in the County of Middlesex Gentleman maketh Oath and Faith that he this Deponent was present on the sixth day of March last and did see the within Named Gustavus Vassa Sign Seal and duly execute in due form of Law the within Release unto the within Named Ann the Wife of Arthur Berry in the presence of this Deponent.

Sworn in Court the 22d day of April 1789} Confession Jas Hunt Hall

8. Letter "To the Lords Spiritual and Temporal, and the Commons of the Parliament of Great Britain," 24 March 1789[12]

My Lords and Gentlemen,
PERMIT me with the greatest deference and respect, to lay at your feet the following genuine Narrative; the chief design of which is to excite your august assemblies a sense of compassion for the miseries which the Slave Trade has entailed on my unfortunate countrymen. By the horrors of that trade I was first torn away from all the tender connexions that were dear to my heart; but these, through the mysterious ways of Providence, I ought to regard as infinitely more than compensated by the introduction I have thence obtained by the knowledge of Christian religion, and of a nation which, by its liberal sentiments, its humanity, the glorious freedom of its government, and its proficiency in arts and sciences, has exalted the dignity of human nature.

I am sensible I ought to entreat your pardon for addressing to you a work so wholly devoid of literary merit; but, as the production of an unlettered African, who is actuated by the hope of becoming an instrument towards the relief of his suffering countrymen. I trust that *such a man*, pleading in *such a cause*, will be acquitted of boldness and presumption.

May the god of Heaven inspire your hearts with peculiar benevolence on that important day when the question of Abolition is to be discussed, when thousands, in consequence [o]f your determination, are to look for Happiness or Misery!

   I am,

  My LORDS and GENTLEMEN,

    Your most obedient,

    And devoted humble servant,

     OLAUDAH EQUIANO,

      OR

     GUSTAVUS VASSA

March 24, 1789.[13]

9. Letter to The Rev. G. Walker and Family, Nottingham, 27 February 1792[14]

Cambridgeshire Archives: R88/74.

London Feby the 27.th–1792

Dr. Revd. & Worthy friends &c.

This with my Best of Respects to you & Wife with many Prayers that you both may ever be Well in Souls & Bodys–& also your Little Lovely Daughter–I thank you for all kindnesses which you w[er]e please[d] to show me, may God ever Reward you for it–Sir, I went to Ireland & was there 8 1/2 months–& sold 1900 copies of my narrative. I came here on the 10th inst.–& now mean as it seem Pleasing to my Good God!–to leave London in about 8–or, 10 Days more, & take me a Wife–(one Miss Cullen–) of Soham in Cambridge shire–& when I have given her about 8 or 10 Days Comfort, I mean Directly to go Scotland–and sell my 5th. Editions–I Trust that my going about has been of much use to the Cause of the abolition of the accu[r]sed Slave Trade–a Gentleman of the Committee the Revd. Dr. Baker has said that I am more use to the Cause than half the People in the Country–I wish to God, I could be so. A noble Earl of Stanhope has Lately Consulted me twice about a Bill which his Ld.ship now mean[s] to bring in to the House to allow the sable People in the wt Indias the Rights of taking an oath against any White Person–I hope it may Pass, tis high time–& will be of much use.

May the Lord Bless all the friends of Humanity. Pray Pardon what ever you here see amiss–I will be Glad to see you at my Wedg.–Pray give my best Love To the Worthy & Revd. Mr. Robinson, & his–also to my friends Coltman–and Mr. & Mrs. Buxton–I Pray that the Good Lord may make all of that family Rich in faith as in the things of this World–I have [a] Great Deal to say if I ever have the Pleasure to see you again–I have been in the uttermust hurry ever since I have be[en] in this wickd. Town.–& I only came now to save if I can, £232, I Lent to a man, who [is] now Dying. Pray Excuse ha[ste] –will be Glad to hear from you–& do very much beg your Prayers as you ever have mine–& if I see you no more here Below may I see you all at Last at Gods Right Hand– here parting will be no more–Glory to God that J. Christ is yet all,

& in all, to my Poor Soul–
    I am with all Due Respects
        yours to Command–
            Gustavus Vassa
                The African
    –at Mr. Hardys No. 4 Taylors Building
    Chandos street, Covent Garden

[Reverse side]
London twenty seventh February 1792
The Revd. G. Walker
P.S. you see how I am confused–Pray excuse this mistake of the
frank–for Mr. Houseman
Pray mind the Africans from the Pulpits

10. Letter to Thomas Hardy, 28 May 1792[15]

National Archives, Kew, England: TS 24/12/2.

Edinburg May 28th.–1792
Dr. Sir, &c. &c.

   With Respect I take this oppertunity to acquaint you (by Mr. Ford–an acquaintance of mine who is to go to Day for London) that I am in health–hope that you & Wife [are] well–have sold books at Glasgow & Paisley, & came here on the 10th. ult. I hope next month to go to Dunde[e], Perth, & Aberdeen.–Sir, I am sorry to tell you that some Rascal or Rascals have asserted in the news pa[r]pers viz. Oracle of the 25th. of april, & the Star. 27th.–that I am a native of a Danish Island, Santa Cruz, in the Wt. Indias. The assertion has hurted the sale of my Books–I have now the aforesaid Oracle & will be much obliged to you to get me the Star, & take care of it till you see or

or hear from me — Pray ask Mr. & mrs Peters who Lodged in the next droom to me, if they have found a Little round Gold brest Buchel, or broach, sett in fine stones. if they have, I will pay them well for it.–& if they have found it pray write to me on that account Directly. & if tis not found you need not write on that account (& the Direction is to me, to be Left at the Post office here) my best respect to my fellow members of your society. I hope they do yet incr ase. I do not hear in this place that there is any such society.–I think Mr. Star Mathews in Glasgow told me that there was (or is) some there —Sir. on Thursday the 24. Inst. I was in the General assembly of the Church of Scotland, now Convened & it was wraped up in a bit of paper.—&

National Archives, Kew, England: TS 24/12/2.

hear from me–Pray ask Mr. & Mrs. Peters who Lodged in the next Room to me, if they have found a Little Round Gold Breast Buckel, or broach, sett in, or with fine stones–if they have, I will pay them well for it.–& if they have found it pray write to me on that account Directly. & if this not found you need not write on that account–(& the Direction is to me, to be left at the Post Office here.) My best Respect to my fellow members of your society. I hope they do yet increase. I do not hear in this place that there is any such societys–I think Mr. Alexr. Mathews in Glasgow told me that there was (or is) some there–Sir. On Thursday the 24th. Inst.– I was in the General assembely of the Church of Scotland, now Convened,

National Archives, Kew, England: TS 24/12/2.

& they agreed unanimously on a petition, or an address to the House of Lords to abolish the Slave Trade–& on which account I gave them an address of thanks in two news papers which is well Recd. I find the Scotchmen is not Like the Irish–or English–nor yet in their Houses–which is to High–Especially here. But thanks to God the Gospel is Plantifully preached here–& the Churches, or Karks[16] is well filled–I hope the good Lord will enable me to

hear & to profit, & to hold out to the end–& keep me from all such
Rascals as I have met with in London–Mr. Lewis wrote me a Letter
within 12 Days after I Left you & acquaintd me of that villain who
owed me above 200£–Dying on the 17th. of April–& that is all the
Comfort

National Archives, Kew, England: TS 24/12/2.

1 got from him since–& now I am again obliged to slave on more than before if possible–as I have a Wife.

May God ever keep you & me from atachment to this evil World, & the things of it–I think I shall be happy when time is no more with me, as I am Resolved ever to Look to Jesus Christ–& submit to his Preordainations.

Dr. Sir, –I am with Christian Love to you & Wife–&c.

Gustavus Vassa
The African
p.s.–pray get me the Gentlemens. Magazine for April 1792 & take Care of it for me.

---

11. Letter "To the Reader," June 1792

AN invidious falsehood having appeared in the Oracle of the 25th, and the Star of the 27th of April 1792, with a view to hurt my character, and to discredit and prevent the sale of my Narrative, asserting that I was born in the Danish island of Santa Cruz, in the West Indies, it is necessary that, in this edition, I should take notice thereof, and it is only needful of me to appeal to those numerous and respectable persons of character who knew me when I first arrived in England, and could speak no language but that of Africa.

Under this appeal, I now offer this edition of my Narrative to the candid reader, and to the friends of humanity, hoping it may still be the means, in its measure, of showing the enormous cruelties practiced on my sable brethren, and strengthening the generous emulation now prevailing in this country, to put a speedy end to a traffic both cruel and unjust.

Edinburgh, June 1792.[17]

12. Letter of Thanks to Quaker Subscriber, Stanley Pumphrey, 1 July 1793[18]

Dr. Friends &c. / This with my best Respts. Hope thou are well–& got the 7 Books I sent on Friday Last if the parcel did not come, pray write to me–Directly be the return of the Post–& Direct to me at Mr. John Mountains–Grocer–& if thou have recd. The above–I think there is no need of Writing–I am exceeding much obliged to thee for thy very kind Letter to the friends here, they have been very kind to me in going about with me–& by Saturday night we had sold (or engaged) 53 Books which is all Delivered to Day. I go from here tomorrow for Gloucester–& are much obliged to thee for all favours & also to those friends here which thou made mention of. & they went with me to several of their neighbours–may my God ever hear my Prayers & reward you all for every Kindness to me & the Sable People–

13. Letter to Josiah Wedgwood, 21 August 1793[19]

London, August 21st, 1793
Dr. & Worthy Sir, &c.

I am with great respects–hope you are Well.

Dr. Sir I hope you do remember that you did once tell me, if that I was to be molested by the press gang to Write to Mr. Phillip Steven–at the Admiralty–I will now take it a great favour to inform me, if I may act so in Case I am molested–I mean next Week to be in Bristol where I have some of my narrative engaged–& I am very apt to think I must have enemys there—on the account of my Publick spirit to put an end to Slavery–or reather [sic] in being active to have the Slave Trade Abolished. Dr. Sir, I leave London on friday the 23d. inst. therefore will take it a particular favour if you will be kind enough as to Direct to me few Lines at the post office—till Calld. for–Bristol.

Worthy sir, &c. &c.

I am with all Due respt.

ever yrs. To Command &c.

Gustavus Vassa

The African

14. Letter to Mr. or Mrs. Liversege, Linen Draper, Ipswich, 20 June 1794[20]

Wellcome Library, London.

Colchester June 20th 94

Very Worthy friends &c.

This with my innate respect to you & Wife–& also to my dear friends Peckovers–pray show them this Letter as he wish'd me to write to him. Give my love to them. Mr. & Mrs. Ransome – &c. & tell them I mean to write to them when I have used their kind Letter to Kelvedon which may be on Thursday next God willing.

I make no doubt but you have heard of the false report which the Sons of Belial have raised of Late in saying that the Kings messengers were in quest of me, & my friends here persuaded me to go to London.

London. – So I did & inquired of Gent. men in Power – & my friends – & they went to the privy Councill & were told yt there was not any messenge. after me – So I went to Soham to see my family which is well. I Left them ten days past & are again Selling the Last 110 Copies of my narrative – which I hope to sell against I go from Chelmsford –

I came here yesterday – & mean to go from here about Tuesday next. & will be glad to hear from any of you my friends – if you write Direct to me at John Banks high Street. Colchester –

Dear friend. I remain with all Due respects ever yrs &c &c.

Gustavus Vassa

The African –

Wellcome Library, London.

—so I did & inquired of Gentlemen in Power–my friends–& they went to the Privy Council & were told that there was not any messengers after me. So I went to Soham to see my family which is well. I left them ten days past & are again selling the Last 110 Copies of my narrative–which I hope to sell against I go from Chelmsford.

I came here yesterday & I mean to go from here about Tuesday next, & will be glad to hear from any of you my friends–if you write direct to me at John Banks High Street, Colchester–

Dear Friends–I remain with all due respects ever yrs &c &c.

Gustavus Vassa
The African

Wellcome Library, London.

Pray give these Lines to Mr William Nortcoft or Mr John Taylor–

Colchester June the 20th. Gust. Vassa send[s] his best respects to Mr. John Taylor & Mr. William Nortcoft & family & the Revd. Mr. L. Atkinson & Wife hope they are well.

Adieu &c.

15. Letter to Reverend Peter Peckard, undated[21]

The Revd Dr. Peckard

Very kind & worthy Sir.–
This with my Dutiful Respect–pray pardon this Liberty of mine in Disturbing you. I will take it a Particular favour if you will be kind enough to see me a minute or two–
Very kind & Worthy Sir–
I am with all Due Respects

Gustavus Vassa

SECTION 2
Vassa and Other Africans

This section features two documents that establish Vassa's relationship with other Africans. Vassa was a prominent member of the group known as the Sons of Africa, which disseminated information about the evils of slavery and racial discrimination. The Sons of Africa wrote letters of thanks to key supporters, such as the Quakers (document 1) and Granville Sharp (document 2).

1. Address of Thanks to the Gentlemen Called Friends or Quakers, in Gracechurch–Court Lombard–Street, 21 October 1785[22]

© Religious Society of Friends in Britain.

To the truly worthy Society of Gentlemen called Friends
GENTLEMEN,

By reading your Book, entitled a Caution to great Britain and her Colonies, concerning the Calamitous State of the enslaved Negroes–We the poor, oppressed, needy, and much–degraded Africans who are here met desire to approach you with this address of thanks, with our inmost love and warmest acknowledgments and with the deepest sense of your benevolence, unwearied labour, and kind interposition and laudible attempts which under God you have made towards breaking the yoke of slavery, and to administer a little comfort and ease to thousands and tens of thousands of very grievously afflicted, and too heavy burthened negroes. Gentlemen, could you, by perseverance, at last be enabled, under God, to lighten in any degree the heavy burthen of the afflicted, no doubt it will, in some measure, be the possible means of saving the souls of many of the oppressors–and, if so, sure we are that the God, whose eyes are ever upon all his creatures, and ever rewards every true act of virtue and regards the prayers of the oppressed, will give to you and yours those blessings which are not in the power of the mortals to express or conceive which we as a part of those captivated oppressed and afflicted people, most earnestly wish and pray for.

Presented by Gustavus Vassa and Seven others the 21st Oct 1785.

2. Address of Thanks of the Sons of Africa to the Honourable Granville Sharp, Esq, 15 December 1787[23]

Honourable and Worthy Sir,   December 15, 1787.

Give us leave to say, that every virtuous man is a truly honourable man; and he doth good hath honour himself: and many blessings are upon the head of the just, and their memory shall be blessed, and their works praise them in the gate.

And we must say, the we, who are in part, or descendants, of the much wronged people of Africa, are peculiarly and greatly indebted to you, for the many good and friendly services that you have done towards us, and which are now even out of our power to enumerate.

Nevertheless, we are truly sensible of your great kindness and humanity; and we cannot do otherwise but endeavour, with the utmost sincerity, and thankfulness, to acknowledge our great obligations to you, and, with the most feeling sense of our hearts, on all occasions to express and manifest our gratitude and love for your long, valuable, and indefatiguable labours and benevolence towards using every means to rescue our suffering brethren in slavery.

Your writings, Sir, are not of trivial matters, but of great and essential things of moral and religious importance, worthy the regard of all men; and abound with many great and precious things, of sacred writ, particularly respecting the laws of God, and the duties of men.

Therefore, we wish, for ourselves and others, that these valuable treatises may be collected and preserved, for the benefit and good of all men, and for an enduring memorial of the great learning, piety, and vigilance of our good friend the worthy Author. And we wish that the laws of God, and his ways of righteousness set forth therein, may be as a path for the virtuous and prudent to walk in, and as a clear shining light to the wise in all ages; and that these and other writings of that nature, may be preserved and established as a monument or beacon to guide or to warn men, lest they should depart from the paths of justice and humanity; and that they may more and more become means of curbing the vicious violators of God's holy law, and to restrain the avarice invaders of the rights and liberties of men, whilever the human race inhabits this earth below.

And every honourable and worthy Sir, may the blessing and peace of Almighty God be with you, and long preserve your valuable life, and make you abundantly useful in every good word and work! And when God's appointed time shall come, may your exit be blessed, and may you arise and for ever shine in the glorious world above, when that Sovereign Voice, speaking with joy, as the sound of many waters, shall be heard, saying, "Well done, thou good and faithful servant: enter thou into the joy of thy Lord!" It will then be the sweetest of all delights for ever, and more melodious than all music! And such honour and felicity will the blessed God and Savior of his people bestow upon all the saints and faithful servants who are redeemed from among men, and saved from sin, slavery, misery, pain, and death, and from eternal dishonour and wrath depending upon the heads of all the wicked and rebellious.

And now, honourable Sir, with the greatest submission, we must beg you to accept this memorial of our thanks for your good and faithful service towards us, and for your humane commiseration of our brethren and countrymen unlawfully held in slavery.

And we have hereunto subscribed a few of our names, as a mark of our gratitude and love. And we are, with the greatest esteem, and veneration, honourable and worthy. Sir, your most obliged and most devoted humble servants.

OTTOBAH CUGOANO.
JOHN STUART.
GEORGE ROBERT MANDEVILLE.
WILLIAM STEVENS.
JOSEPH ALMAZE.
BOUGHWA GEGANSMEL.

JASPER GOREE.
GUSTAVUS VASSA.
JAMES BAILEY.
THOMAS OXFORD.
JOHN ADAMS.
GEORGE WALLACE.

SECTION 3
Letters to Vassa

This section contains three examples of letters that Vassa received. The letter to Vassa from the Officers and Commissioners of His Majesty's Navy is about his employment as Commissary of Provisions and Stores for the Black Poor to Sierra Leone (document 1). The letter from Susannah Atkinson expresses her disappointment at not meeting Vassa while he was in Mould Green (document 2). Lastly, Josiah Wedgwood's letter expresses concern for Vassa's safety (document 3).

1. Letter "By the principal Officers and Commissioners of his Majesty's Navy," 16 January 1787[24]

WHEREAS you were directed, by our warrant of the 4th of last month, to receive into your charge from Mr. Irving the surplus provisions remaining of what was provided for the voyage, as well as the provisions for the support of the black poor, after the landing at Sierra Leone, with the cloathing, tools, and all other articles provided at government's expense; and as the provisions were laid in at the rate of two months for the voyage, and for four months after the landing, but the number embarked being so much less than was expected, whereby there may be a considerable surplus of provisions, cloathing, &c. These are, in addition to former orders, to direct and require you to appropriate or dispose of such surplus to the best advantage you can for the benefit of government, keeping and rendering to us a faithful account of what you do herein. And for your guidance in preventing any white persons going, who are not intended to have the indulgences of being carried thither, we send you herewith a list of those recommended by the Committee for the black poor as proper persons to be permitted to embark, and acquaint you that you are not to suffer any others to go who do not produce a certificate from the committee for the black poor, of their having their permission for it. For which this shall be your warrant. Dated at the Navy Office, January 16, 1787.

To Mr. Gustavus Vassa, Commissary of Provisions and Stores for the Black Poor to Sierra Leona.
J. HINSLOW,
GEO. MARSH,
W. PALMER.

---

2. Letter from Susannah Atkinson, Mould Green, 29 March 1791[25]

Since my much valued Friend did not receive the few lines directed to Halifax—and since my Husband has come Home and informed me you wish'd to have a few lines from me—I could not think of going to Manchester without leaving you a few lines—hoping you are *here* to receive it for tho' your Friend Susannah Atkinson will not be here to see you—yet she leaves her *Law* who will always meet *you,* my Friend[,] with pleasure—nor will *he* be the only one who will see you here with pleasure—Miss Frith who is so kind as to become my housekeeper—will be also glad to see you—I am sorry to hear you are low—suffer yourself not to be hurt with triffles *[sic]* since you must in this transitory and deceitful World [you must CROSSED OUT] meet with many unpleasing changes—I was sorry we should be so unfortunate as to recommend you to any who should in the least slight you—which seem'd to be the case at Elland—but I sincerely hope you have since experienced that friendship and civility from those you have been with—which has amply made up for the treatment you there received—but you have a friend above who can afford you more *real* comfort than Mortals here can give—not but friends are a Blessing—and afford that comfort—which I hope you will *never* want—but it is I believe absolutely necessary that we should meet with rebuffs—otherwise our Affections would be wholly placed *here*—which would in the end prove our destruction—but I ought to check my pen, as you have seen more of the World than me—and must of course know how to place a proper dependence on both God and Man—may he ever direct and watch over you—fear not—those who depend on *him* he will defend—and also in *the end befriend*—should I ever be so happy to see you again—(and I hope and trust I shall) I hope I need not say how happy I shall always be to see you—this I flatter myself you are assured of—I thank you for your picture—believe me we shall value it much—we will have it Framed—and hung with our own Family who are doing now—I hope you *may* see it— it wont be done the next time you come—but hope you will see it the time *after* next—till then may God preserve and Guide you— and believe me to be *ever* sincerely your well wisher—and Friend—Susannah Atkinson N.B. Miss Haigh and Cousin Tinkler [?] leave their Respects.

---

3. Letter from Josiah Wedgwood, 19 September 1793[26]

[Endorsed Sept. 19, 1793]

Dear Sir

Your letter of the 21st of Augt came here in due course & would have been answd sooner but I have been from home for five weeks.

When I was in London if you had been molested by any press gang I would have applied personally to Mr Stevens in your behalf,

& might have procured you relief before they had time to carry you away, but your writing from Bristol[27] in case of an accident of that kind would not I fear have the same effect.

I hope you will not be in any danger, but if it should be otherwise you may direct a letter to Mr. Byerley No. 5 Greek St. Soho acquainting him with your situation & he will take the necessary steps with Mr Stevens in your favor.

With best wishes for your health & safety

I am Sr. your frd & servt

JW

SECTION 4

Character References, Letters of Introduction, and Letters of Recommendation

This section includes fourteen character references, letters of introduction, and letters of recommendation. Robert King wrote a reference for Vassa on 26 July 1767 (document 1), and Dr. Charles Irving wrote another in mid-June 1777 (document 2). These references were evidence of Vassa's status as a free man, eligible to be hired in various capacities. In March of 1779, former Governor of the Province of Senegambia, Mathias Macnamara, and Macnamara's assistant, Thomas Wallace, both wrote references in support of Vassa's application to the Right Rev. Robert Lowth, Lord Bishop of London, for an appointment as missionary to Africa (documents 3 and 4). These character references and the numerous letters of introduction and recommendation attest to the acceptance of Vassa, his qualifications, and his cause. Vassa included these documents in the prefaces to the various editions of his *Interesting Narrative*.[28]

The letters of reference reveal that he visited Cambridge in 1789 (document 5) and Cambridge, Birmingham, Sheffield, and Nottingham in the following year (documents 6, 7, 8, and 9). From these letters, we also know that Vassa was in Belfast on Christmas day 1791 (document 10), that he visited Durham and Hull in 1792 (documents 11 and 12), that he was at Bath and Devizes in 1793 (document 13), and that he was in Sudbury in 1794 (document 14).

1. Character Reference from Robert King, 26 July 1767[29]

Montserrat, 26th of July, 1767.

The bearer hereof, Gustavus Vasa, was my slave for upwards of three years, during which he has always behaved himself well, and discharged his duty with honesty and assiduity.

ROBERT KING

To all whom this may concern

2. Character Reference from Dr. Charles Irving, mid-June 1776[30]

The bearer, Gustavus Vassa, has served me several years with strict honesty, sobriety, and fidelity. I can therefore, with justice recommend him for these qualifications; and indeed in every respect I consider him as an excellent servant. I do hereby certify that he always behaved well, and that he is perfectly trust–worthy.

CHARLES IRVING.

3. Character Reference from Mathias MacNamara, Former Governor, Province of Senegambia, 11 March 1779[31]

My Lord,

I have resided near seven years on the coast of Africa, for most part of the time as commanding officer. From the knowledge I have of the country and its inhabitants, I am inclined to think that the within plan will be attended with great success, if countenanced by your Lordship. I beg leave further to represent to your Lordship, that the like attempts, when encouraged by other governments, have met with uncommon success; and at this very time I know a very respectable character, a black priest, at Cape Coast Castle. I know the within named Gustavus Vassa, and believe him a moral good man.

I have the honour to be,
    My Lord,
        Your Lordship's
            humble and obedient servant,
Grove, 11th March, 1779.
MATT. MACNAMARA.

4. Character Reference from Thomas Wallace, Former Employee of the Province of Senegambia, 13 March 1779[32]

March 13, 1779.

My Lord,
    I have resided near five years on Senegambia on the coast of Africa, and have had the honour of filling very considerable employments in that province. I do approve of the within plan, and think the undertaking very laudable and proper, and that it deserves your Lordship's protection and encouragement, in which case it must be attended with the intended success. I am, My Lord,
    Your Lordship's
        Humble and obedient servant,
        THOMAS WALLACE
Ninth edition, 1794

5. Letter of Introduction from Thomas Clarkson to the Reverend Thomas Jones, Master of Trinity College, Cambridge University, 9 July 1789[33]

Dear Sir

I take the Liberty of introducing to your Notice Gustavus Vassa, the Bearer, a very honest, ingenious, and industrious African, who wishes to visit Cambridge. He takes with him a few Histories containing his own Life written by himself, of which he means to dispose to defray his Journey. Would you be so good as to recommend the Sale of a few and you will confer a Favour on your already obliged and obedt Servt

Thomas Clarkson

6. Letter of Recommendation from Reverend Peckard of Cambridge to the Chairmen of the Committee for the Abolition of the Slave Trade, 26 May 1790[34]

Magdalen College, Cambridge, May 26 1790.
GENTLEMEN,

I TAKE the liberty, as being joined with you in the same laudable endeavours to support the cause of humanity in the Abolition of the Slave Trade, to recommend to your protection the bearer of this note, GUSTAVUS VASSA, an African; and to bed the favour of your assistance to him in the sale of his book.

I am, with great respect,

GENTLEMEN,

Your most obedient servant,

P. PECKARD.

7. Letter of Recommendation from Thomas Walker, 23 July 1790[35]

THOMAS WALKER has the great pleasure in recommending the sale of the NARRATIVE of GUSTAVUS VASSA to the friends of justice and humanity, he being well entitled to their protection and support, from the united testimonies of the Rev. T. Clarkson of London; Dr. Peckard, of Cambridge; and Sampson and Charles Lloyd, Esqrs. of Birmingham.

Manchester, July 23, 1790.

8. Letter of Recommendation to the Friends of Humanity in the Town and Neighbourhood of Sheffield, 20 August 1790[36]

In consequence of the recommendation of Dr. Peckard, of Cambridge; Messrs. Lloyd, of Brimingham; the Rev. T. Clarkson, of London; Thomas Walker, Thomas Cooper, and Isaac Moss, Esqrs. of Manchester, we beg leave also to recommend the sale of the NARRATIVE of GUSTAVUS VASSA to the friends of humanity in the town and neighbourhood of Sheffield.

Dr. Brown,   Rev. Ja. Wilkinson,
Wm Shore, Esq.   Rev. Edw. Goodwin,
Samuel Marshall,   John Barlow.

Sheffield, August 20, 1790.

9. Letter of Recommendation, Nottingham, 17 January 1791[37]

IN consequence of the respectable recommendation of several gentlemen of the first character, who have born testimony to the good sense, intellectual improvements, and integrity of GUSTAVUS VASSA, lately of that injured and oppressed class of men, the injured Africans; and further convinced of the justice of his recommendations, from our own personal interviews with him, we take the liberty also to recommend the said GUSTAVUS VASSA to the protection and assistance of the friends of humanity.

Rev. G. Walker,	F. Wakefield,
John Morris,	T. Bolton,
Joseph Rigsby, Rector St. Peter's,	Thomas Hawksley,
Samuel Smith,	S. White, M.D.
John Wright,	J. Hancock.

10. Letter to Mr. O'Brien, Carrickfergus, Per Favour of Mr. Gustavus Vassa, from Thomas Atwood Digges, 25 December 1791[38]

Belfast, December 25, 1791
Dear Sir,

The bearer of this, Mr. GUSTAVUS VASSA, an enlightened African, of good sense, agreeable manners, and of an excellent character, and who comes well recommended to this place, and noticed by the first people here, goes to–morrow for your town, for the purpose of vending some books, written by himself, which is a Narrative of his own Life and Sufferings, with some account of his native country and its inhabitants. He was torn from his relatives and country (by the more savage white men of England) at an early period in life; and during his residence in England, at which time I have seen him, during my agency for the American prisoners, with Sir William Dolben, Mr. Granville Sharp, Mr. Wilkes, and many other distinguished characters; he supported an irreproachable character, and was a principal instrument in bringing about the motion of the repeal of the Slave–Act. I beg leave to introduce him to your notice and civility; and if you can spare the time, your introduction of him personally to your neighbours may be of essential benefit to him.

>   I am,
>   SIR,
>   Your obedient servant,
>   THOS. DIGGES

---

11. Letter to Rowland Webster, Esq. Stockton (Per Favour of Mr. Gustavus Vassa), 25 October 1792[39]

DEAR SIR,

I TAKE the liberty to introduce to your knowledge Mr. GUS-TAVUS VASSA, an African of distinguished merit. He has recommendations to Stockton, and I am happy in adding to the number. To the principal supporters of the Bill for the Abolition of the Slave Trade he is well known; and he has, himself, been very instrumental in promoting the plan so truly conducive to the interests of religion and humanity. Mr. VASSA has published a Narrative which clearly delineates the iniquity of that unnatural and destructive commerce; and I am able to assert, from my own experience, that he has not exaggerated in a single particular. This work has been mentioned in very favourable terms by the Reviewers, and fully demonstrates that genius and worth are not limited to country or complexion. He has with him some copies for sale, and if you can conveniently assist him in the disposal thereof, you will greatly oblige,

> DEAR SIR,
> Your friend and humble servant,
> WILLIAM EDDIS.

Durham, October 25, 1792.

12. Letter of Recommendation to the Friends of Humanity In Hull, 12 November 1792[40]

Hull, November 12, 1792

THE bearer hereof, Mr. GUSTAVUS VASSA, an African, is recommended to us by the Rev. Dr. Peckard, Dean of Peterborough, and by many other very respectable characters, as an intelligent and upright man; and as we have no doubt but the accounts we have received are grounded on the best authority, we recommend him to the assistance of the friends of humanity in this town, in promoting the subscriptions to an interesting Narrative of his Life.

John Sykes, Mayor,   R.A. Harrison, Esq.
Thomas Clarke, Vicar,   Jos. R. Pease, Esq.
William Hornby, Esq. Of Gainsborough.

13. Letter to William Hughes, Esq. Devizes, 10 October 1793[41]

DEAR SIR,

WHETHER you will consider my introducing to your acquaintance the bearer of this letter, OLAUDAH EQUIANO, the enlightened African, (or GUSTAVUS VASSA) as a liberty or favour, I shall not anticipate.

He came recommended to me by men of distinguished talents and exemplary virtue, as an honest and benevolent man; and his conversation and manners as well as his book do more than justice to the recommendation.

The active part he took in bringing about the motion for a repeal of the Slave Act, has given him much celebrity as a public man; and, in all the varied scenes of chequered life, through which he has passed, his private character and conduct have been irreproachable.

His *business* in your part of the world is to promote the sale of his book, and [it] is a part of *my business*, as a friend to the cause of humanity, to do all the little service that is in my poor power to a man who is engaged in so noble a cause as the freedom and salvation of his enslaved and unenlightened countrymen.

The simplicity that runs through his Narrative is singularly beautiful, and that beauty is heightened by the idea that it is *true*; this is all I shall say about this book, save only that I am sure those who buy it will not regret that they have laid out the price of it in the purchase.

Your notice, civility, and personal introduction of this fair minded black man, to your friends in Devizes, will be gratifying to your own feelings, and laying a considerable weight of obligation on.

DEAR SIR,

Your most obedient and obliged servant,

WILLIAM LANGWORTHY.

Bath, October 10, 1793.

14. Letter to the Inhabitants of Coggeshall, Halstead, and Bocking in Essex from John Mead Ray, Introducing Vassa and His Book, 19 June 1794[42]

Cambridgeshire Archives: 132/B3.

Sudbury, June 19, 1794

The Bearer of this / Mr. Gustavus Vassa / is a native of Africa was carried into slavery at an early period of Life has passed Through scenes most distressing and interesting is truly intelligent was recommended to me by my friend Mr. Buck of Bury who has long known him as a person of great moral worth and in this judgment of charity as a genuine disciple of our common Lord.–

The object of his journey is the disposal of a Book which contains the narrative of his life. I shall consider it as a favour if you will give him such assistance as you think proper in promoting the sale of his publication in doing which you will at the same time render very as capable assistance to a worthy man where sufferings and services (in my judgment) give him some claim on the patronage of the community.–

I am with sincere regard.
Your ob.t. Servt.
John Mead Ray

CHAPTER
III

Newspapers

This chapter comprises seven sections, all featuring documents pertaining to Vassa's interactions with the press. Section 1 contains eight documents relating to the Sierra Leone Commission. Section 2 includes nine letters and writings by Vassa and the "Sons of Africa" against the slave trade. Section 3 consists of four book reviews Vassa published in the press. Section 4 contains sixteen advertisements for his *Interesting Narrative* published in newspapers across Britain. Section 5 contains four reviews of *The Interesting Narrative* published by Vassa's contemporaries. Section 6 consists of seven letters Vassa wrote to newspapers, addressed in particular to printers and town inhabitants in the places that he had visited. Lastly, Section 7 includes nine additional documents relating to the press.

SECTION 1
Vassa and the
Sierra Leone Commission

This section contains eight documents relating to Vassa's appointment as Commissary for the Black Poor. His position was announced in December 1786 in *The Morning Herald* (document 1). Three months later, Thomas Thompson wrote a letter denouncing his conduct (document 2), after which Vassa was dismissed. The debate that ensued in the press is indicated in the 4 April 1787 article published in the *Public Advertiser* (document 4). Vassa's letter to Ottobah Cugoano (known by the name of Mr. John Stewart), dated 24 March 1787 (document 3), was also published in the *Public Advertiser* on 4 April 1787, as were two criticisms of his behavior on 11 and 14 April (documents 5 and 6). He responded to these criticisms on 12 May 1787 (document 7). Two months later, Reverend Patrick Fraser published a letter in the press that accused Vassa of "antiwhite racism."[1] Vassa responded to these accusations on 14 July 1787 (document 8).

1. *The Morning Herald*, 29 December 1786[2]

We hear from authority that a Meeting of the Black Poor was to have been held in Whitechapel on Wednesday [27 December], composed of those who are ... to go to Africa. ... The Committee [for the Relief of the Black Poor] and Agent [Irwin], however, interfered, and prevented their intended discussion of that Subject, in such great numbers. ... Some of them applied again yesterday to Lord George Gordon. ... A ministerial paper having denied that our intelligence on this subject is not true, it now behooves us to mention the name of the person. ... It is Gustavus Vasa, an African from Guinea ... the Commissary of the Expedition.

2. Letter from Thomas Boulden Thompson, 21 March 1787[3]

Nautilus, Plymouth Sound, March 21, 1787.

Gentlemen,

I am sorry to be under the necessity of complaining to you of the conduct of Mr Gustavus Vasa, which has been, since he held the situation of Commissary, turbulent, & discontented, taking every means to actuate the minds of the Blacks to discord: & I am convinced that unless some means are taken to quell his spirit of sedition, it will be fatal to the peace of the settlement; & dangerous to those intrusted with the guiding it.

I am equally chagrined to say that I do not find Mr Irwin the least calculated to conduct this business; as I have never observed any wish of his to facilitate the sailing of the ships, or any steps taken by him which might indicate that he has the welfare of the people the least at heart —

305

National Archives, Kew, England: T 1/643, no. 681, f. 87.

Nautilus, Plymouth Sound, March 21st, 1787.

Gentlemen,

I am sorry to be under the necessity of complaining to you of the conduct of Mr. Gustavus Vasa, which has been, since he held the situation of Commissary,–turbulent, & discontented, taking every means to actuate the minds of the Blacks to discord: & I am convinced that unless some means are taken to quell his spirit of sedition, it will be fatal to the peace of the settlement, & dangerous to those intrusted with the guiding it.

I am equally chagrined to say that I do not find Mr. Irwin the least calculated to conduct this business: as I have never observed any wish of his to facilitate the sailing of the Ships, or any steps taken by him which might indicate that he had the welfare of the people the least at heart.–

The general conduct of the Blacks, since the Transports have been under my orders, has been troublesome & discontented, I have taken such methods as I could, to keep them in order, but as these have yet failed, I fear, as I am not authorized to take any rigorous steps, unless You interfere, the people who are instructed with the care of them, will be inadequate to accomplish the designs of Government. As Mr. Irwin the director, has declared to me his intention of leaving the Ships, & going immediately to London, I beg to know your instructions how I am to act, & have the honor to be, Gentlemen, &c. &c. &c.

Tho B.n Thompson.

Attested
Geo. March

To the Principal Officers
& Commissioners of His Majesty's Navy.

National Archives, Kew, England: T 1/643, no. 681, f. 87.

The general conduct of the Blacks, since the Transports have been under my orders, has been troublesome & discontented, I have taken such methods as I could, to keep them in order, but as these have yet failed, I fear, as I am not authorized to take any rigorous steps, unless You interfere, the people who are instrusted with the care of them, will be inadequate to accomplish the designs of Government.

As Mr. Irwin the director, has declared to me his intention of leaving the Ships, & going immediately to London, I beg to know your instructions how I am to act, & have the honor to be, Gentlemen, &c: &c: &c:

Tho[mas] B[oulde]n Thompson
Attested.
Geo[rge] Marsh
to The Principal Officers
& Commissioners of His Majesty's Navy.

---

3. *The Public Advertiser*, 4 April 1787[4]

We are sorry to find that his Majesty's Commissary for the African Settlement [Vassa] has sent the following letter to Mr. John Stewart [Ottobah Cugoano], Pall Mall:

At Plymouth, March 24, 1787.

Sir,

These with my respects to you. I am sorry you and some more are not with us. I am sure [Joseph] Irwin, and [Patrick] Fraser the Parson, are great villains and Dr. Currie. I am exceeding much aggrieved at the conduct of those who call themselves gentlemen. They now mean to serve (or use) the blacks the same as they do in the West Indies. For the good of the settlement I have borne every affront that could be given, believe me, without giving the least occasion, or even yet resenting any.

By Sir Charles Middleton's letter to me, I now find Irwin and Fraser have wrote to the Committe and the Treasury, that I use the white people with arrogance, and the blacks with civility, and stir them up to mutiny: which is not true, for I am the greatest peace–maker that goes out. The reason for this lie is, that in the presence of these two I acquainted Captain [Thomas Boulden] Thompson of the Nautilus sloop, our convoy, that I would go to London and tell of their roguery; and further insisted on Captain Thompson to come on board of the ships, and see the wrongs done to me and the people; so Captain Thompson came and saw it, and ordered the things to be given according to contract–which is not yet done in many things–and many of the black people have died for want of their due. I am grieved in every respect. Irwin never meant well to the people, but self–interest has ever been his end: twice this week [the Black Poor] have taken him, bodily to the Captain, to complain of him, and I have done it four times.

I do not know how this undertaking will end; I wish I had never been involved in it, but at times I think the Lord will make me very useful at last.

I am, dear Friend,
With respect, yours,
"G. VASA."
The Commissary for the Black Poor.

---

4. *The Public Advertiser*, 4 April 1787[5]

We find his Majesty's servants have taken away the Commissary's commission from Vasa. He came up from Plymouth to complain, and is now gone back again to take his effects on shore. The memorials [written petitions and/or statements of facts] of all the Black people, which they have sent up from Plymouth, represent that they are much wronged, injured, and oppressed natives of Africa, and under various pretences and different manners, have been dragged away from London, and carried captives to Plymouth, where they have nothing but slavery before their eyes, should they proceed to Africa or the West–Indies under the command of the persons who have the charge of them–That many of them served under Lord Dunmore, and other officers in America, in the British army–Also on board the British Fleet in the West–Indies–That the contract on Mr. Smeathman's plan to settle them in Africa, has not been fulfilled in their favour, but a Mr. Irwin has contrived to monopolize the benefit to himself–That they fear a right plan has not been formed to settle them in Africa with any prospect of happiness to themselves, or any hope of future advantage to Great–Britain.–They cannot conceive, say they, that Government would establish a free colony for them, whilst it supports its forts and factories to wrong and ensnare, and to carry others of their colour and country into slavery and bondage–They are afraid that their doom would be to drink the bitter water, and observe that it would be their prudence and safety to take warning from the cautions in Scripture:–"Doth a fountain send forth at the same place sweet water and bitter?"–That they say the design of some in sending them away, is only to get rid of them at all events, come of them afterwards what will.–In that perilous situation they see themselves surrounded with difficulties and danger; and what gives them the most dreadful presage of their fate is that the white men set over them have shewn them no humanity or good–will, but have conspired to use them unjustly before they quitted the English coast–And that they had better swim to shore, if they can, to preserve their lives and liberties in Britain, than to hazard themselves at Sea with such enemies to their welfare, and the peril of settling at Sierra Leona under their government.

5. *The Public Advertiser*, 11 April 1787[6]

The Public will naturally suspend their disbelief as to the improbable tales propagated concerning the Blacks, especially as the cloven foot of the author of these reports is perfectly manifest. That one of the persons employed in conducting those poor people is discharged, is certainly true, his own misconduct having given too good reason for his dismission. The blacks have never refused to proceed on the voyage but the ships have been delayed at Plymouth by an accidental damage which one of them received in a gale of wind. To sum up all, should the expedition prove unsuccessful, it can only be owing to the over–care of the committee, who, to avoid the most distant idea of compulsion, did not even subject the Blacks to any government, except such as they might choose themselves. And among such ill–informed people, this delicacy may have fatal consequences.

X

6. *The Public Advertiser*, 14 April 1787[7]

The expedition of the Blacks to Sierra Leone is not the least retarded by the dismission of V–the Black who was appointed to superintend the Blacks.

The assertions made by that man that the Blacks were treated as badly as the West–India blacks, and that he was discharged to make room for the appointment of a man who would exercise tyranny to those unfortunate men, show him to be capable of advancing falsehoods as deeply as black as his jetty face. The true reason for his being discharged, was gross misbehaviour, which had rendered him not only disagreeable to the officers and crew, but had likewise drawn on him the dislike of those over whom he had been appointed.

The person since appointed is the purser, a man of good character and unimpeached humanity, under whose care, for control it cannot be called, the Blacks, so far from entertaining any apprehensions, are perfectly happy.[8]

The cloven foot, as observed by a judicious correspondent X in Wednesday's paper, is perfectly manifest in the tales propagated on account of the above discharge. No man endowed with common sense can credit for a moment that the committee (all men of acknowledged humanity and honour) would give any countenance to the least ill-treatment of objects of their compassion, for whom they have endeavoured to snatch from misery and place in comfortable situations.

The proceedings of the committee do them the greatest honour and as Christians they have provided for the poor Blacks every necessary of life, and will on their arrival at Sierra Leone place them in such a situation as to enable them to live happily. Another provision they have also made for those men, and one which ought not to be forgotten; they have provided for them schoolmasters[9] to instruct them in reading and writing, and have sent out books to have them instructed in the Christian religion.[10]–Are such the measures which would have been pursued if the intention had been to enslave them? Would inculcating the principles of the Christian religion cause the so instructed tamely to submit to unchristian oppression? Or does it not seem far more probable that such measures were adopted for the purpose of inspiring the intended settlers with such elevated ideas of the blessings of liberty, as to induce them to resist any endeavour which may hereafter be made to encroach on their freedom? Let us hear no more of these *black* reports which have been industriously propagated; for if they are continued, it is rather more probable that most of the dark transactions of a *Black* will be brought to *light*.

7. Extract of Letter from Reverend Patrick Fraser on Board the Ship *Atlantic*, off Santa Cruz, Teneriffe, *London Chronicle* and the *Morning Chronicle*, 2–3 July 1787[11]

I take this opportunity of informing you, that we arrived here on Saturday last, after a most pleasant passage of 13 days from Plymouth. I have the pleasure to inform you, that we are well, and that the poor blacks are in a much more healthy state than when we left England. Vasa's discharge and the dismission of [William] Green and [Lewis] Rose [two of the black settlers], are attended with the happiest effects. Instead of that general misunderstanding under which we groaned through their means, we now enjoy all the sweets of peace, lenity, and almost uninterrupted harmony. The odious distinction of colours is no longer remembered, and all seem to conspire to promote the general good. The people are now regular in their attendance upon divine service on the Sundays, and on public prayers during the week; they do not, as formerly, absent themselves purposely on such occasions, for no other reasons whatever than that I am white. … In short, Sir, our affairs upon the whole are so much changed for the better, that I flatter myself with the pleasing hope that we may still do well, and enjoy the blessing of Providence in the intended settlement.

8. *The Public Advertiser*, 14 July 1787[12]

An extract of a letter from on board one of the ships with the Blacks, bound to Africa, having appeared on the 2nd and 3nd inst. in the public papers, wherein injurious reflexions, prejudicial to the character of Vasa, the Black Commissary, were contained, he thinks it necessary to vindicate his character from these misrepresentations, informing the public, that the principal crime which caused his dismission, was an information he laid before the Navy Board, accusing the Agent [Irwin] of unfaithfulness in his office, in not providing such necessaries as were contracted for the people, and were absolutely necessary for their existence, which necessaries could not be obtained from the Agents. The same representation was made by Mr. Vasa to Mr. Hoare, which induced the latter, who had before appeared to be Vasa's friend, to go to the Secretary of the Treasury, and procure his dismission. The above Gentleman impowered the Agent to take many passengers in, contrary to the orders given to the Commissary.

(Mr. Vasa).

SECTION 2
Vassa's Campaign against the Slave Trade

This section contains newspaper articles by Vassa and the Sons of Africa. They relate to the slave trade, were published in the press between 1788 and 1792, and are addressed to the leaders of the abolition movement. Part A contains five newspaper articles written by Vassa. He thanks members of Britain's Senate (documents 1 and 2), encourages Lord Sydney to change his position on the slave bill (document 3), and thanks both the Committee for the Abolition of the Slave Trade at Plymouth (document 4) and members of the General Assembly of the Church of Scotland (document 5).

Part B contains four articles by Vassa and the Sons of Africa. On behalf of themselves and other Africans, they praise William Dickson for his book publication (document 9), and thank William Dolben (document 6), William Pitt (document 7), and Charles James Fox (document 8).

Part A. Vassa

---

1. Letter from "Aethiopianus," *The Public Advertiser*, 13 February 1788[13]

To the Senate of GREAT BRITAIN.

Gentlemen,

May Heaven make you what you should be, the dispensers of light, liberty and science to the uttermost parts of the earth; then will be glory to God on the highest—on earth peace and goodwill to man:—Glory, honour, peace, &c. To every soul of man that worketh good; to the Britons first (because of them the Gospel is preached) and also to the nations: To that truly immortal and illustrious advocate of our liberty, Granville Sharp, Esq., the philanthropist and justly Reverend James Ramsay, and the much to be honoured body of gentlemen called *Friends*, who have exerted every endeavour to break the accursed Yoke of Slavery, and ease the heavy burthens of the oppressed Negroes. "Those that honour their Maker have mercy on the Poor";—and many blessing are upon the heads of the just.—May the fear of the Lord prolong their days, and cause their memory to be blessed, and may their numbers be increased, and their expectations filled with gladness, for commiserating the poor Africans, who are counted as beasts of burthen by base–minded men. May God ever open the mouths of these worthies to judge righteously, and plead the cause of the poor and the needy—for the liberal devise liberal things, and by liberal things shall stand; and they can say with the pious Job "Did I not weep for him that was in trouble? Was not my soul grieved for the Poor?"

It is this righteousness exalteth a nation, but sin is a reproach to any people.—Destruction shall be to the workers of iniquity—and the wicked shall perish by their own wickedness.—May the worthy Lord Bishop of London be blessed for his pathetic[14] and human sermon on behalf of the Africans, and all the benevolent gentlemen who are engaged in the laudable attempt to abolish Slavery, and thereby prevent many savage barbarities from being daily committed by the enslavers of men, to whom the Lord has pronounced wrath, anguish, and tribulation, &. To the sons of Britain first (as having the Gospel preached against them) and also to the nations–.

AETHIOPIANUS[15]

2. Letter from Vassa to J.R. and T.C., *The Public Advertiser*, 19 June 1788[16]

To the Honourable and Worthy Members
of the BRITISH SENATE.

Gentlemen,

Permit me, one of the oppressed natives of Africa, thus to offer you the warmest thanks of a heart glowing with gratitude for your late humane interference on behalf of my injured countrymen. May this and the next year bear record of deeds worthy of yourselves! May you then complete the glorious work you have so humanely begun in this, and with the public voice in putting an end to an oppression that now so loudly calls for redress! The wise man saith, *Prov.* xiv. 34, "Righteousness exalteth a nation, but sin is a reproach to any people." May all the noble youths I hear speak in our favour in the Senate, be renowned for illustrious deeds, and their aspiring years crowned with glory! May the all bountiful Creator, the God whose eyes are ever upon all his creatures, who ever rewards all virtuous acts, and regards the prayers of the oppressed, make you that return, which I and my unfortunate countrymen are not able to express, and shower on you every happiness this world can afford, and every fulness of which Devine Revelation has promised us in the next! Believe me, Gentlemen, while I attended your debate on the Bill for the relief of my countrymen, now depending before you, my heart burned within me, and glowed with gratitude to those who supported the cause of humanity. I could have wished an opportunity of recounting to you not only my own sufferings, which, though numerous, have been nearly forgotten, but those of which I have been a witness to for many years, that they might have influenced your decision; but I thank God, your humanity anticipated my wishes, and rendered such recital unnecessary. Our cries have at length reached your ears, and I trust you already in some measure convinced that the Slave Trade is as impolitic as inhuman, and as such must ever be unwise. The more extended our misery is, the greater claim it has to your compassion, and the greater pleasure you must feel in administering to its relief. The satisfaction, which, for the honour of human nature, this distinguished act of compassion gave you, was as visible as felt, and affected me much. From the particular favours shewed me by many of your worthy Members, especialy your honourable Chairman Mr. Whitbread, Sir P. Burrell, Sir William Dolben, the Hon. G. Pitt, &. &. I beg thus to express my most grateful acknowledgements, and I pray the good and gracious God ever to distinguish them by his choicest blessings!–And if it should please Providence to enable me to return to my estate in Elese, in Africa, and to be happy enough to see any of these worthy senators there, as the Lord liveth, we will have such a libation of pure virgin palm–wine, as shall make their hearts glad!!!–And we will erect two altar[s]–one to Pity–the other to Freedom–to perpetuate their benevolence to my countrymen.

I am, with the most devoted respect, Honourable and Most Worthy Senators, Your graceful and lowly Servant, GUSTAVUS VASSA, the African.

Baldwin's Gardens, June 18, 1788.   *J.R. and T.C.[17]

3. Letter from Vassa to Lord Sydney, *The Public Advertiser*, 28 June 1788[18]

To the Right Hon. LORD SYDNEY.[19]

My Lord,

Having been presnt last Wednesday [25 June] at the debate on the Slave Bill, now depending in the House of Lords, I with much surprize heard your Lordship combat the very principle of the Bill, and assert that it was founded in mistaken humanity. At the first, such assertion would appear rather paradoxical. If imposing a restraint on the cruelties practised towards wretches who never injured us, be mistaken humanity, what are the proper channels through which it ought to be directed? However, as your Lordship gave reasons for your opinion, I not wish either to tax your humanity or candour, but on the contrary believe you were misled by your information. Your Lordship mentioned you had been told by Captain Thompson, under whose convoy the natives of Africa were lately sent out to Sierra Leona, that shortly after their arrival there, some of them embraced the first opportunity of embarking for the West Indies, some of the Lascars, rather than work, lay down among the bushes and died, and that the humane intentions of the Government were frustrated, and the expectations of all concerned in the enterprise disappointed. Now, my Lord, without impeaching the veracity of that gentleman, or controverting the facts he related, permit me to explain the cause of the ill success of that expedition, which I hope will sufficiently obviate the interferences your Lordship drew from them.

When the intention of sending those people to Sierra Leona was first conceived, it was thought necessary by Government to send a Commissary on their part to Superintend the conduct of the Agent who had contracted for carrying them over, and I being judged a proper person for that purpose was appointed Commissary by the

Commissioners of the Navy, the latter end of 1786. In consequence I proceeded immediately to the execution of my duty on board one of the vessels destined for the voyage, where I continued till the March following.

During my continuance in the employment of the Government, I was struck with the flagrant abuses committed by the Agent, and endeavoured to remedy them, but without effect. One instance, among many which I could produce, may serve as a specimen: Government had ordered to be provided all necessaries (slops as they are called included) for 750 persons; however not being able to muster more than 426, I was ordered to send the superfluous slops, & to the King's stores at Portsmouth, but when I demanded them for that purpose from the Agent, it appeared they had never been bought, tho' paid for by the Government.–But that was not all, Government were not the only objects of peculation; these poor people suffered infinitely more–their accommodations were most wretched, many of them wanted beds, and many more cloathing and other necessaries.–For the truth of this, and much more, I do not seek credit on my assertion. I appeal to the testimony of Captain Thompson himself, to whom I applied in February 1787, for a remedy, when I had remonstrated to the Agent in vain, and even brought him to a witness of the injustice and oppression I complained of.–I appeal also to a letter written by these wretched people, so early as the beginning of the preceeding January, and published in *The Morning Herald* of the 4th of that month, signed by twenty of their Chiefs.

My Lord, I could not silently suffer Government to be thus cheated, and my countrymen plundered and oppressed, and even left destitute of the necessaries for almost their existence–I therefore informed the Commissioners of the Navy of the Agent's proceedings–but my dismission was soon after procured by means of a friend, a Banker in the City, possibly his partner in contract. By this I suffered a considerable loss in my property, and he, it is said, made his fortune; however, the Commissioners were satisfied with my conduct, and wrote to Captain Thompson, expressing their approbation of it.

Thus provided, they proceeded on their voyage, and at last worn out by treatment, perhaps not the most mild, and wasted by sickness, brought on by want of medicine, cloathes, and beddings, &. &. They reached Sierra Leone, just at the commencement of the rains–At that season of year, it is impossible to cultivate lands; their provisions therefore were exhausted before they could derive benefit from agriculture.–And it is not surprising that many, especially the Lascars, whose constitutions are very tender, and who had been cooped up in a ship from October to June, and accommodated in the manner I have mentioned, should be so wasted by their confinement as not long to survive it.–As for the native Africans who remained, there was no object for their industry; and, surely, my Lord, they shewed a much less indulgent spirit in going to the West–Indies than staying at Sierra Leona to starve.

The above facts and many more instances of oppression and injustices, not only relative to the expedition to Sierra Leona, but to the Slave Trade in general, I could incontrovertibly establish, if at any time it should be judged necessary to call upon me for that purpose.

I am, my Lord,
Your Lordship's most respectful and
Obedient Servant,
GUSTAVUS VASSA, the African.

Tottenham Street No. 13, June 26.

4. Letter from Gustavus Vassa to the Committee for the Abolition of the Slave Trade at Plymouth, *The Public Advertiser*, 14 February 1789[20]

To the Committee for the Abolition of the Slave Trade at Plymouth.

Gentlemen,

Having seen a plate representing the form in which Negroes are stowed on board the Guinea ships, which you are pleased to send to the Rev. Mr. [Thomas] Clarkson, a worthy friend of mine,[21] I was filled with love and gratitude towards you for your humane interference on behalf of my oppressed countrymen. Surely this case calls aloud for redress! May this year bear record of acts worthy of a British Senate, and you have the satisfaction of seeing the completion of the work you have so humanely assisted us in. With you I think it the indispensable duty of every friend of humanity, not to suffer themselves to be led away with the specious but false pretext drawn from the supposed political benefits this kingdom derives from the continuance of this iniquitous branch of commerce. It is the duty of every man, every friend to religion and humanity, to assist the different Committees engaged in this pious work; reflecting that it does not often fall to the lot of individuals to contribute to so important a moral and religious duty as that of putting an end to a practise which may, without exaggeration, be stiled one of the greatest evils now existing on earth.–The wise man saith, "Righteousness exalteth a nation, but sin is a reproach to any people." Prov. Xiv. 34.

Permit me, Gentlemen, on behalf of myself and my brethren, to offer you the warmest effusions of hearts over flowing with gratitude for your pious efforts, which it is my constant prayer may prove successful.

With the best wishes for health and happiness,

I am, Gentlemen,
Your obedient, humble Servant,
GUSTAVUS VASSA, the African
Feb. 7, 1789, No. 10, Union Street,
Middlesex Hospital.

---

5. Letter of Gustavus Vassa to the General Assembly of the Church of Scotland, *The Edinburgh Evening Courant*, Saturday, 26 May 1792[22]

To the GENERAL ASSEMBLY of the CHURCH OF SCOTLAND now convened.

GENTLEMEN,

PERMIT me, one of the oppressed natives of Africa, to offer you the warmest thanks of a heart glowing with gratitude on the unanimous decision of your debate of this day–It filled me with love towards you. It is no doubt the indispensable duty of every man, who is a friend to religion and humanity, to give his testimony against that iniquitous branch of commerce the slave trade. It does not often fall to the lot of individuals to contribute to so important a moral and religious duty, as that of putting an end to a practice which may, without exaggeration, be stiled one of the greatest evils now existing on the earth.–The Wise Man saith, "Righteousness exalteth a nation, but sin is a reproach to any people." Prov. xiv. 34. Gentlemen, permit me, on behalf of myself and my much oppressed countrymen, to offer you the warmest effusions of a heart overflowing with hope from your pious efforts. It is my constant prayer that these endeavours may prove successful–And with best wishes for your health, happiness temporal and spiritual, I am,

Gentlemen,

Your most respectful humble servant, &c. &c.
GUSTAVUS VASSA the African.

At Mr. M'Laren's, turner, second stair above Chalmers's Close,
High Street–where my Narrative is to be had.
Edinburgh, May 24, 1792.

Part B. Vassa and the Sons of Africa

6. Letter from Gustavus Vassa et al. to Sir William Dolben, *The Morning Chronicle, and London Advertiser*, 15 July 1788[23]

To the Honourable Sir WILLIAM DOLBEN, Bart.[24]
Sir,

We beg your permission to lay in this manner our humble thank-fulness before you, for a benevolent law obtained at your motion, by which the miseries of our unhappy brethren, on the coast of Africa, may be alleviated, and by which the lives of many, though destined for the present to a cruel slavery, may be preserved, as we hope, for future and for greater mercies.

Our simple testimony is not much, yet you will not be displeased to learn, that a few persons of colour, existing here, providentially released from the common calamity, and feeling for their kind, are daily pouring forth their prayers for you, Sir, and other noble and generous persons who will no (as we understand) longer suffer the rights of humanity to be confounded with ordinary commodities, and passed from hand to hand, as an article of trade.

We are not ignorant, however, Sir, that the best return we can make is, to behave with sobriety, fidelity, and diligence in our different stations, whether remaining here under the protection of the laws, or colonizing our native soil, as most of us wish to do, under the dominion of this country; or as free labourers and artizans in the West Indian islands, which, under equal laws, might become to men of colour places of voluntary and very general resort.

But in whatever station, Sir, having lived here, as we hope, without reproach, so we trust that we and our whole race shall endeavour to merit, by dutiful behaviour, those mercies, which, humane and benevolent minds seem to be preparing for us.

THOMAS COOPER.
GUSTAVUS VASSA.
OTTOBAH CUGOANA STEWARD.
GEORGE ROBERT MANDEVIL.
JOHN CHRISTOPHER.
THOMAS JONES.

For ourselves and Brethren

Sir W. DOLBEN is highly gratified with the kind of acceptance his endeavours to promote the liberal designs of the Legislature have met from the worthy natives of Africa; whose warm sense of benefits, and honourable resolution of showing their gratitude by their future conduct in steadiness and sobriety, fidelity, and diligence, will undoubtedly recommend them to the British Government, and he trusts, to other Christian powers, as most worthy of their further care and attention; yet as he is but one strong among many who are equally zealous for the accomplishment of this good work, he must earnestly desire to decline any particular address upon the occasion. Duke Street, Westminister, 1788.

7. Letter from Gustavus Vassa et al. to William Pitt, *The Morning Chronicle, and London Advertiser*, 15 July 1788[25]

To the Right Honourable WILLIAM PITT.

Sir,

We will not presume to trouble you with many words. We are persons of colour, happily released from the common calamity, and desirous of leaving at your door, in behalf of our Brethren, on the Coast of Africa, this simple, but graceful acknowledgement of your goodness and benevolence towards our unhappy race.

THOMAS COOPER.
GUSTAVUS VASSA.
OTTOBAH CUGOANA STEWARD.
GEORGE ROBERT MANDEVIL.
JOHN CHRISTOPHER.
THOMAS JONES.

For ourselves and Brethren.

8. Letter from Gustavus Vassa et al. to Charles James Fox, *The Morning Chronicle, and London Advertiser*, 15 July 1788[26]

To The Right Honourable CHARLES JAMES FOX.

Sir,

    We are men of colour, happily, ourselves, emancipated from a general calamity by the laws of this place, but yet feeling very sensibly of our kind, and hearing, Sir, that, in their favour, you have cooperated with the minister [Pitt], and have nobly considered the rights of humanity as a common cause, we have thereupon assumed the liberty (we hope, without offense) of leaving this simple, but honest token of our joy and thankfulness at your door.

THOMAS COOPER.
GUSTAVUS VASSA.
OTTOBAH CUGOANA STEWARD.
GEORGE ROBERT MANDEVIL.
JOHN CHRISTOPHER.
THOMAS JONES.

For ourselves and Brethren.

---

9. Letter from Gustavus Vassa et al. to William Dickson, *The Diary; or Woodfall's Register*, 25 April 1789[27]

To Mr. WILLIAM DICKSON, formerly Private Secretary to the Hon. Edward Hay, Governor of the Island of Barbadoes.[28]

Sir,

We who have perused your well authenticated Book, entitled LETTERS ON SLAVERY, think it a duty incumbent on us to confess, that in our opinion such a work cannot be too esteemed; you have given but too just a picture of the Slave Trade, and the horrid cruelties practised on the poor sable people in the West Indies, to the disgrace of Christianity. Their injury calls aloud for redress, and the day we hope is not far distant, which may record one of the most glorious acts that ever passed the British Senate—we mean an Act for the total Abolition of the Slave Trade.

It is the duty of every man who is a friend to religion and humanity (and such you have shewn yourself to be) to shew his detestation of such inhuman traffick. Thanks to God, the nation at last is awakened to a sense of our sufferings, except the Oran Otang philosophers, who we think will find it a hard task to dissect your letters. Those who can feel for the distresses of their own countrymen, will also commiserate the case of the poor Africans.

Permit us, Sir, on behalf of ourselves and the rest of our brethren, to offer you our sincere thanks for the testimony of regard you have shewn for the poor and much oppressed sable people.

With our best wishes that your praise–worthy publication may meet with the wished–for success, and may the all–bountiful Creator bless you with health and happiness, and bestow on you every blessing of time and eternity.

We are,
Sir,
Your most obedient humble servants,

OLAUDAH EQUIANO, or GUSTAVUS VASSA.
OTTOBAH CUGOANA, or JOHN S[T]UAR[T].
YAHNE AELANE, or JOSEPH SANDERS.
BROUGHWAR JOGENSMEL, or JASPER GOREE.
COJOH AMMERE, or GEORGE WILLIAMS.
THOMAS COOPER.
WILLIAM GREEK.
GEORGE MANDEVILLE.
BERNARD ELLIOT GRIFFITHS.

SECTION 3
Book Reviews by Vassa

This section comprises four reviews of books on the slave trade and issues of race—reviews that Vassa published in the press. It includes his reviews of Samuel Jackson Pratt's *Humanity, or the Rights of Nature, a Poem: in Two Books* (document 4), James Tobin's *Cursory Remarks & Rejoinder* (document 1), Gordon Turnbull's *Apology for Negro Slavery* (document 2), and Raymond Harris's *Scripture Researches on the Licitness of the Slave Trade* (document 3).

1. *The Public Advertiser*, 28 January 1788[29]

To J. T. [James Tobin] Esq; Author of the BOOKS called CUR-SORY REMARKS & REJOINDER

Sir,

That to love mercy and judge rightly of things is an honour to man, no body I think will deny; but "if he understandeth not, nor sheweth compassion to the sufferings of his fellow–creatures, he is like the beasts that perish." Psalm lix verse 20.

Excuse me, Sir, if I think you in no better predicament than that exhibited in the latter part of the above cause; for can any man less ferocious than a tiger or a wolf attempt to justify the cruelties inflicted on the negroes in the West Indies? You certainly cannot be susceptible of human pity to be so callous to their complicated woes! Who could but the Author of the Cursory Remarks so debase his nature, as not to feel his keenest pangs of heart on reading their deplorable story? I confess my cheek changes colour with resentment against your unrelenting barbarity, and wish you from my soul to run the gauntlet of Lex Talionis[30] at this time; for as you are so fond of flogging others, it is no bad proof of your deserving a flagellation yourself. Is it not written in the 15th chapter of Numbers, the 15th and 16th verses, that there is the same law for the stranger as for you?

Then, Sir, why do you rob him of the common privilege given to all by the Universal and Almighty Legislator? Why exclude him from the enjoyment of benefits which he has an equal right to with yourself? Why treat him as if he were not of like feeling? Does civilization warrant these incursions upon natural justice? No.– Does religion? No.–Benevolence to all is its essence, and do unto others as we would others do unto us, its grand precept–to Blacks as well as Whites, all being the children of the same parent. Those, therefore, who transgress those sacred obligations, and here, Mr. Remarker, I think you are caught, are not superior to brutes which understandeth not, nor to beasts which perish.

From your having been in the West Indies, you must know the facts stated by the Rev. Mr. [James] Ramsay are true; and yet regardless of the truth, you controvert them. This surely is supporting a bad cause at all events, and brandishing falsehood to strengthen the hand of the oppressor. Recollect, Sir, that you are told in the 17th verse of the 19th chapter of Leviticus, "You shall not suffer sin upon your neighbour"; and you will not I am sure, escape the upbraidings of your conscience, unless you are fortunate enough to have none; and remember also, that the oppressor and the oppressed are in the hands of the just and awful God, who says, Vengeance is mine and will repay–repay the oppressor and the justifier of the oppression. How dreadful then will your fate be? The studied and torturing punishments, inhuman, as they are, of a barbarous planter, or a more barbarous overseer, will be tenderness compared to the provoked wrath of an angry but righteous God! who will raise, I have the fullest confidence, many of the sable race to the joys of Heaven, and cast the oppressive white to that doleful place, where he will cry, but will cry in vain, for a drop of water!

Your delight seems to be in misrepresentation, else how could in page 11 of your Remarks, and in your Rejoinder, page 35, communicate to the public such a glaring untruth as that the oath of a free African is equally admissible in several courts with that of a white person? The contrary of this I know is the fact at every one of the islands I have been, and I have been at no less than fifteen. But who will dispute with such an invective fibber? Why nobody to be sure; for you'll tell, I wish I could say truths, but you oblige me to use ill manners, you lie faster than Old Nick can hear them. A few shall stare you in the face:

What is your speaking of the laws in favour of the Negroes?

Your description of the iron muzzle?

That you never saw the infliction of severe punishment, implying thereby that there is none?

That a Negro has every inducement to wish for a numerous family?

That in England there are no black labourers?

That those who are servants, are in rags or thieves?

In a word, the public can bear testimony with me that you are a malicious slanderer of an honest, industrious, injured people!

From the same source of malevolence the freedom of their inclinations is to be shackled–it is not sufficient for their bodies to be oppressed, but their minds must also? Iniquity in the extreme! If the mind of a black man conceives the passion of love for a fair female, he is to pine, languish, and even die, sooner than an intermarriage be allowed, merely because the complexion of the offspring should be tawny–A more foolish prejudice than this never warped a cultivated mind–for as no contamination of the virtues of the heart would result from the union, the mixture of colour could be of no consequence. God looks with equal good–will on all his creatures, whether black or white–let neither, therefore, arrogantly condemn the other.

The mutual commerce of the sexes of both Blacks and Whites, under the restrictions of moderation and law, would yield more benefit than a prohibition–the mind free–would not have such a strong propensity toward the black females as when under restraint: Nature abhors restraint, and for ease either evades or breaks it. Hence arise secret amours, adultery, fornication and other evils of lasciviousness! hence the most abandoned boasting of the French Planter, who, under the dominion of lust, had the shameless impudence to exult at the violations he had committed against Virtue, Religion, and the Almighty–hence also spring actual murders on infants, the procuring of abortions, enfeebled constitution, disgrace, shame, and a thousand other horrid enormities.

Now, Sir, would it not be more honour to us to have a few darker visages than perhaps yours among us, than inundation of such evils? and to provide effectual remedies, by a liberal policy against evils which may be traced to some of our most wealthy Planters as their fountain, and which may have smeared the purity of even your own chastity?

As the ground-work, why not establish intermarriages at home, and in our Colonies? And encourage open, free, and generous love upon Nature's own wide and extensive plan, subservient only to moral rectitude, without distinction of colour of a skin?

That ancient, most wise, and inspired politician, Moses, encouraged strangers to unite with the Israelites, upon this maxim, that every addition to their number was an addition to their strength, and as an inducement, admitted them to most of the immunities of his own people. He established marriage with strangers by his own example–The Lord confirmed them–and punished Aaron and Miriam for vexing their brother for marrying the Ethiopian–Away then with your narrow impolitic notion of preventing by law what will be a national honour, national strength, and productive of national virtue–Intermarriages!

Wherefore, to conclude in the words of one of your selected texts, "If I come, I will remember the deeds which he doeth, prating against us with malicious words."

I am Sir,
Your fervent Servant,
GUSTAVUS VASSA, the Ethiopian and the King's late Commissary for the African settlement.
Baldwin's Garden, Jan. 1788.

---

2. *The Public Advertiser*, 5 February 1788[31]

To MR. GORDON TURNBULL, Author of an "Apology for NEGRO SLAVERY."

Sir,

I am sorry to find in your Apology for oppression, you deviate far from the Christian precepts, which enjoin us to do unto others as we would others should do unto us. In this enlightened age, it is scarcely credible that a man should be born educated, in the British dominions, especially, possessed of minds so warped as the author of the Cursory Remarks and yourself. Strange that in a land which boasts of the purest light of the Gospel, and the most perfect freedom, there should be found advocates of oppression–for the most abject and iniquitous kind of slavery. To kidnap our fellow creatures, however they may differ in complexion, to degrade them into beasts of burthen, to deny them every right but those, and scarcely those we allow to a horse, to keep them in perpetual servitude, is a crime unjustifiable as cruel; but to avow and defend this infamous traffic required then ability and modesty of you and Mr. Tobin. Certainly, Sir, you were perfectly consistent with yourself attacking as you did that friend to the rights of mankind, the Rev. James Ramsay. Malignity and benevolence do not well associate, and humanity is a root that seldom flourishes in the soil of a planter. I am not therefore surprised that you have endeavoured to depreciate his noble Essay on the Treatment and Conversion of African

Slaves &c. That learned and elegant performance written in favour of a much injured race of men, we are happy to think has had a good effect in opening the eyes of many of his countrymen to the sufferings of the African brethren; for the Apostle calls us brethren; but if I may form a conjecture from your writings; the Apostles have very small credit either with you or your worthy partner in cruelty, Mr. Tobin; for can any man be a Christian who asserts that one part of the human race were ordained to be in perpetual bondage to another? Is such an assertion, consistent with that spirit of meekness, of justice, of charity, and above all, that brotherly love which it enjoins? But we trust that in spite of your *hissing* zeal and impotent malevolence against Mr. Ramsay, his noble purpose of philanthropy will be productive of much good to many, and in the end through the blessing of God, be a means of bringing about the abolition of Slavery. To the Reverend Gentleman we return our most unfeigned thanks and heartfelt gratitude, and we also feel ourselves much indebted to all those gentlemen who have stepped forward in our defence, and vindicated us from the aspersions of our tyrannical calumniators.

You and your friend, J. Tobin, the cursory remarker, resemble Demetrius, the silversmith, seeing your craft in danger, a craft, however, not so innocent or justifiable as the making of shrines for Diana, for that though wicked enough, left the persons of men at liberty, but yours enslaves both body and soul–and sacrifices your fellow-creatures on the altar of avarice.[32] You, I say, apprehensive that the promulgation of truth will be subversive of your infamous craft, and destructive of your iniquitous gain, rush out with the desperation of assassins, and attempt to wound the reputation of the reverend Essayist by false calumnies, gross contradictions of several well-known facts, and insidious suppression of others. The character of that reverend Gentleman to my knowledge (and I have known him well before here and in the West Indies for many years) is irreproachable. Many of the facts he relates I know to be true, and many others still more shocking, if possible, have fallen within my own observation, within my feeling; for were I to enumerate even my own sufferings in the West Indies, which perhaps I may one day offer to the public,[33] the disgusting catalogue would be almost too great for belief. It would be endless to refute all your false assertions respecting the treatment of African slaves in the West Indies; some of them, however, are gross; in particular, you say in your apology page 30, "That a Negro has every inducement to wish a numerous family, and enjoys every pleasure he can desire." A glaring falsehood! But to my great grief, and much anguish in different islands in the West Indies, I have been a witness to children torn from their anguished parents, and sent off wherever their merciless owners please, never more to see their friends again. In page 34 of the same elaborate and pious work, you offer an hypothesis, that the Negro race is an inferior species of mankind: Oh fool! See the 17th chapter of the Acts, verse 26, "God hath made of one blood all nations of men, for to dwell on all the face of the earth, &c." Therefore, beware of that Scripture, which says, Fools perish for lack of knowledge.

GUSTAVUS VASSA, *the Ethiopian,*
and late Commissary for the African Settlement

Baldwin's Gardens

---

3. *The Public Advertiser*, 28 April 1788[34]

To the Rev. Mr. RAYMOND HARRIS, *the* Author *of the* Book *called*–"Scripture Researches on the *Licitness* of the *Slave Trade*."[35]

SIR,
    THE Subject of Slavery is now grown to be a serious one, when we consider the buying and selling of Negroes not as clandestine

or piratical business, but as an open public trade, promoted by Acts of Parliament. Being contrary to religion, it must be deemed a national sin, and as such may have a consequence that ought always to be dreaded.–May God give us grace to repent of this abominable crime before it be too late! I could not have believed any man in your office would have dared to come forth in public in these our days to vindicate the accursed Slave Trade on any ground; but least of all by the law of Moses, and by that of Christ in the Gospel. As you are so strenuous in bringing in that blessed and benevolent Apostle, Paul, to support your insinuations, with respect to Slavery, I will here attack you on the Apostle's ground. The glorious system of the Gospel destroys all narrow partiality, and makes us citizens of the world, by obliging us to profess universal benevolence; but more especially are we bound, as Christians, to commiserate and assist, to the utmost of our power, all persons in distress, or captivity. Whatever the Worshipful Committee of the Company of Merchants trading to Africa, and their hirelings, may think of it, or their advocate, the Rev. Mr. Harris, we are not to do evil that good may come, though some of our Statesmen and their political deceivers may think otherwise. We must not for the sake of Old England, and its African trade, or for the supposed advantage or imaginary necessities of the American colonies, lay aside our Christian charity, which we owe to all the rest of mankind; because whenever we do so we certainly deserve to be considered in no better light than as an overgrown society of robbers–a mere banditti, who perhaps may love one another, but at the same time are at enmity with all the rest of the world. Is this according to the law of Nature? For shame! Mr. Harris. In your aforesaid book I am sorry to find you wrest the words of St. Paul's Epistle to Philemon. St. Paul did not entreat Philemon to take back his servant Onesimus in his former capacity, as you have asserted, in order to render bondage consistent with the principles of revealed religion; but St. Paul said expressly, not now as a servant, but above a servant, a brother beloved, &c. –So, Mr. Harris, you have notoriously wrested St. Paul's words; in the other texts, where St. Paul recommends submission to servants for conscience sake, he at the same time enjoins the master to entertain such a measure of brotherly love towards his servant, as must be entirely subversive of the African trade, and West Indian slavery. –And though St. Paul recommends Christian Patience under servitude; yet at the same time he plainly insinuates, that it is inconsistent with Christianity. –The apostle's right to have detained Onesimus, even without the master's consent, is sufficiently implied in the 8th verse. –The dignity of Christ's kingdom doth not admit of Christians to be slaves to their brothers. –Canst thou be made free, says the apostle to the Christian Servant, choose it rather; for he that is called of the Lord being a servant, is the free man of the Lord; ye are brought with a price, be not therefore the servants of men. –Sir, to me it is astonishing, you should in the open face of day, so strangely pervert the apostle's meaning in the 16th verse. –Of this epistle, which you cite strongly in favour of slavery, when the whole tenor of it is in behalf of the slave, I think if you were not hired, you must necessarily observe and acknowledge this matter beyond dispute: and if you were well acquainted with the Bible, you would have seen the very time St. Paul sent Onesimus back to his former master. He then was a Minister or a Preacher of the Gospel. This is corroborated by a variety of circumstances; pray see the epistle to the Colossians. –Surely every reasonable Christian must suppose St. Paul mad, according to the doctrine presumed in your book, to send Onesimus to be a slave and private property the very time when the Christians had all one heart, one mind, and one spirit; and all those who had property sold it, and they had all things common amongst them. You, Sir, as a Clergyman ought to have considered this subject well; I think you have done no credit to the doctrine of Christ, in asserting, that Onesimus was to be received by Philemon for ever as a slave. –St. Paul in his epistles enjoins servants to submission, and not to grieve on the account of their temporal estate. For if, instead of this, he had absolutely declared the iniquity of slavery, tho' established and authorised by the laws of a temporal government, he would have occasioned more tumult than reformation: among the multitude of slaves there would have been more striving for temporal than spiritual happiness; yet it plainly appears by the insinuations which immediately follow, that he thought it derogatory to the honour of Christianity, that men who are bought with the inestimable price of Christ's blood, shall be esteemed slaves, and the private property of their fellow-men. And had Christianity been established by temporal authority in those countries where Paul preached, as it is at present, in this kingdom, we need not doubt but that he would have urged, nay, compelled the masters, as he did Philemon, by the most pressing arguments, to treat their quondam slaves, not now as servants, but above servants–a brother beloved–May God open your eyes while it is called to-day, to see aright, before you go hence and be no more seen. –Remember the God who has said, Vengeance is mine, and I will repay not only the oppressor, but also the justifier of the oppression.

SIR,

I am fervently thine,

GUSTAVUS VASSA, The African.

Baldwin's Gardens.

4. *The Morning Chronicle, and London Advertiser*, 27 June 1788[36]

To the Author of the POEM OF HUMANITY.[37]

Worthy Sir,

In the name of the poor injured Africans, I return you my innate thanks; with prayers to my God ever to fill you with the spirit of philanthropy here, and hereafter receive you into glory. During time may you exert every endeavour in aiding to break the accursed yoke of slavery, and ease the heavy burthens of the oppressed Africans. Sir, permit me to say, "Those that honour their Maker have mercy on the poor"; and many blessings are upon the heads of the Just. May the fear of the Lord prolong your days, and cause your memory to be blessed, and your expectations filled with gladness, for commiserating the poor Africans, who are counted as beasts of burthen by base-minded men. May God ever enable you to support the cause of the poor and the needy. The liberal devise liberal things, and by liberal things shall stand; and may you ever say with the pious Job, "Did not I weep for him that was in trouble? Was not my soul grieved for the poor?" May the all-seeing God hear my prayers for you and crown your works with abounding success! pray you excuse what you here see amiss. I remain with thanks and humble respect.

Yours to Command,

GUSTAVUS VASSA,

The Oppressed African.

Now at No. 13 Tottenham-Street,

Wednesday June 25, 1788.

Editorial note:

We cannot but think the letter a strong argument in favour of the *natural abilities*, as well as *good feelings*, of the Negro Race, and a solid answer in their favour, though manifestly written in haste, and we print it exactly from the original. As to the question of their *stupidity*, we are sincere friends to commerce, but we would have it flourish without *cruelty*.

SECTION 4
Advertisements for
The Interesting Narrative

This section contains sixteen advertisements for *The Interesting Narrative*. Vassa registered the first edition of *The Interesting Narrative* at Stationers' Hall in London on 24 March 1789. He would go on to publish nine editions. Between November 1788 and February 1794, dozens of advertisements—including names of subscribers—informed inhabitants of the stops on his book tour. The following examples appeared in newspapers across England.

1. Printed Solicitation for Subscriptions to the First Edition of *The Interesting Narrative*, November 1788[38]

London, November, 1788.

TO THE NOBILITY, GENTRY, AND OTHERS.
PROPOSALS
For publishing by Subscription
THE INTERESTING
NARRATIVE
OF THE
LIFE
OF
Mr. Olaudah Equiano,
OR

Gustavus Vasa,
THE AFRICAN.
WRITTEN BY HIMSELF:
Who most respectfully solicits the Favour of the Public.

The Narrative contains the following Articles:

The Author's Observations on his Country, and the different Na-
tions in Africa; with an Account of their Manners and Customs,
Religion, Marriages, Agriculture, Buildings, &c. –His Birth–The
Manner how he and his Sister were kidnapped, and of their acci-
dentally meeting again in Africa–His Astonishment at sight of the
Sea, the Vessel, White Men, Men on Horseback, and the various
Objects he beheld on his first Arrival in England; particularly a
Fall of Snow–An Account of Five Years Transactions in the Wars,
under Admiral Boscawen, &c. from 1757 to the Peace in December
1762–Of his being immediately after sent into Slavery, in the West
Indies–Of the Treatment, and cruel Scenes of punishing the
Negroes–The manner of obtaining his Freedom–The verification
of Five remarkable Dreams, or Visions; particularly in being shipwrecked in 1767, and picking up Eleven miserable Men at Sea in
1774, &c.–The wonderful Manner of his Conversion to the Faith
of CHRIST JESUS , and his Attempt to convert an Indian Prince–
Various Actions at Sea and Land, from 1777 to the present Time,
&c. &c.

CONDITIONS.

I. This Work shall be neatly printed on a good Paper, in a Duodecimo, or Pocket Size, and comprized in two handsome Volumes.

II. Price to Subscribers Seven Shillings bound, or Six Shillings
unbound; one half to be paid at subscribing, and the other on the
delivery of the Books, which will be very early in Spring.

III. A few Copies will be printed on Fine Paper, at a moderate advance of Price. It is therefore requested, that those Ladies and Gentlemen who may choose to have paper of that quality, will please to signify the same at subscribing.

IV. In Volume I, will be given an elegant Frontpiece of the Author's Portrait.

SUBSCRIPTIONS *are taken by the following Booksellers:*

Mr. [John] Murray, Fleet-Street; Mess. [James] Robson and [William] Clark[e], Bond Street; Mr. [Lockyer] Davis, opposite Gray's Inn, Holborn; Messrs. [John] Shepperson and [Thomas] Reynolds, Oxford-Street; Mr. [James] Lackington, Chiswell-Street; Mr. [David] Mathews, Strand; Mr. [David or John] Murray, Prince's Street, Soho; Mr. Taylor and Co. South Arch, Royal Exchange; Mr. Thomson, Little Pultney-Street, Golden Square; Mr. [William] Harrison, No. 154. Borough; Mr. Hallowell, Cockhill, Ratcliff; Mr. [William?] Button, Newington Causeway; Mr. Burton, over the Brook, Chatham; and by the Booksellers in Dover, Sandwich, Exeter, Portsmouth, and Plymouth.

---

2. *The World*, 24 March 1789[39]

On Thursday, March 26, will be published,
In 2 Vols. 12mo. Price 7s.
The Interesting NARRATIVE of the LIFE of OLAUDAH EQUIANO, or GUSTAVUS VASA, the African. Written by Himself.

London: Printed for and sold by the Author, No. 10, Union-street, Middlesex Hospital; sold also by Mr. Johnson, St. Paul's Church Yard; Mr. Murray, Fleet-street; Messrs. Robson and Clark,

Bond-street; Mr. Davis, opposite Gray's-Inn, Holborn; Messrs. Shepperdson and Reynolds, and Mr. Jackson, Oxford-street; Mr. Lackington, Chiswell-street; Mr. Mathews, Strand; Mr. Murray, Prince's-street, Soho; Mr. Taylor and Company, South Arch, Royal Exchange; Mr. Parsons, Pater-noster-row; Mr. Hallowell, Cockhill, Ratcliff; Mr. Button, Newington-Causeway; Mr. Burton, over the Brook, Chatham; Mr. Walter Row, Great Marlborough-street; Mr. Bateman, Devonshire-street, Queen's-square; and may be had of all the Booksellers in town and country.

3. *The Morning Star*, 29 April–1 May 1789[40]

29 APRIL, 1 MAY, 1789.
This Day is published,

The Interesting Narrative of the Life of
OLAUDAH EQUIANO;
OR,
GUSTAVUS VASSA, THE AFRICAN,
Written by himself.

THIS Work is neatly printed on a good paper, in a duodecimo, or pocket size, and comprised in two handsome volumes. Price 7s. unbound.

In Vol. I is given an elegant Frontpiece of the Author's Portrait. Vol. II. A plate shewing the manner the Author was shipwrecked in 1767.

The Narrative contains the following Articles:

The Author's observations on his country, and the different nations in Africa; with an account of their manners and customs, religion, marriages, agriculture, buildings, &c. his birth, the manner how he and his sister were kidnapped, and of their accidentally meeting again in Africa. His astonishment at sight of the sea, the vessel, white men, men on horseback, and the various objects he beheld on his first arrival in England; particularly a fall of snow. An account of five years transactions in the wars, under Admiral Boscawen, &c. from 1757 to the Peace in December, 1762. Of his being immediately after sent into slavery, in the West Indies. Of the treatment, and the cruel scenes of punishing the negroes; the manner of obtaining his freedom; the verification of five remarkable dreams or visions; particularly in being shipwrecked in 1767, and picking up eleven miserable Men at Sea in 1775, &c. The wonderful manner of his conversion to the Faith of Christ Jesus, and his attempt to convert an Indian Prince. Various actions at sea and land, from 1777, to the present time.

The books are sold by the Author, No. 10, Union-street, Middlesex Hospital; and by the following Booksellers: Mr. [Joseph] Johnson, St. Paul's Church Yard; Mr. [John] Murray, Fleet-Street; Mess. [James] Robson and [William] Clark[e], Bond Street; Mr. [Lockyer] Davis, opposite Gray's Inn, Holborn; Messrs. [John] Shepperson and [Thomas] Reynolds, Oxford-Street; Mr. [James] Lackington, Chiswell-Street; Mr. [David] Mathews, Strand; Mr. [David or John] Murray, Prince's Street, Soho; Mr. Taylor and Co. South Arch, Royal Exchange; Mr. Hallowell, Cockhill, Ratcliff; Mr. [William?] Button, Newington Causeway; Mr. Burton, over the Brook, Chatham; Mr. S[hirley]. Woolmir [Woolmer], Exeter; Mr. [John] Parsons, Paternoster-row; and Mr. H[enry]. Trapp, No. 1, Paternoster-row.

4. *The General Evening Post,* 20 February 1790[41]

This Day was published,
The SECOND EDITION of
The Interesting Narrative of the LIFE of OLAUDAH EQUIANO,
or GUSTAVUS VASA, the AFRICAN.
Written by HIMSELF.

This work is neatly printed on a good paper, in a duodecimo, or pocket size, and comprised in Two handsome Volumes, price 6s. unbound.

In Volume I. is given an elegant Frontispiece of the Author's Portrait. Volume II. a Plate, shewing the manner the Author was shipwrecked in 1767.

Printed and sold for the Author by T. Wilkins, Aldermanbury; sold also by Mr. Johnson, St. Paul's Church-yard; Mr. Buckland, Paternoster row; Messrs. Robson and Clark, Bond-street; Mr. Davis, opposite Gray's-Inn, Holborn; Mr. Matthews, Strand; Mr. Stockdale, Piccadilly; Mr. Richardson, Royal Exchange; Mr. Kearsley, Fleet street; and the Booksellers in Oxford and Cambridge; and by the Author, No. 10, Union-street, Middlesex Hospital.

5. *Aris's Birmingham Gazette,* 14 June 1790[42]

December 24, 1789,

This Day is published,
The Second, and corrected Edition of
The interesting NARRATIVE of the LIFE of OLAUDAH
EQUIANO, or GUSTAVUS VASSA, the African.
Written by himself.

From the Reception this Work has met with, from above Seven Hundred Persons of all Denominations—the Author humbly Thanks his numerous Friends for past Favours; and as a new Edition is now out, he most respectfully solicits the Favour and Encouragement of the candid and unprejudiced Friends of the Africans.

This Work is neatly printed on a good Paper, in a Duodecimo, or Pocket Size, and comprised in two handsome Volumes. Price 6s. unbound–and 4s. 6d. if six Copies are taken.

In Volume I. is given an elegant Frontispiece of the Author's Portrait. Volume II a Plate shewing the Manner the Author was shipwrecked in 1767.

The Narrative contains the following Articles–The Author's Observations on his Country, and the different Nations in Africa; with an Account of their Manners and Customs, Religion, Marriages, Agriculture, Buildings, &c.–His Birth–The Manner how he & his Sister were kidnapped, and of their accidentally meeting again in Africa–His Astonishment at the Sight of the Sea, the Vessel, White Men, Men on Horseback, and the various Objects he beheld on his first Arrival in England, particularly a Fall of Snow– An Account of five Years Transactions in the Wars, under Admiral Boscawen, &c. from 1757 to the Peace in December, 1762–Of his being immediately after sent into Slavery in the West Indies–Of the Treatment and the cruel Scenes of punishing the Negroes–The Manner of obtaining his Freedom.–The Verification of five remarkable Dreams or Visions; particularly in being shipwrecked in 1767, and picking up eleven miserable Men at Sea in 1775, &c.–The wonderful Manner of his Conversion to the Faith of Christ Jesus, and his Attempt to convert an Indian Prince–Various Actions at Sea and Land, from 1777 to the present Time.

Sold by the Author, at Mr. [William] Bliss's, Grocer, Aston– street; T[homas]. Pearson, and M[yles]. Swinney, Printers, in High– street; and Mr. [Edward] Piercy, Bull-street, Birmingham; likewise by Mr. [J.W] Piercy, Printer, in Coventry.[43]

6. *The Manchester Mercury, & Harrop's General Advertiser*, 20 July 1790[44]

This Day is Published
The second and corrected EDITION of the interesting
Narrative of the
LIFE of OLAUDAH EQUIANO;
Or GUSTAVUS VASSA, the AFRICAN.
Written by himself.

From the reception this work has met with, from above seven hundred persons of all denominations, the Author humbly thanks his numerous friends, for past favours; and as a New Edition is now out, he most respectfully solicits the favour and encouragement of the candid and unprejudiced friends of the Africans.

This work is nearly printed on a good paper, in a duodecimo, or pocket Size, and comprised in two handsome volumes. Price 6s. unbound–and 4s. 6d. to those who take six copies.

In volume I. is given an elegant frontispiece of the Author's Portrait. Volume II a plate shewing the manner the Author was shipwrecked in 1767. The narrative contains the following articles

The Author's observation on his country, and the different nations in Africa; with an account of their manners and customs, religion, marriages, agriculture, buildings, &c.–His birth–The manner how he & his Sister were kidnapped, and of their accidentally meeting again in Africa–His astonishment at the sight of the sea, the vessel, white men, men on horseback, and the various objects he beheld on his first arrival in England; particularly a fall of snow–An account of five years transactions in the wars, under Admiral Boscawen, &c. from 1757, to the peace in December 1762– Of his being immediately after sent into slavery in the West-Indies –Of the treatment, and the cruel scenes of punishing the Negroes– The manner of obtaining his freedom. –The verification of five remarkable dreams or visions; particularly in being shipwrecked in 1767, and picking up eleven miserable men at sea, in 1775, &c.– The wonderful manner of his conversion to the faith of Christ Jesus, and his attempt to convert an Indian Prince.–Various actions at sea and land, from 1777 to the present time.

The above narrative is to be had of Mr. Harrop, printer, & J. Thompson, bookseller, Market–street–lane, Manchester; and of the Author, at Mrs. Lord's, No. 12, Spring gardens.[45]

7. The Sheffield Register, Yorkshire, Derbyshire, & Nottinghamshire Universal Advertiser, 20 August 1790[46]

This Day was published
A SECOND AND CORRECTED EDITION,
Of the interesting Narrative of
THE LIFE OF OLAUDAH EQUIANO,
OR
GUSTAVUS VASSA, THE AFRICAN,
Written by himself.

The Author humbly thanks his numerous friends for the reception this Work has met with from above Seven Hundred Persons of all denominations; and as a New Edition is now out, he most respect-fully solicits the Favour and Encouragement of the candid and un-prejudiced Friends of the AFRICANS. This Work is neatly printed on a good Paper, in a Duodecimo, or Pocket Size, and comprised in two handsome Volumes. Price 6s. unbound.

In Vol. I. is given an elegant Portrait of the Author; in Vol. II a Plate shewing the Manner in which the Author was shipwrecked in 1767.

The Narrative contains the following Articles. The Author's Observations on his Country, and the different Nations in Africa; with an Account of their Manners and Customs, Religion, Marriages, Agriculture, Buildings, &c.–His Birth–The Manner how he & his Sister were kidnapped, and of their accidental Meeting again in Africa-His Astonishment at the Sight of the Sea, the Vessel, white Men, Men on Horseback, and the various Objects he beheld on his first Arrival in England; particularly a Fall of Snow–An Account of five Years Transactions in the Wars, under Admiral Boscawen, from 1757 to the Peace in December, 1762–Of his being immediately after sent into Slavery in the West Indies–Of the Treatment, and the cruel Scenes of punishing the Negroes–The Manner of obtaining his Freedom.–The Verification of five remarkable Dreams or Visions; particularly in being shipwrecked in 1767, and picking up eleven miserable Men at Sea in 1775, &c.–The wonderful Manner of his Conversion to the Faith of Christ Jesus, and his Attempt to convert an Indian Prince.–Various Actions at Sea and Land, from 1777, to the present Time.

Sold by the Printer [Joseph Gales] hereof, and by the Author, at the Rev. Mr. [Thomas] Bryant's, in Sheffield—who makes Allowance to Booksellers.[47]

---

8. The St. James's Chronicle; or, British Evening–Post, 23–25 November 1790[48]

This Day was published,
(In One handsome Volume, Twelves, on good Paper,
Price Four Shillings, sewed)
The THIRD EDITION, corrected and enlarged, of
THE INTERESTING NARRATIVE of the LIFE of
OLAUDAH EQUIANO,
or

GUSTAVUS VASSA, the AFRICAN.
Written by himself.

With an elegant Print of the Authour [*sic*]; and a Plate showing the manner in which he was shipwrecked.

Printed for, and sold by, the Authour [*sic*]; and by Mr. Johnson, St. Paul's Church–yard; Mr. Robson and Mr. Clark, Bond-Street; Mr. Davis, opposite Gray's–Inn, Holbo[ur]rn; Mr. Matthews, Strand; Mr. Richardson, Royal Exchange; Mr. Thomson, Manchester; and the booksellers in Oxford and Cambridge.

---

9. *The York Chronicle*, 22 April 1791[49]

This day is published,
In one handsome volume, twelves, on good paper,
Price Four Shillings sewed.
The THIRD EDITION, CORRECTED and ENLARGED,
of the Interesting
NARRATIVE of the LIFE of
OLAUDAH EQUIANO,
or
GUSTAVUS VASSA,
THE AFRICAN.
Written by himself.—With an elegant PRINT of the AUTHOR;
and a plate shewing the manner in which he was ship-wrecked.

The kind reception which this Work has met with from many hundred persons of all denominations, demands the Author's most sincere thanks to his numerous friends; and he most respectfully solicits the favour and encouragement of the candid and unprejudiced friends of the Africans.

The General Magazine and Impartial Review, for July 1789,

characterizes this Work in the following terms:–"This is 'a round unvarnish'd Tale' of the chequered adventures of an African, who early in life was torn from his native country by those savage dealers in a trade disgraceful to humanity, and which has fixed a stain on the legislature of Britain. The narrative appears to be written with much truth and simplicity.–The Author's account of the manners of the natives of his own province (Eboe) is interesting and pleasing."

The Book may be had of the Author at Mr. [William] Tuke's Castlegate, and of Mr. [Robert] Spence in Ousegate, York.[50]

---

10. *The Freeman's Journal,* 31 May–2 June 1791[51]

This day is published,
In one handsome volume, Twelves, on good Paper,
Price Four Shillings, sewed:
The FOURTH EDITION, corrected and enlarged, of the
Interesting Narrative of the Life of
OLAUDAH EQUIANO,
Or GUSTAVUS VASSA–the AFRICAN.
Written by himself–With an elegant Print of the
AUTHOR; and a Plate shewing the manner
in which he was shipwrecked.

The kind reception which this Work has met with in England, from many hundred persons of all denominations, demands the Author's most sincere thanks to his numerous Friends; and he most respectfully solicits the favour and encouragement of the candid and unprejudiced friends of the Africans.

The General Magazine and Impartial Review, for July 1789, characterizes this Work in the following terms:–"This is 'a round unvarnished tale' of the chequered adventures of an African who early in his life was torn from his native Country by those savage dealers in a traffic disgraceful to humanity and which has fixed a stain on the Legislature of Britain. The narrative appears to be written with much truth and simplicity.–The Author's account of the manners of the natives of his own province (the Eboes) is interesting and pleasing."

The book will be had of the Author at 151 Capel–street; Mr. William Sleater [11]28 Dame–street; and by P[atrick] Byrne.[52]

11. *The Belfast News–Letter,* 20 December 1791[53]

This Day is published, (in one handsome Volume, Twelves, on good Paper, Price 4s. sewed) the 4th Edition, corrected and enlarged, of the interesting Narrative of the Life of OLAUDAH EQUIANO: or, GUSTAVUS VASSA, the AFRICAN; Written by himself. With an elegant Print of the Author; and a Plate shewing the Manner in which he was shipwrecked.–The–Narrative contains

The Author's Observations on his Country, and the different Nations in Africa; with an Account of their Manners and Customs, Religion, Marriages, Agriculture, Buildings–The Manner how he and his Sister were kidnapped, and of their accidentally meeting again in Africa–His Astonishment at the Sight of the Sea, the Vessel, white Men, and the various Objects he beheld on his first Arrival in England, particularly a Fall of Snow–An Account of five Years Transactions in the Wars.

The General Magazine and Impartial Review, for June 1789, characterizes this Work in the following Terms:–"This is 'a Round unvarnish'd Tale' of the chequered Adventures of an African, who, early in Life, was torn from his native Country by those savage

Dealers in a Traffic disgraceful to Humanity, and which has fixed a Stain on the Legislature of Britain.–The Narrative appears to be written with much Truth and Simplicity.–The Author's Account of the manners of the Natives of his own Province (Eboe) is interesting and pleasing."

To be had of the Author, at Mr. Mullan's on the Quay; at Mr. Samuel Neilson's, Waring–street; and the Booksellers in Town.[54]

---

12. *The Glasgow Advertiser and Evening Intelligencer*, 27 April–30 April 1792[55]

This day is published.
(In one handsome Volume Twelves,
on good paper, price 4s. sewed)
The FOURTH Edition of the interesting NARRATIVE
of the LIFE of
OLAUDAH EQUIANO;
Or,
GUSTAVUS VASSA, THE AFRICAN:
Written by himself.
With an elegant Print of the Author, and a Plate
shewing the Manner In which he was ship-wrecked.

The Narrative contains the following Articles:

The Author's observations on his country, and the different nations in Africa; with an account of their Manners and Customs, Religion, Marriages, Agriculture, Buildings–The manner how he and his Sister were kidnapped, and of their accidentally meeting again in Africa-His astonishment at the sight of the Sea, the Vessels, White Men, and the various objects he beheld on his first arrival in England, particularly a Fall of Snow–An account of five years Transactions in the Wars.

The General Magazine and Impartial Review, for July 1787 [*sic*], characterizes this work in the following terms:–"This is 'a round unvarnished tale' of the chequered adventures of an African, who, early in life, was torn from his native country by those savage dealers in a traffic disgraceful to humanity, and which has fixed a stain on the Leglslature of Britain. The narrative appears to be written with much truth and simplicity. The author's account of the manners of the natives of his own province (Eboe) is interesting and pleasing."

To be had of the Author, at the King's Arms Inn, Trongate, and of the Booksellers in this city.[56]

---

13. *The Caledonian Mercury*, 21 May 1792[57]

This day is published,
In one handsome volume 12mo,
on good paper, Price 4s. sewed
The Fourth Edition of the Interesting Narrative
of the Life of
OLAUDAH EQUIANO;
Or GUSTAVUS VASSA, THE AFRICAN:
Written by Himself.
With an elegant Print of the Author, and a Plate shewing
the Manner in which he was ship-wrecked.

The Narrative contains the following Articles:

The Author's Observations on his Country, and the different Nations in Africa' with an Account of their Manners and Customs, Religion, Marriages: Agriculture, Buildings; the manner how he and his sister were kidnapped, and of their accidentally meeting again in Africa. His astonishment at the sight of the sea, the vessels, white men, and the various objects he beheld on his first arrival in

England, particularly a fall of snow. An account of five years transactions in the Wars.

The General Magazine and Impartial Review, for July 1787 [*sic*], characterizes this work in the following Terms:–"This is a round unvarnish'd Tale of the Chequered Adventures of an African, who early in life, was torn from his native country, by those savage dealers in a traffic disgraceful to humanity, and which has fixed a stain on the Legislature of Britain. The Narrative appears to be written with much truth and simplicity. The Author's Account of the manners of the natives of his own province (Eboe) is interesting and pleasing."

To be had of the Author, at Mr. Wilson's Hair-dresser, Anchor Close, and the Booksellers in town.

14. *The Aberdeen Journal*, 20 August 1792[58]

This Day is published,
(In one handsome Volume Twelves,
on good Paper, price 4s. sewed)
The FIFTH Edition of the interesting NARRATIVE
of the LIFE of
OLAUDAH EQUIANO;
OR,
GUSTAVUS VASSA, THE AFRICAN:
Written by himself.
With an elegant Print of the Author, and a plate shewing
the manner in which he was shipwrecked.

The narrative contains the following articles:

The Author's observations on his country, and the different nations in Africa; with an account of their Manners and Customs, Religion, Marriages, Agriculture, Buildings–The manner how he and his Sister were kidnapped, and of their accidentally meeting again in Africa-His astonishment at the sight of the Sea, the vessels, White Men, and the various objects he beheld on his first arrival in England, particularly a Fall of Snow—An account of five years Transactions in the Wars.

The General Magazine and Impartial Review, for July 1789, characterizes this work in the following terms:—"This is 'a round unvarnish'd tale' of the chequered adventures of an African, who, early in life, was torn from his native country by those savage dealers in traffic disgraceful to humanity, and which has fixed a stain on the Legislature of Britain. The narrative appears to be written with much truth and simplicity. The author's account of the manners of the natives of his own province (Eboe) is interesting and pleasing."

To be had, on Thursday next, of the Author, at Mr. Spalding's, Marishal Street; of Messrs Angus and Son, Mr. Brown, and the other booksellers.

---

15. *The Newcastle Chronicle, or Weekly Advertiser, and Register of News Commerce, and Entertainment* (Newcastle), 15 September 1792[59]

This Day is published,
(In one handsome Volume Twelves,
on good Paper, Price 4s. Sewed)
THE FIFTH EDITION of the interesting
NARRATIVE of the LIFE of
OLAUDAH EQUIANO;
or,
GUSTAVUS YASSA, THE AFRICAN:
WRITTEN BY HIMSELF.

With an elegant PRINT of the AUTHOR.
And a PLATE shewing the Manner
in which he was ship-wrecked.

The Narrative contains the following Articles:

The Author's Observations on his Country, and the different Nations in Africa; with an Account of their Manners and Customs, Religion, Marriages, Agriculture, Buildings–The Manner how he and his Sister were kidnapped, and of their accidentally meeting again in Africa–His Astonishment at the Sight of the Sea, the Vessels, white Men, and the various Objects he beheld on his first Arrival in England, particularly a Fall of Snow–An Account of five Years Transactions in the Wars.

The General Magazine and Impartial Review, for June 1789, characterizes this Work in the following Terms: – "This is 'a round unvarnish'd Tale' of the chequered Adventures of an African, who, early in Life, was torn from his native Country by those savage Dealers in a Traffic disgraceful to Humanity, and which has fixed a Stain on the Legislature of Britain.–The Narrative appears to be written with much Truth and Simplicity. The Author's Account of the Manners of the Natives of his own Province (Eboe) is interesting and pleasing."

To be had of the Author, Gustavus Yassa, at Mr. Robert Denton's, opposite the Turk's Head, Bigg–Market, Newcastle, and of the Booksellers in this Town.

16. *The Norfolk Chronicle*, 22 February 1794[60]

IN THE PRESS
And will be published, ready to be delivered on the 12th of
March next,
The EIGHTH EDITION, enlarged,
OF
THE
LIFE
Of OLAUDAH EQUIANO;
OR,
Gustavus Vassa,
THE AFRICAN
WRITTEN BY HIMSELF.

Containing the Author's observations on his country, the manner in which he and his Sister were kidnapped, of the treatment he received during the term of his slavery, and the manner of obtaining his freedom, &c. &c. With a portrait of the Author, and a View of his being shipwrecked.

The work will be printed in one handsome volume twelves, price 4s. (Formerly sold for 7s.) on a good paper.

Subscriptions taken in by the Author, at Mr. [Jacob] Johnson's, bridgestreet, St. George's [Colegate parish]; and by Mr. [William] Stevenson, at the Norfolk Arms, in the Market-place, Norwich. As it is intended to publish a List of Subscribers, the Author would be happy to have the names of such friends as mean to subscribe by the 6th of March at farthest.

For the Character of this Narrative see the Monthly Review for June; and also General Magazine, or Impartial Review for July 1789.

Reviews of *The Interesting Narrative*

This section contains reviews of *The Interesting Narrative*. Mary Wollstonecraft (document 1), Richard Gough (document 2), and two anonymous authors (documents 3 and 4) each published reviews of the first edition of the *Narrative* in 1789.[61]

---

1. Mary Wollstonecraft, *The Analytical Review,* May 1789[62]

The life of an African, written by himself, is certainly a curiosity, as it has been a favourite philosophic whim to degrade the numerous nations, on whom the sun-beams more directly dart, below the common level of humanity, and hastily to conclude that nature, by making them inferior to the rest of the human race, designed to stamp them with the mark of slavery. How they are shaded down, from the fresh colour of northern rustics, to the sable hue seen on the African sands, is not our task to inquire, nor do we intend to draw a parallel between the abilities of a negro and European mechanic; we shall only observe, that if these volumes do not exhibit extraordinary intellectual powers, sufficient to wipe off the stigma, yet the activity and ingenuity, which conspicuously appear in the character of Gustavus, place him on a par with the general mass of men, who fill the subordinate stations in a more civilized society than that which he was thrown into at his birth.

The first volume contains, with a variety of other matter, a short description of the manners of his native country, an account of his family, his being kidnapped with his sister, his journey to the sea

124

coast, and terror when carried on shipboard. May anecdotes are simply told, relative to the treatment of his family, his being kidnapped with his sister, his journey to the sea coast, and terror when carried on shipboard. Many anecdotes are simply told, relative to the treatment of male and female slaves, on the voyage, and in the West Indies, which makes the blood turn its course; and the whole account of his unwearied endeavours to obtain his freedom, is very interesting. The narrative should have closed when he once more became his own master. The latter part of the second volume appears flat; and he is entangled in many, comparatively speaking, insignificant cares, which almost efface the lively impression made by the miseries of the slave. The long account of his religious sentiments and conversion to methodism, is rather tiresome.

Throughout, a kind of contradiction is apparent: many childish stories and puerile remarks, do not agree with some more solid reflections, which occur in the first pages. In the style also we observed a striking contrast: a few well written periods do not smoothly unite with the general tenor of the language.

2. Richard Gough, *The Gentleman's Magazine*, June 1789[63]

Among other contrivances (and perhaps one of the most innocent) to interest the national humanity in favour of the Negro slaves, one of them here writes his own history, as formerly another [Ignatius Sancho] of them published his correspondence....–These memoirs, written in a very unequal style, place the writer on a par with the general mass of men in the subordinate stations of civilized society, and prove that there is no general rule without an exception. The first volume treats of the manners of his countrymen, and his own adventures till he obtained freedom; the second, from that period to the present, is uninteresting; and his conversion to Methodism oversets the whole.

3. Anonymous, *Monthly Review*, June 1789[64]

WE entertain no doubt of the authenticity of this very intelligent African's story; though it is not improbable that some English writer has assisted him in the compilement, or, at least, the correction of his book; for it is sufficiently well-written. The Narrative wears an honest face; and we have conceived a good opinion of the man, from the artless manner in which he has detailed the variety of adventures and vicissitudes which have fallen to his lot. His publication appears very seasonable, at a time when the negro–slavery is the subject of public investigation; and it seems calculated to increase the odium that has been excited against the West–India planters, on account of the cruelties that some are said to have exercised on their slaves, many instances of which are here detailed.

The sable author of this volume appears to be a very sensible man; and he is, surely, not the less worthy of credit from being a convert to Christianity. He is a Methodist, and has filled many pages towards the end of his work, with accounts of his dreams, visions, and divine influences; but all this, supposing him to have been under any delusive influence, only serves to convince us that he is guided by principle, and that he is not one of those poor converts, who, having undergone the ceremony of baptism, have remained content with that portion only of the christian religion; instances of which are said to be almost innumerable in America and the West Indies.

GUSTAVUS VASSA appears to possess a very different character; and, therefore, we heartily wish success to his publication, which we are glad to see has been encouraged by a very respectable subscription.

4. Anonymous, *The General Magazine and Impartial Review*, July 1789[65]

This is 'a round and unvarnished tale'[66] of the chequered adventures of an African, who early in life, was torn from his native country, by those savage dealers in a traffic disgraceful to humanity, and which has fixed a stain on the legislature of Britain. The Narrative appears to be written with much truth and simplicity. The Author's account of the manners of the natives of his own province (Eboe) is interesting and pleasing; and the reader, unless, perchance he is either a West–India planter, or Liverpool merchant, will find his humanity often severely wounded by the shameless barbarity practiced towards the author's hapless countrymen in all our colonies: he feels, as he ought, the oppressed and the oppressors will equally excite his pity and indignation. That so unjust, and iniquitous a commerce may be abolished, is our ardent wish; and we heartily join in our author's prayer, 'That the God of Heaven may inspire the hearts of our Representatives in Parliament, with peculiar benevolence on that important day when so interesting a question is to be discussed; when thousands in consequence of their determination, are to look for happiness or misery!'

SECTION 6
Letters to Local Newspapers and Towns

This section features the letters Vassa sent to local newspapers while on his book tours from 1789 to 1794. He addressed the printers of the *Cambridge Chronicle* (document 1), *Aris's Birmingham Gazette* (document 2), *Manchester Mercury* (document 3), *Sheffield Register* (document 4), and *Leeds Mercury* (document 5). The final two letters are addressed to the inhabitants of Newcastle (document 6) and Norwich (document 7).

---

1. *The Cambridge Chronicle and Journal; and General Advertiser* for The Counties of Cambridge, Huntingdon, Lincoln, Rutland, Bedford, Herts, Isle of Ely, &c., 1 August 1789[67]

Printed by Francis Hodson, at the Comer of Green-Street, Cambridge.

To the Printer of the CAMBRIDGE CHRONICLE.
SIR,
Having received particular marks of kindness from the Gentlemen of the University, and the inhabitants of this town, I beg you to suffer me thus publickly to express my grateful acknowledgements to them for their favours. I have been more particularly delighted with that fellow-feeling they have discovered, for my very poor and much oppressed countrymen. Here I experience true civility with-

out respect to colour or complexion. Nor have even the amiable fair–sex refused to countenance the sooty African. These acts of kindness and hospitality have filled my grateful heart with longing desires to see these worthy friends on my own estate, where the richest produce of Africa should be devoted to their entertainment: they should there partake of the luxuriant Pine-apple, and the well savoured virgin-palm-wine. And to heighten the bliss, I would burn a certain kind of tree that would afford us a light, as clear and brilliant as the virtues of my guests. Such shall be our joy, if it please God I am ever restored to my lost estate, and meet these my friends in my native country.

I am, Sir,
Your humble Servant
GUSTAVUS VASSA,
The African.
CAMBRIDGE, *July* 30th, 1789.

2. *Aris's Birmingham Gazette,* Monday, 28 June 1790[68]

To the Printer of the Birmingham Gazette

SIR,   June 19, 1790
HAVING received great Marks of Kindness from the under-mentioned Gentlemen of this Town, who have subscribed to my Narrative: particularly from Mess. Charles and Sampson Lloyd, and Families, and Dr. [William] Gilby.

Dr. [Edward] Johnstone   Mess. John Hammonds
John Taylor, Esq.   James Osborn
Sam[uel] Garbet, Esq.   William Sprigg

Sam[uel] Galton, Esq.

W[illia]m Russell, Esq.

Rev. Dr. [Joseph] Priestley

Rev. Mr. [J.] Riland

Rev. Mr. Pearce

Rev. Mr. Bass

William Smith

Samuel Ford

Peter Capper

Joseph Randell

Joseph Gibbons

Thomas Robinson

Thomas Laurence

John Ward

Thomas Price

James Bingham

John Jukes

Matt[hew] Boulton, Esq.

Edward Palmer, Esq.

Mess. Henry Perkins

George Simcox

Thomas Green

Thomas Parkes

Sam[uel] Pemberton

John Lee

John Dickenson

Thomas Ketland

John Lowe, Jun.

John Freer, Jun.

S. Ryland

John Harwood

Thomas King

Wm. Humphreys

G. Humphreys

Thomas Colemore

Samuel Colemore

Richard Gibbs

James Bedford

William Medley

William Hicks

John Cope

John Robbins

Mess. Cockle

Joseph Rabone

Edward Webb

Samuel Baker

William Hunt

Mrs. Wiggin

William Cope

John Biddle

Thomas Francis

William Reynolds

Joseph Cotterell

James Gottington

Benjamin Freeth

I beg you to suffer me, thus publicly to express my grateful Acknowledgments to them for their Favours, and for the Fellow-feeling they have discovered for my very poor and much oppressed Countrymen; these Acts of Kindness and Hospitality, have filled me with a longing Desire to see these worthy Friends on my own

Estate in Africa, when the richest Produce of it should be devoted to their Entertainment; they should there partake of the luxuriant Pine-apples, and the well flavoured virgin Palm-wine; and to heighten the Bliss I would burn a certain Kind of Tree, that would afford us a Light as clear and brilliant as the Virtues of my Guests.

I am Sir, your humble Servant,
GUSTAVUS VASA, the African.

The Narratives are Sold by the Author, at Mr. Bliss', Grocer, Astonstreet, and by T. Pearson, and T. Wood, Booksellers, in High–street, Birmingham, at 6s. a Copy, and 4s. 6d. to those who take six Copies.[69]

---

3. *The Manchester Mercury, & Harrop's General Advertiser*, 31 August 1790[70]

p. 1
To the Printer of the Manchester Mercury.
SIR,
Having received Great Marks of Kindness from many Ladies and Gentlemen here, (who have subscribed to my Interesting Narrative) particularly Thomas Walker, Esq; the Rev. Dr. Bayley, Mr Ralph Kirkham, Mr Isaac Moss, jun., Mr Richard Routh, Mr John Lowe, jun. & Family, & Mr Lloyd, I beg you to suffer me thus publickly to express my grateful Acknowledgement to them for their Favours, and for the Fellow-feeling they have discovered, for my very poor and much oppressed Countrymen; these acts of Commisseration have fill'd my Heart with Gratitude, therefore, permit me Sir, on Behalf of myself and the rest of my Brethren, to offer this sincere Thanks, for the Testimony of your Regard to the Sable People.

May your endeavours meet with the desired Success, and may the all–bountiful Creator bless you all, in Time and Eternity.

                                        I am, Gentlemen,
Manchester   Your obedient humble Servant,
August 18, 1790.   GUSTAVUS VASA, THE AFRICAN

---

4. *Sheffield Register, Yorkshire, Derbyshire, & Nottinghamshire Universal Advertiser,* 2 September 1790[71]

Printed by Joseph Gales, in the Hartshead.

TO THE PRINTER OF THE SHEFFIELD REGISTER.
SIR,

Having received very great Marks of Kindness from many of the inhabitants of this Town–particularly the under-mentioned Gentlemen, who have generously subscribed to my interesting Narrative, viz.

   Dr. Browne, Wm. Shore Esq., Samuel Marshall, Rev. James Wilkinson, Rev. E. Goodwin, John Barlow, Rev. Mr. Bryant. I beg you to suffer me thus publicly to express my grateful Acknowledgments for their Favours, and the fellow-feeling they have discovered for my very poor and much oppressed Countrymen. For these Acts of Hospitality, I pray God to bless them all with every Blessing of Time and Eternity.

       I am, Sir
           Your humble servant,
                GUSTAVUS VASSA,
                THE AFRICAN
Sheffield, Sept. 2.

5. *The Leeds Mercury*, Following Notice of a Subscription Drive to Support the London Abolition Society, 19 April 1791[72]

To the PRINTER of the LEEDS MERCURY.

Leeds, April 16th.

Having received particular marks of kindness from Mr. Law Atkinson and Family, of Huddersfield, and many Gentlemen and Ladies, &c., of and near this town, who have purchased my genuine and interesting Narrative; I beg to offer them my warmest thanks; and also to the friends of humanity here, on behalf of my much oppressed countrymen, whose case calls aloud for redress–May this year bear record of acts worthy of a British Senate, and you have a satisfaction of seeing the completion of the work you have so humanely assisted in:–'Tis now the duty of everyone, who is a friend to religion and humanity, to assist the different Committees engaged in this pious work. Those who can feel for the distresses of their own countrymen, will also comiserate the case of the poor Africans. Since that it does not often fall to the lot of individuals to contribute to so important a moral and religious duty, as that of putting an end to a practice, which may, without exaggeration, be stiled one of the greatest evils now existing on the earth, it may be hoped, that each one will now use his utmost endeavours for that purpose. The Wise Man saith–"Righteousness exalteth a nation, but sin is a reproach to any people."

Permit me, dear friends, on behalf of myself and countrymen, to offer you the warmest effusions of a heart replete with gratitude.

I am, with constant prayers for your health and happiness,
Worthy friends,
Your respectful humble Servant,
GUSTAVUS VASSA,
The African.

6. *Newcastle Chronicle and Newcastle Courant,* 6 October 1792[73]

GUSTAVUS VASSA; the AFRICAN
To the Inhabitants of this Town and its Environs.

GENTLEMEN,
PERMIT me, one of the oppressed Natives of Africa, to offer you the warmest Thanks of a Heart glowing with Gratitude to you, for your Fellow-feeling for the Africans and their Cause. Having received Marks of Kindness from you who have purchased my interesting Narrative, (particularly from George Johnson, Esq. of Byker) I am therefore happy that my Narrative has afforded Pleasure in the Perusal; and heartily wish all of you every Blessing that this World can afford, and every Fulness of Joy which Divine Revelation has promised us in the next.
    Gentlemen,
    I am, with profound Respect and Gratitude, &c. &c.
GUSTAVUS VASSA
Newcastle, October 4th, 1792.

7. *The Norfolk Chronicle,* 15 March 1794[74]

GUSTAVUS VASSA, the AFRICAN.
To the Inhabitants of this City and its Environs,
And also of Bury St. Edmund.

GENTLEMEN,
PERMIT me, one of the oppressed Natives of Africa, to offer you the warmest thanks of a heart glowing with gratitude to you for your fellow feeling for the Africans and their cause:–Having

received marks of kindness from you who have subscribed to my interesting Narrative, I heartily wish all of you every blessing that this world can afford, and all fullness of joy in the next world.

Gentlemen,

I am, with profound respect and gratitude, &c.

GUSTAVUS VASSA.

Norwich, March 14th, 1794.

N.B. Subscribers and others may now have the Narrative of the Author, at Mr. [Jacob] Johnson's, Bridge–street, St. George's [Colegate], and of Mr. [William] Stevenson, at the Norfolk Arms, in the Market–place, price 4s.

SECTION 7
Other Documents
Relating to the Press

The following nine documents, which were printed in the press between July 1788 and November 1796, do not fall into a specific category. They are all about Vassa, but all but one were neither written nor sent by him.

The biographical sketch of Vassa (document 1) describes his reception in July 1788. His *Morning Post, and Daily Advertiser* comment reveals that he was a well-known public figure prior to the publication of his *Narrative* (document 2). The advertisement for a city debate involving Vassa on the issue of the slave trade (document 3) and the reference to his testimony at the first sight of a fall of snow in the *Oracle Bell's New World* (document 4) attest to his status as a public figure in 1789. Joseph Gale's article (document 5) defends Vassa and his brethren against a racist attack. The article in the *Derby Mercury* (document 6) provides context about proceedings in the Senate and an informal endorsement not only of Vassa's autobiography and book tour but also of him as an intelligent, good person, working to end the slave trade. We are made aware of Vassa's activities in Edinburgh in May of 1792 through a notice in the *Gazetteer and New Daily Advertiser* (document 7). Lastly, we learn through the press that Vassa was a subscriber to defray the expenses of defendants in their trials for high treason in Britain, and that he made observations about the slave trade following the acquittal of his friend Thomas Hardy (documents 8 and 9).

1. *The Morning Chronicle, and London Advertiser*, 1 July 1788[75]

Gustavus Vasa, who addressed a letter in the name of his oppressed countrymen, to the author of the popular poem on Humanity, which devotes several pages to that now universal subject of discussion, the Slave Trade, is, notwithstanding its romantic sound, the real name of an Ethiopian now resident in the metropolis, a native of Eboe, who was himself twice kidnapped by the English, and twice sold to slavery. He has since been appointed the King's Commissary for the African settlement, and besides having an irreproachable moral character, has frequently distinguished himself by occasional essays in the different papers, which manifest a strong and sound understanding.

2. *The Morning Post, and Daily Advertiser*, 5 July 1788[76]

To the Author of Sable Soup and Black Bouille, who belied GUSTAVUS VASA in yesterday's paper–thus sayeth the Almighty–"No Lyars, nor *Devourers* of *human* Rights, shall have any Inheritance in the Kingdom of Heaven." GUTAVUS [*sic*] VASA, the African.

3. *The Gazetteer and New Daily Advertiser* (London), 9 May 1789[77]

CITY DEBATES, CAPEL–COURT,
Bartholomew–Lane, opposite the Bank.

Held every Monday Evening.

Chair taken at Half past Eight o'Clock. Admission Sixpence.

AFRICAN SLAVE TRADE.

"Can the Legislators of this Country, consistently with its true interests, consent to the total Abolition of the Slave Trade?"

The abilities of Gentlemen who speak in this Society having raised it to public estimation, superior to every other, several respectable Citizens have desired the above Question to be debated on Monday next. The Managers respectfully hope the following circumstances will ensure an early attendance: The African Prince, who lately spoke in this Society, has promised to be present; the celebrated Oubladah [sic] Equiano, or Gustavus Vassa, who has lately published his Memoirs, will speak; and the Lady, whose abilities are the ornament of this Institution, and the admiration of the Public, positively will deliver her sentiments. The united efforts of such genius and abilities were never before expected in one evening, and the Managers are happy it is on a subject the most important in the whole annals of this country.

Next question, on the Repeal of the Test and Corporation Acts, proposed by an eminent Dissenting Clergyman.

4. *Oracle Bell's New World*, 12 August 1789[78]

A certain beautiful DUTCHESS, lately emerging at Margate, exposed to the stolen glances of an Officer, the *centaur* of a Venus, heightened by the more than *Lybian* contrast of her attendant Nymphs. The military *Actaeon*, being perceived, was glad to make a precipitate retreat; declaring, that the sight of such a model of perfection inspired equal admiration in him (though sensations of a warmer kind) as the first sight of a fall of *snow* did in *Olaudah Equiano*, on his arrival in England.

5. *Sheffield Register, Yorkshire, Derbyshire, & Nottinghamshire Universal Advertiser,* 27 August 1790[79]

Printed by Joseph Gales, in the Hartshead.

The arrows of ridicule should be pointed by wit, and shot from the bow of truth, to produce the desired effect; as wit and ingenuity must ever be perverted when they attempt to laugh at laudable purposes. The most *pitiful* thing we have lately seen, appeared in the London papers of last week, in the form of a petition from the "Ourang Outangs, Jackoos, and other *next of kin* to the African Negroes," attempting to prove them of the same species; and under the appearance of admiration, ridiculing the favourers of the abolition. Surely this unfortunate race is sufficiently degraded by being the objects of an iniquitous traffic, without being in *every* degree levelled with the beasts that perish. With a little alteration, what Shakespeare says of a Jew may, with propriety, be applied to the sable race.–"Hath not an African eyes, hands, organs and dimensions, senses, affections, passions? fed with the same food, hurt by the same weapons, subject to the same diseases, healed by the same means, warmed and cooled by the same winter and summer as an European?"–Can this be denied? and yet there are people who are weak or base enough, to *affect* disbelief.–Should any within the circle of our readers doubt the truth of this comparison, let them see GUSTAVUS VASA, the free African, now in Sheffield–his manners polished, his mind enlightened, and in every respect on a par with Europeans.

6. Comment on the poem "Slavery and the Slave Trade," *Derby Mercury*, 10 February 1791[80]

Affecting as the above lively description of the sorrows of Slavery is, we would refer our readers to the Narrative of the Life of Gustavus Vassa, the African, (written by himself) who arrived in Derby a few days since, for a striking picture of the situation of the poor Negro, torn from the most tender ties of Friendship and Affection; suffering under the accumulated afflictions of Tyranny and Barbarity; and at length rejoicing in the blessings of Liberty, which he has finely, yet artlessly portrayed – This Narrative is another very strong evidence of the good mental powers of the natives of Africa, and leaves not the most distant room to doubt that they would, with European cultivation, exhibit equal instances of Ability and Humanity – And the proceedings of the British Senate, (see opposite page) give the most flattering hopes, that this unnatural traffic will not long disgrace the British name.

7. Notice of Vassa's activities in Edinburgh, *Gazetteer and New Daily Advertiser* (London), 30 May 1792[81]

GUSTAVUS VASA, with his *white* wife, is at Edinburgh, where he has published a letter of thanks to the General Assembly of the Church of Scotland, for their just and humane interference upon the question of the SLAVE TRADE.

8. *The Morning Post and Fashionable World,* 19 May 1795[82]

STATE TRIALS–SUBSCRIPTIONS

At a Meeting of the COMMITTEE of the SUBSCRIBERS for defraying the Expence of Defendants in the late Trails for HIGH TREASON, held at the house of Messrs. Clarkson, Essex-street, Strand, London, on Thursday the 7th May, 1795,
ROBERT KNIGHT, Esq. in the Chair.

Resolved, That a General Meeting of the Subscribers be held at the Crown and Anchor Tavern, in the Strand, on Thursday the 21st instant, at One o'Clock precisely, to report the sums received, and deliberate on the best mode of more effectually carrying their designs into execution.

The friends to this measure who have not subscribed, are earnestly requested to forward their Subscriptions before the General Meeting.

[In addition to the 990£. 4s. 6d. received "by last advertisement," the 37 "SUBSCRIPTIONS since received" include "Gustavus Vassa 0 5 0.," one of only two giving that little, and one of only four giving less than 1£.]

Subscriptions are received in London by Mr. Johnson, Bookseller, St. Paul's Church-yard; Mr. John Arnold, jun. No. 102, Cornhill; Mr. Simkin, Crown and Anchor, Strand; Mr. J.S. Jordan, Bookseller, 166, Fleet-street; at the Morning Post and Fashionable World Office, opposite Somerset-Place, Strand; Messrs. Foulkes and Cooke, Hart-street, Bloomsbury; and Messrs. Clarkson, Essex-street.

In the Country by John Simmons, Esq; Rochester; Mr. John March, Printer, Norwich; Messrs. Grigby and Cork, Bankers, Bury St. Edmund's; Mr. Stephen Johnson, Leicester; John Kerrich, Esq. Harleston, Norwich; Mr. Benjamin Flower, Printer, Cambridge; Mr. Strutt, Derby; Mr. F. Jollie, Carlisle; Mr. Solomon Hodgson,

Printer, Newcastle upon Tyne; Mr. Robert Dennison, Nottingham; Mr. Charles Danvers, in Stones Croft, Bristol; Mr. James Gray, Soap Manufacturer, Banff, North Britain.

---

9. *The Telegraph*, 7 November 1796[83]

TRIAL BY JURY

Saturday being the Anniversary of the memorable acquittal of THOMAS HARDY, a numerous meeting of the Friends of Freedom was held at the Crown and anchor Tavern, in the Strand, to celebrate that triumph of Liberty so propitious for the Rights of the People–so honourable to English Juries.

Dinner was on the table at five o'clock, and about 700 persons dined in the adjoining rooms.

WILLIAM BOSVILLE in the Chair.

[detailed description of proceedings]

Gustavus Vasa, the celebrated African, made some observations respecting the Slave Trade.

One of the Company said, "General Tarleton, all the battles you have hitherto fought have been against Liberty–I hope that when you fight again it will be for Liberty."

[Tarleton explains his earlier vote, as representative of Liverpool to sustain the slave trade.]

CHAPTER

IV

Possible Attributions

There are a number of items that either may have been written by or were attributed to Vassa, but whose attribution to Vassa is not established. The first section of this chapter features ten letters signed "Gustavus Vassa" that were published between 24 July 1777 and 10 July 1778 in *The Morning Post, and Daily Advertiser.* Section 2 includes an anonymous letter he may have written in 1783. Lastly, Section 3 consists of three letters from the 1790s that are difficult to ascribe to Vassa.

July 1777–July 1778

Documents 1 through 10 below were signed "Gustavus Vassa," and appeared in the *Morning Post, and Daily Advertiser* during a period when Vassa was in London.

---

1. *The Morning Post, and Daily Advertiser,* 24 July 1777[1]

Had Great Britain turned her political views to the extention of colonies, in the West Indies, instead of enlarging her territorial dominations upon the continent of America, to secure the great avenues of trade, and commerce to her in-land colonies, or the continent from falling into the hands of France, and Holland, our only rivals in commerce, this nation would for ages to come have remained the *metropole* of the commercial world, and *mart* of general trade for all Europe, Asia, Africa, and America; as well as the most formidable naval power upon earth. A limited commercial monarchy should always have had in view the colonization of countries, where her marine power could not only command the respect, and obedience of the inhabitants, but also where the current of trade, and produce of her colonies, centered in the mother country. Such is the nature of our West India establishments; first because they are islands; and secondly, because they never can, from their situation, become either manufacturers, mechanics, or artists, that could anyway affect the consumption of merchandize from Britain; and, thirdly, because all their produce, and labour, must come to this mart for sale.

It would have required but very little sagacity to have penetrated the views of a growing people, extending their settlements over a waste fertile continent; nor is the design of this essay, to enter into reasoning upon the ingratitude of a people, which owe their existence to the parent state–I shall only observe, that even in domestic life, when children grow to maturity, they shake off gradually their dependency upon their parents, however they may otherwise respect them; what happens in private life, arises comparatively, and bears an allusion to the actions of men in an aggregate situation. America has now declared her independency of the mother; it is the duty of every honest man, who has the real good of his country at heart, to wish a reconciliation, that will prove of equal advantage to Britain, and her colonies;–those who wish otherwise, if any there should be, are enemies of the state, and traitors to their King and country.

The great misfortune that attended this nation at the end of the last war, which was carried on so successfully, and ended so gloriously to the honour of the British arms, was the inadequateness of the peace, which was concluded between Great-Britain, France and Spain; the arrangements of territorial cession, and division, therein established, are too conspicuous for a total ignorance of geographical knowledge in the British Ministry, and their negotiations, to require a comment.

The ratification of the treaty of Paris, was a more desperate wound to the commercial glory of this country, than any that had ever before been given; and it was from that moment that America began to think seriously of independancy, and that France beheld the sun-shine of commercial splendor, breaking in upon her empire.

It was then that the French administration displayed to all Europe their penetration and superior wisdom, in establishing a treaty of peace, after an unsuccessful war, that would not only repay the nation the many millions they had lost, but they also saw an ample field opening to their view, that would soon gratify their

revenge upon this country without drawing a sword against her:–
they now exult, and glory, that their hopes are come to pass.

It is neither the virtue, nor piety of the Prince, nor his Ministers,
that can secure wisdom to his Councils; and this is not the age of
inspiration,–without a competent share of acquired, and experi-
mental knowledge.–Natural abilities eminently improved, produce
great men in their different walks of life:–but a minister of state,
who takes upon him the arduous task of guiding the helm of public
affairs, should weigh well in his own mind, the stupendous work
he undertakes for the public;—for upon his conduct may depend
the utter ruin, or the glory of his country.

If I can point at some outlines for the future conduct of Ministers, to regain the immense loss we have sustained by the late treaty
of peace with France, and offer a few leading, and permanent observations, respecting a reconciliation, which timely attended to,
may yet take place, I shall deem my time exceedingly well spent,
as well as think myself entitled to the name of

GUSTAVUS VASSA

Anderton's Coffee–house, July 19

2. *The Morning Post, and Daily Advertiser*, 18 August 1777[2]

For the MORNING POST
AMERICA

Mr. EDITOR,

There never was a period in the annals of this country, that required
more wisdom, resolution, and spirit, in the administration, than our
present situation with America, France, and Spain; notwithstanding
the universal complaint of indifference, inactivity, and inapposite-
ness, there appear in all the measures adopted by our present race

of statesmen for ascertaining the natural rights and maintaining the dignity of the empire.

To illustrate this truth, we need only take a back view of their measures, which gendered the soul of rebellion in America, by the stipulations agreed to, and ratified by the last treaty of peace with France, and Spain: the same perseverance in a chain of false politics, with an equal degree of supineness, and self-sufficiency which characterized our peace makers, seem hereditary in their successors.

The plan adopted for sending legions of foreign troops to the American continent, is so pregnant of a profound ignorance of the real interest of Britain in those regions, that even the most superficial speculator who looks but a little forward, can at once discover the injurious tendency of sending foreign mercenaries to aid us in the reduction of our colonies.

The numberless proofs, which may be adduced from ancient as well as modern history, of the evils brought upon empires, kingdoms, and states, who made use of mercenary strangers to assist them in the conquest of distant countries, are so many and striking, that it would be needless to quote them in this place.

German auxiliaries in Flanders, Mr. Editor, where it is the interest of the different sovereigns to take care, that at the end of a peace, each division of foreigners shall return to their own country, differ widely from Germans, or Russians transported from slavery, penury, and an ungrateful soil, into a land of *Canaan* flowing with milk, and honey. Where they are not only far removed from their tyrant masters, but invited by the very people they are sent to conquer, not only to join, and share with them those rights, and privileges set up for, but also offering them a most liberal share of the property of a rich extensive fertile country; where they behold with astonishment in every province they pass, a luxuriance of nature they never beheld before;—where they daily meet with townships, and settlements of numbers of their own countrymen, who either quitted their land for want of bread, or were traffick'd for, and sent thither as bond servants, but now having regained their freedom, they find thousands of them settled in properties, estates, and farms of their own, living in comfort, ease, and even luxury in comparison with their former miserable and indigent state.

These, with numberless other reasons improper to be exposed in the speculations of a public paper, ought to have had some weight with administration before they had agreed to send armies of foreigners into our continental colonies.

Indeed had the spirit of true wisdom, and flood policy guided their resolutions, and councils in disposing of a number of foreign troops, to aid in the conquest of *islands,* and such situations as sagacity, and true policy could have suggested, and have often but in vain been pointed out to our demagogues in power; instead of pouring in an addition of strength to the cause of rebellion, and furnishing new vigour by virtue of veteran adventurers to the spirit of independancy,–we might by this time have not only negotiated an honourable reconciliation with the refractory colonies,–and even had the flower of their army, and navy, to have joined Great Britain in such conquests as would have repaid us the expences of the war, but restored harmony to the continent, and re-united our former friendship with these people upon a lasting, solid, and mutual foundation of commercial, alliance, and dependancy on each other.

But what can be expected in a country where every natural good is sacrificed to partial views, and schemes of interest merely calculated to prolong the calamities of an unprofitable, and unnatural war, by which a few are enriched, and the nation perhaps effectually ruined?

Twenty or thirty thousand foreign troops might be happily, and advantageously employed, with the power of the British navy, to superintend round *islands,* where they might answer the end of garrisons from *Cape Devarde* islands, to the *Hvannah,* there, Sir, is a field for employing both the wisdom, and genius of a capacitated, spirited, and liberal minded administration?–The dominion of the seas, and the possession of islands, which are the grand, and lead-ing avenues to the *East Indies, South Seas,* and *West Indies*, is the only empire Britain should contend for;–troops drafted into islands, where from the nature of the climate, and establishment of the in-habitants, they cannot mingle with the people, nor in any shape quit, or refuse their duty,–may answer a great, and good end, as auxiliaries; but once set upon a continent, and initiated, as well as invited to all the advantages of wide extended dominions, where they can settle *ad libitum,* are considerations worthy of much more attention than has yet distinguished our present ministers.–If these observations can point out to their conviction some errors, which have crept into their most recent measures with respect to the mode of carrying on the continental war in America;–there may yet be pointed out a line of turning the current of war into an advanta-geous channel to Britain, before the opening of another campaign.

The number of adventuring foreigners, which have emigrated from Europe, to join the American cause is astonishing, Mr. Editor, and they continue to flock thither, particular[ly] from Germany, France, and Holland, as well as from Great Britain, and Ireland, the views of France, and Spain are deep, and interested in this scheme, because if they can lengthen out the war until a third power genders, and takes root on the continent, it answers every end to them they wish, which is division;–they are ready, or nearly so, in their West India colonies, to take the first advantage they see will answer the purpose of distressing Britain in those regions. Their present mode of encouraging piracy and depredations by their own people, fitted out under American colours, and the dis-tresses our trade and plantations suffer in those seas, are too alarm-ing not to merit more attention, and some spirited measures. One thousand eight hundred foreign emigrants, within these three years have joined the American cause. This is a fact I have, Mr. Editor, in my power, if necessary, to ascertain. It is therefore high time for this country to act with resolution and vigour, to defeat the views and purposes of her hereditary natural foes, and to come to speedy

measures to re-unite, if possible, the mother country with her natural offspring by means adequate and honourable to both,–is the
ardent wish and prayer of

GUSTAVUS VASSA

Anderton's Coffee House, August 4

---

3. *The Morning Post, and Daily Advertiser,* 7 November 1777[3]

For the MORNING POST

Mr. EDITOR,

Last Tuesday, between two and three o'clock in the afternoon,
going from St. Paul's to Charingcross, in Fleet–street I perceived
the passengers on each side the street looking earnestly, with a mixture of surprise that bespoke amazement, indignation, contempt,
and such other sensations as different minds are agitated with on
beholding an object that calls up immediate astonishment from its
appearance. This *phenomenon,* which called forth the attention of
every creature that beheld it, and seeing every eye directed to the
street behind me, I, of course, turned around,–and was in a moment
planet-struck at the object which thus attracted every eye.–The
windows and doors were as full of gazers as if it had been Lord
Mayor's day, or any new solemn procession.–The subject of their
astonishment was indeed new,–and to me appeared to be an *exotic*
of the neuter gender; for no one, to behold it, could possibly deter-
mine in their own mind whether it was *male* or *female,* and yet it
had something of the resemblance of a production, wherein some
of the human species had a share in its formation.–A good looking
old *English Gentleman,* who stood by me, said, It was a young
British Nobleman, who had lately returned from his travels. On
which an honest *Hibernian* who stood near us, exclaimed, By
Jasus, Sir, I beg your pardon for contradicting you (quoth Paddy);

for by my shoul [soul] I take it to be one of the new animals brought home by some of your curious voyagers; who, as is said, have *crossed* round the world, and have brought home some of the strange creatures found in their way when they came through the northwest passage, by the *Archipellago of St. Lazarus.*–The creature must be the production of a southern climate, for sure I am such a beast never was vegitated in a northern soil!' 'Troth (said a studious looking *Scot,* who overheard the Irish Gentleman) I am entirely of your opinion, Sir; for I will be crucified if there is a single atom of the human composition of either of our country folk in [such] a strange monster as that thing is; for although it has at first sight a something of the human species in its figure, on a close view of its features you will find yourself disappointed, and on contemplating a little more, you will perceive that from its stupid, indolent look, mixed with the appearance of a self consequence in its mode of gazing upon the spectators, as it is carried along; that it has nothing of the *vive risible* features of any of the monkey, or mangumbo kind.' At which my Hibernian befriend cried, 'Stop, stop! I did not tell you it was a monster! and see, my jewels, the owner drives it in that *phaeton* round the streets, as Astley does his great little horse, before he advertises it for a public shew.' Thus ended our conversation.—The being, Mr. Editor, whatever it was, sat upon the left hand of an old man, whose features denoted that of a worn out *Compagnion de Voyage*, and lover of *virtu.* The creature had a man's hat on its head, which was covered, in appearance, with human hair dressed in the *degage* courtesan taste, plaited up behind, and its locks carelessly flowing on each side;–over its carcase was thrown a long mantle, seemingly of fine white freeze cloth, a large cape round its shoulders, with a broad gold lace, and down its breast, or foreside, the lace was continued to its *hoofs* or *toes.* Its face, as already mentioned, had something of a human cast, but of a mixture of features entirely new; its nose was longer than *common*, its complexion seemed made up with *fucus's*, or cosmetics of different kinds; but there broke thro' their colourings a species of sallowness that bespoke its natural *hue,* between the copper and brass–looking skins of old people, who had been long used to paint, notwithstanding the creature cannot be old; its eyes looked something like those of a dead cod,–its mouth rather large, and it grinned not to laugh, but to shew its teeth, which appeared tolerable white. Behind the phaeton stood two well dressed footmen, in green liveries; on the carriage was a coat armour of distinction, and a crest on a *chapeau.* It seemed to chatter to the person who drove it slowly along, as if to give time to the spectators to examine it. The only thing it moved was its lips and head, which it turned from side to side, and seemed to stare at the people with an un-meaning, cold, contemptuous look, as if they were creatures below its notice. This makes me think it is an animal of pitiful pride, full of its own consequence, and deeply in love with itself; for it appears fretful and surly.–These hints may lead some of your learned readers, and lovers of natural history, to inquire into this animal's species and generation, as well as into its place of nativity; whether it be an *amphibi,* or a terrestrial; whether quadruped, or aduped; or whether it may really be a young person of fashion of these times, or what it really is.–I am not, upon my honour, Mr. Editor, any way concerned in the property of this creature, and therefore I hope you will think I do not send you this, in order to get money, by raising the public curiosity, before it be advertised for exhibition,–if it is brought hither for that purpose from beyond seas. I remain,

Sir, your most humble servant,
GUSTAVUS VASSA

Peel's Coffee-house
Fleet-street, October 30th

4. *The Morning Post, and Daily Advertiser,* 1 January 1778[4]

For the MORNING POST

To Lord NORTH

LETTER I

My Lord,

The turn American affairs have taken, notwithstanding the variety of advice, and information your Lordship has received from the New England pensioners, to which so much ear has been given, and in whom so much confidence has been trusted, proves that error, or something worse has operated amongst those who followed, and abetted the system adopted for bringing back to their duty the rebellious Americans.

It is a matter of little consequence to the aggregate body of the British empire, whether your Lordship, or Lord Germaine, or any other is officially *ostensible* for measures immediately issuing from their departments in the administration since his Majesty consigns the superintendency of the whole administration to a Premier, your Lordship is that chief of the King's Ministers.

It is therefore that no scheme, no plan, nor no measure can meet with approbation, or success or be in any way adopted, without your knowledge and concurrence.

A time draws near, when a justification of the fatal measures pursued during the course of this unlucky war will be demanded (I speak not, my Lord, as a modern *patriot,* for I despise the tribe) of Administration; and I am well aware, *Sir,* will be had.

A people who, by excess of freedom, are daily approaching to the verge of slavery, are, my Lord, more formidable than, I fear, your wisdom and sagacity have penetrated.

And however well cloathed Administration may be, by the united sovereign power and concurrence of Parliament, it is nothing new, in this country, to see Ministers deserted, and reduced to pitiful plight:–The present mode of parliamentary representation sufficiently authorizes this suggestion.–I blame not your Lordship for having any hand in changing to corruption and venality, either the spirit of the *electors,* or those they make a choice of to represent them. These premises drawn, we need not wonder at the clamours of the present demagogues of opposition; their political refinement on our constitution, with other like great changes, we owe to the glorious, immortal revolution, which opposition so much idolize.

As the Premier of the day, my Lord, it is a matter of surprize, and wonder, you should not be better informed respecting the original, and true state of America; as a man of business,—of calculator,—-and an adept in financing, it is strange you do not yet understand the great commercial *line of interest* between *America* and *Great Britain,*—To have been led into such chimerical schemes, and plans, as have been adopted in your *reign*, discovers at least a want of superior abilities. This, my Lord, is not the season of mediocrity; I shall not conceive an idea of your having any other view than that of being a faithful servant of the Crown, and a good Briton.

Look for a moment to the rise of this war, behold that dreadful supineness, which conducted its first campaigns in America; the war began in New England, in New England it should have immediately *ended.*–No reason can be given for breeding, fostering, and abetting *rebellion*.

General Gage either sacrificed, or had it not in his command to exert his strength, and power, or rebellion never would have been what it is;–why was not *Boston* afterwards supplied with sufficient troops to keep that important *station.*

The retreat to *New York,* and the plans afterwards adopted to send such an expedition as went through Canada, is full of ignorance, full of absurdity, and I wish they may not turn out designs inimical to the sovereign dignity of this country in its contrivance; when New York was in our possession, a few troops from Canada were sufficient to possess them of *Ticonderoga;* that post gained, they need attempt no further.–The British arms could with ease have reached Albany, and its environs; but great Ministers, my Lord, do not think it worth their while to become *geographers*.— Why did not Gen. Sir William Howe attack Mr. General Washington, with nearly equal numbers? You will perhaps say, Sir William Howe is of the *Fabian* line; if so Mr. Washington is no bastard;– but it was necessary to wear out the war, to sacrifice to avarice, not only this country, but many thousands of excellent subjects;—and those who gain by *legal spoil,* if they survive, will laugh at poor old England, as do, my Lord, your modern chiefs of patriotism for whom you care not a button,—because they only gull the credulous, ignorant, and unwary with the tale of a *tub*; who labour to sell those whom they have bought for seven years,–and indeed that is the only plausible excuse which can be made for them: I speak only of those chiefs, who bring in auxiliary adventurers to assist them in their parliamentary opposition.–A few enthusiasts, who have native interest, are to be pitied for their folly, and imbecility.

Had an expedition from New York taken place, in concert with the taking of *Ticonderoga*, Mr. General Gates's army would, if they would have stood, have been in the same humiliating state, which Gen. Burgoyne's army is in now.–The principal expedition necessary to forward the King's interest, and the service of this country, should have been carried on from New York to *Albany*, and *further*, for a tenth part of the expence it has cost from *Quebec,* to where the British *army* were made prisoners; but that would not have answered the end of those, who contrived this diabolical plan.

I address this to your Lordship as *Premier* only; when I have done with you, my Lord, I will of course address your colleagues.

December 27, 1777

GUSTAVUS VASSA

5. *The Morning Post, and Daily Advertiser,* 4 March 1778[5]

For the MORNING POST

Mr. EDITOR,

FACTION, opposition, and mock patriotism are at last drove into confusion, by Lord North's Reconciliation Bill.–Whatever serious effect Administration may hope to derive from it, I know not: but I trust the wisdom of the Ministry foresaw, that before it is published in America, those Colonies in rebellion will be convinced thoroughly, it is their interest to reunite themselves, upon liberal terms, to the mother country.–It is high time not only to shew the world, that wisdom only guides the helm of the state, but that resolution, and a speedy exertion of power, shall convince our natural enemies of the national indignation for their perfidy and infidelity to *Britain,* for the part they have so long acted with impunity, to aid, supply, and support the Rebels in America.–By cutting off all communication between the rebellious *Americans,* and *France* and *Spain,* or any further intercourse, either in *Europe,* or the *West Indies,* these deluded people will soon return to their duty, and they may yet make *Britain* amends for the losses sustained during this disagreeable war.–No man, but an enemy to the *British monarchy,* can wish *America* to be independant, merely because our Ministers may not have been so fortunate, and successful as those who directed the last war.–I own I have felt very sensibly for the loss of many opportunities I have seen slip, since the commencement of the *American* troubles, by which they might have been ended; but I have the charity to believe, that our Ministers have done as much as their line of abilities could lead them to do.–It is not every age that produces a *Sully,* or a *Marlborough,* nor so fortunate a Minister as *Pitt.* The current of fortune drove furiously for a time in the last Minister's favour; but, *alas!* he has lived to see that his former system of politics, altho', in war–successful, became, when reduced into a *peace,* the means of blasting all the laurels he had acquired for his country.–May the present set of Ministers profit by his example! May they be able to conquer from the common, and hereditary foes of *Britain,* with equal rapidity, all those valuable islands, which were sacrificed, at the end of the last war, for Mr. *Pitt's* favourite *Canada. Britain* is formed by nature to be the Empress of the Main, and the Sovereign of Islands; but it is contrary to every idea, that even common sense can form, to imagine a commercial, limited monarchy, should grasp at the unlimited empire of a continent like *America.*–If the Commissioners, who are to carry the Reconciliation Bill to *America*, can announce, that *Britain* is determined to revenge herself immediately on her perfidious enemies, where she can at once crush their marine power, I should not be surprized to hear of Gen. *Washington*, and his whole army having joined the Royal Standard at *Philadelphia*, or *New* York, by the middle of *May* next; otherwise the Commissioners, and their Missionaries may, if they please, use all the Acts of Parliament they carry to *America*–for a certain purpose!

GUSTAVUS VASSA

---

6. *The Morning Post, and Daily Advertiser,* 10 March 1778[6]

For the MORNING POST
To Lord NORTH
Is e Mian Naduir gu Graidhamid ar Duthick[7]
LETTER II

My Lord,
We are taught by nature the love of our country! Such was the reply of *Galgus* to *Caesar, w*hen he accused the *British Prince* of temerity, and boldness, for driving the Romans out of *Caledonia;*

but, *alas,* my Lord, what shall we say of you, at a time when the soul of loyalty, native valour, and love of their country, animated every gallant spirit that breathes the air of free born Britons, from utmost *Thule* to Dover *Cliffs,* when the Sovereign had it in his power to command the lives and fortunes of every real lover of constitutional liberty, to support, and sustain the dignity of the British Empire, and to reduce audacious disobedience, and rebellion to a state of lawful, and natural obedience?

At a moment when the torrent of good fortune was breaking in upon the efforts of your Sovereign, to bring back to their duty a race of unnatural, and ungratefull bastards, in order that they might be in due time legitimised;–at such a crisis to offer, in the face of a British Parliament, *terms of humiliating reconciliation*, beggars, my Lord, in my mind, all description *of pusilanimity,* if not depravity in the management of the public cause.

The bill you have brought into parliamemt, as a measure of reconciliation between Britain, and her revolted Colonies, lays down a precedent for any, or all the nations of Europe, to consider them as an independent people, confessing by your own tacit acknowledgement, that they are invincible.–It was all they wanted, my Lord; and they will speedily shew you, that they have the wisdom, and gratitude to despise your measures, notwithstanding they are sanctified by the consent of parliament.

I have long seen, and lamented, my Lord, that you little know the people you have to deal with, and that you will not be advised by men who are really willing, and able to give you a true idea of American virtue.–If the terms you offer are accepted by the Congress, you may live to see the most populous streets in London overgrown with grass. The Americans only wanted an opportunity to depopulate Britain and Ireland. Your reconciliation bill, my Lord, effectually opens a new avenue to the grateful Americans,– to draw from this country every subject worthy of their acceptance. It were a thousand degrees better for Britain, that America was separated from us for ever, than for them only to be nominal subjects.

Take courage, my Lord! Carry on the war with spirit, only change its present channel.–The Americans will sue for *mercy, peace,* and *protection.*–Revive again the fire of true patriotism, which you have nearly extinguished. Let the British lion once more be fairly roused; Give the command of the army, and navy to men of spirit, courage, and abilities;–let the fury of our revenge fall where it ought to do, on the perfidious House of Bourbon:–then, my Lord, you will truly merit the name of a great, and good Minister!

March 5

GUSTAVUS VASSA

---

7. The Morning Post, and Daily Advertiser, 11 June 1778[8]

For the MORNING POST

Mr. EDITOR,

DURING this vacancy of politics, the following essay may afford many of your enlightened readers some amusement,–The other day I was agreeably entertained by the conversation of some ingenious gentlemen of the *British,* and *Irish* nations.

The discourse turned upon the antiquity, and origin of the inhabitants of their different countries. Woes me! quoth I, who am not a native of either of the happier isles, but a continental spawn of accident; I can only be an humble hearer in this grand dispute.–The Englishman, as a matter of right, began; said he, I am firmly of opinion, whatever innovations have crept in amongst us, by the propensity of our mothers to novelty, the original inhabitants of Britain were all of them *True-born Englishmen;* and as to the people called by *Tacitus* and other Historians *Aborigines,* I am, with that illustrious author, of opinion, their origin is very difficult to trace.

A *Scotch gentleman,* with great humour, agreed with the English

gentleman, that *Tacitus* was very just in his remarks upon the difficulty of tracing, with any degree of certainty, the origin of *True-
born Englishmen*; for, said he, altho' no nation on earth produced
more originals than Old England, she might challenge all that ever
wrote of antiquity, or that ever may write, to give any thing like a
true account, who were the *Aborigines* of that part of South Britain
called *England.*–A gentleman of Ireland, happy to find an apt occasion to speak of his *Milesian* descent, "By my shoul, said he,
you have hit him home: I will soon shew you, gentlemen, how your
whole nation of Britain was originally peopled by the descendants
of *Milesius*;–first of all, we peopled Scotland out of Ireland with
Milesians, and then we sent a few tribes over to England, in order
to people that country too: You may therefore rest satisfied, that
all of you are originally of Irish Aborigine, for there is no doubt
but the Irish nation was the first, and only nation in those seas
whose first people was taught to walk upright, or as I may say, go
upon their *hind legs.*"

An ancient *Briton,* who was rather impatient to hear the Irish
Gentleman's mode of peopleing Great Britain, said, "Sir, I allow
that no nation on earth satisfies their appetite with false, and un-
founded notions of their antiquity more than those Irish, who call
themselves *Milesians*; for the truth is, you have no documents of
any date that can be said to savour of antiquity: all your accounts
of yourselves are merely tales of a *tub. Look you,* my friend—for
we have undeniable records, and stubborn facts to prove, that
Wales did people all South-Britain, as the original *Albions* did that
of *North–Briton*; for to be plain, and pleasant with you, we never
had any great notion of your *Milesians*, as you call them; and as to
you, Mr. True–born Englishman, it is nothing new from your mot-
ley tribe, to speak with ingratitude of your founders, since ye know
not one in ten thousand of ye who were your *mothers*, much less
who were your *fathers*.

"Moreover it is clear that neither *Scotland* nor *Wales*, could possibly have been peopled from southern climes. Who the devil

would quit a land of *milk* and *honey,* to live upon *clifted rocks,* and mountains of *ice* and *snow*? Besides there is nothing but the dialect, that affords the least divinity between the fat, brawny, fleshy *Milesian*, and the iron-faced hardy *Scot*, or the short, stout, athletic rawboned *Welshman.* The true spirit of the north is perseverance, and conquest. The northern nations have often re-peopled all Europe; and as ungrateful as their colonies and children have ever been to them, after they planted them in rich soils, and forgetting their origin by being sunk in luxury and vice, they always find fresh supplies of natural veterans to guard them in times of danger, and secure their legal freedom. Another proof that no people of the north could ever originate from the south, is, that even the Roman empire with all her legions, never could entirely subdue *Wales*, nor did they ever get above a third of Scotland; when they were so tired of their futile attempt during near 400 years, that at last they evacuated Britain, as an unconquerable nation. In what period of history can the Milesian valour speak to such a subject, I would be glad to know look you," said the ancient Briton?

"We have no instance since the Romans of any nation of spirit coming from the south to the north, to conquer barren mountains and leave fertile fields. It is much more likely, that the Scots bordering upon Ireland, made at various times descents into that rich country, and finding it a happier climate and soil than their own, remained amongst the natives; and hence the old Irish acquired their barbarous language; for the *Erse* affords not any thing to discover its affinity with any southern ancient languages, but continues to be spoken in all the remote parts of the northern nations, particularly among the Delicarlians of *Sweden*, and thence to the northern *Tartars*."

GUSTAVUS VASSA

Hungerford Coffee-house,
June 9, 1778

8. *The Morning Post, and Daily Advertiser,* 23 June 1778[9]

For the MORNING POST

A MILITARY PARALLEL

Mr. EDITOR,

YOU have lately indulged me with a place in your paper; I could not therefore resist my propensity for sending yon the following short *Gallic* piece of history, as it does honour to the chief who commanded the *Gauls* at that time.

But it brought into my mind a groupe of things, which a short essay can but poorly explain, To tell you, that I have been a *Soldier,* would be of no consequence, unless I told you, that I have been a commander of men. Battles and sieges I have frequently been in; and sometimes I have been eminently successful, Mr. Editor. I never quitted the field unsuccessfully but once–that fatal day ended all my hopes of glory! And I soon beheld myself in a different point of view to what I had looked at myself before. Indeed it may have been for me a happier change, otherwise unavailing pride, loaded with vanity, and embroidered with self-conceit, might in time have made a very ridiculous fellow of me.

You may remember I long ago reprobated the idea of an expedition from *Canada* across the Lakes. There were but two principles upon which I could possibly see it founded: the one was speculation, without a shadow of real knowledge of the undertaking; the other was a superficial knowledge of some flattering parts, supported by an amazing fund of self-applause, in imagining the possession of superlative ability merely because of being by the stroke of the hand of Providence, the child of Good Fortune. I would not have dared to have solicited my Sovereign for such command, much less, Mr. Editor, professed the imbecility of planning so moonshine-like an expedition. You will perhaps say no, because you profess yourself an old soldier: I say that is not the fault of those who set the Canadian expedition on foot as it was carried into execution.–But to the story of Belgius the Gaul.

Belgius with his clans having left their native country in search of a more favourable clime, (for they had little or nothing to eat at home) undertook, without any heavy *artillery,* to traverse the alps; a region which nought but *Hercules* ever had attempted, and for which *Hercules* was deemed a god. The glory of the *Gallic Chief* was only to be thought amongst the first of men. Pardon the reflection, Mr. Editor; those Gauls were called Barbarians; alas! how they differed from our modern heroes. Our great moderns write long letters, and tell you a story that fills two or three sheets of paper about taking a few old iron guns, and killing some forties or fifties of men. Oratory, and senatorial eloquence, are necessary to make a Christian General of our day. But a General of Gaul could neither read, nor write, else why call them Barbarians? yet they could manage such expeditions, and make such conquests, that no nation before them, nor since their time, have equalled. Had *Belgius* been at Saratoga, I should not have had occasion to have quoted this part of his history. *Ptolomy,* King of *Macedonia,* was the only monarch who "treated the irruptions of the Gauls into *Italy* and Greece with contempt. The Gauls having sacked *Rome,* and laid the *capitol* in *ashes,* turned their face to *Greece*, having heard of *Alexander's* fame; they were told *Macedonia* was rich with the spoils of the world!–Quoth *Belgius*, 'my brothers, friends, and fellow soldiers, let us find out those *Macedonians*, and share at least the plunder of the universe with them.–I wish to meet a brave people in arms, it is no mark of a true soldier to look with indignation and contempt on an enemy with whom he is not at war!' 'None,' said he to *Mulucha Minichan,* his companion, 'are invincible but the Gods! We are my fellow soldier, but men! and it is beneath a chief of *Gauls*, my brother, to be proud, and full of mean arrogance, because the Gods may have occasionally crowned him with fortune, and fame. A man of pride is but a shadow, which perishes as he rises into fortune's lap; but wisdom, modesty, and perseverance will crown the possessor with endless glory!'–The Gauls were now on the borders of *Macedon,* and *Belgius,* their leader, sent ambassadors to *Ptolamy,* who treated them with disrespect and arrogance, because their mission was to offer peace, provided the Macedonian King would give a moderate price for it! *Ptolomy's* vanity was raised to such a pitch at the demand of peace, that he told his people, the *Gauls* after their long march and great fatigues, were afraid to come to a battle. 'Besides,' said he, 'they dread the very name of a *Macedonian* soldier': and to the ambassadors, he answered, 'ye shall have no peace unless your principal officers are left as hostages, that your people shall lay down their arms!' The ambassadors returned to *Belgius*, and told him what had passed; that *Ptolomy* in a rage, cried out, 'What shall *Macedon,* who gave to the wide and extended world, treat for a peace with a few tribes of undisciplined bare ar[se]d Gauls? no! away, away!'–The Gauls could not forbear a general laugh throughout the army at this reply!

"'*Ah*!' said *Belgius*, 'is it so *Ptolomy* replies to us?—The Gallic legions will teach the mistaken proud *Ptolomy* manners and humility, to his superiors;' and turning to his army, says, 'Gauls, will ye fight, or will ye become captives of *Macedon*? What say ye, my children of the North! will ye follow me and make your way through the mighty phalanx of Macedonia, or will ye afford them a triumph, and become their slaves?',–The *Gauls,* shouting with one voice, cried, 'Conquest, or death!–*Belgius* lead on!'"–The Gauls were not more than 30,000, the Macedonians 200,000: the Gauls were far from home, ill cloathed, ill fed with no arms but the short black spear and a lance: The Macedonians were armed with all the new–invented arms of Alexander the Great, and every other invention of defence used in those days; well cloathed, and well fed,–For all this the Gauls gained a compleat victory, and *Belgius* immortal honour!

GUSTAVUS VASSA

---

9. *The Morning Post, and Daily Advertiser,* 2 July 1778[10]

For the MORNING POST

REVERSE OF FORTUNE

Mr. EDITOR,

AN illustrious person, whose early misfortunes, from the mistaken zeal, and principle of his predecessors, obliged him to become a man of the world, and to endeavour the enquirement of such treasure, as no mortal power could deprive him of, while life remained, travelled Europe, Asia, Africa, and America, as a merchant, and philosopher; both honourable characters, and both of infinite advantage to society!

In his youth he was bred to arms, and bore a distinguished rank before he was twenty years old. A series of misfortunes changed his turn of mind, and he felt a secret pleasure in pursuing, unknown, a scheme of life becoming a private gentleman.

At Cairo, in Egypt, he fell in with the following adventure, amongst many others which he met with; and, as it brought him to the possession of a friend, whose misfortunes in youth arose from the same cause with his own, their meeting may afford many feeling hearts a sympathy unknown but to virtuous minds, and a contemplation, which none but the wise can reach.

Our traveller had an interpreter, Mordecai, an Armenian Jew, who was likewise a child of sorrow, having once been a merchant of great worth, and reputed a man of honour, tho' a *Jew.* He lost his fortune by the hand of Providence, in a storm, and now for bread became an interpreter.

As they were passing in the streets of Cairo, a great multitude stood round an old, venerable, tall man, whose hair, as white as the milk-white lamb, hung careless round his shoulders: he sung, with a melodious voice, a melancholy tune, in a tongue which none round him could understand; but so powerful and fascinating was his harmony, and so commanding of respect was his countenance, and manner, that the rude rabble of Cairo stood with an awful muteness round him, which at once bespoke a mixture of pleasure and venerable admiration!

"Mordecai," (said the traveller,) "who is that fine old prophet, whom the ruffian mob of Cairo stand so silent to hear?" "Ah! my Lord," (said Mordecai)," he is like me, a child of dire fortune!– That venerable wanderer, Sir, was once in a most exalted line of life, tho' now he earns his *quotidien,* by singing his mournful, pleasing, harmonious ditties to the ruffian tribes of Cairo. When I was in India, in the days of my prosperity, that noble Christian was prime Minister, and General to one of the first Sovereigns in the East. His wisdom, and valour, rendered him the admiration of all good men, Mahometans, Gentoos, Jews, or Christians, as he was the dread, and envy, of all villains, of either sect or religion. Tho' generally victorious, he never appeared lifted with pride; nor at reverses, some of which he met with, was he ever dejected. I have seen him at the head of 50,000 victorious troops. Once I saw a letter he wrote after a battle to his Sovereign,–*'I have vanquished the enemy, by the valour of your soldiers!'*–After a series of long services, his Prince permitted him to retire, with a vast treasure, acquired by honourable means, and the liberality of his sovereign. He loaded a very large ship with his treasures, which he designed for Egypt, from thence to remit them to France, where be intended to go, altho' he is a native of some northern nation.–But, alas! how uncertain is human grandeur!–he fell in with a nest of pirates, who attacked his ship, who after a desperate engagement took her, with all his wealth, stripped him naked, and put him on shore, covered only with wounds!–The very barbarians of our Egyptian shore took pity on him! and you behold him now, fallen from what he was, to what he is!"–The traveller let fall the sweet tear of sympathetic compassion! Mordecai, with uplifted eyes, and hands, exclaimed. "O God of Abraham, what a poor creature is man!"

The traveller drew near the subject of their observation. In his countenance, tho' furrowed with age, and sorrow, he could trace the lines of a face at once familiar to his *ken*. It was the companion of his youth, the illustrious son of—.

This meeting would be too tender a tale for me to relate; but, after an absence of thirty years, two sincere friends met, and now enjoy, with each other, the satisfaction of retirement, and that happiness, which virtue can only afford.

The song he sung to the tawney mobility of Cairo was, the following, to the tune of *"Lochaber no more!"*

LET mortals take warning whom splendor adorn,
Nor virtue, nor valour, secures them from *scorn*;
When *Fate* has decreed them to pay an auld score,
Like me, they may wander on some foreign shore!
If virtue's allied to a life without blame,
And laurels obtain'd, without thirst of fame;
'Tho' Fortune's turn'd cruel, I had them *galore;*
E'er plunder'd and ruin'd, on Egypt's fam'd shore.
Wherever I pilgrim, whate'er comes of me,
Fair *Albion!* may blessings show'r ever on thee,
Mav thy sons fam'd for valour, as always of *Yore,*
Maintain their great fame,—and from conquest their *shore!*
And, oh! may that from whence I'm exil'd.
Still flourish in virtue, tho' barren and wild;
Her sons rich in honour, far distant explore,
More worth than the di'monds on India's bright shore.
Ye daughters of ALBION, whose beauties disclose
More sweets than the lillies, or soft blushing rose;
Whose honour preserves you, from tainture or guile,
Preserve that bold race, who will guard the *old isle!*

GUSTAVUS VASSA

Hungerford Coffee-house,
June 27, 1778.

10. *The Morning Post, and Daily Advertiser,* 10 July 1778[11]

For the MORNING POST

The arrival of General Howe has awakened the public anxiety, with an expectation of his reasons being made public for so long, and passive a conduct to the rebels in America. Mr. Howe, as a military man, will no doubt, for his own honour, give his reasons for not having given a decisive blow to rebellion during so many campaigns, and so many unavailing movements of his army.

All the military men of experience, and judgment throughout Europe, are puzzled to account for those delays, and procrastinations to a decisive action with Gen. Washington, which have marked the British General's operations through the different campaigns of his command. The intent of this essay is not to enter into the *minutiae* of Mr. Howe's generalship; but it is hoped he will step forth, and satisfy those, whose judgement, experience, and profession, entitle them to be satisfied of some doubts, that naturally hang round them at so unprecedented a mode of conducting a war.

I may venture to affirm, that no period of ancient, or modern history will furnish the most ingenious speculator with any thing that can be brought forward, as a parallel to the campaigns of which General Howe has had the command, for inactivity, and decision!

This war having been carried on upon entire new principles, military men of course are anxious to know its political, and military ratios: the British army has, on all hands, been acknowledged to have been every way qualified for attack, or defence; they were likewise the flower of our veterans,—soldiers, who had already traversed America, although not with the same Commander in Chief at their head. The rebel army, in opposition to them, admitting for a moment they were thrice the number of the British, were not in fact any way equal to them, either in experience, discipline, appointment, arms, ammunition, artillery, or implements of war, for attack, and defence. Let their bravery be deemed as high as possible, there is a want of steadiness in irregular troops, which nothing but a military command, and the habit of war will diffuse through an army, so as to make them equal to stand a long and obstinate engagement. The British soldiers were equal to that; and with no disrespect to the Americans, I may say they had not yet acquired the necessary time by war to make them such veterans.

It is true, the mode in which they have been treated by the British army, has given them every encouragement which such an army could wish, to set a high value upon their own valour, and superiority; at a time, when in a manner destitute of arms, ammunition, cloathing, money, or permanent alliance, they were let lie a whole winter in camp within a few miles of the royal army unmolested, is sufficient reason for them to judge highly of their consequence in the eyes of the enemy.

What would the Roman Senate, or that of Carthage, have said to *Flaminius,* or *Hannibal,* and the one returned from *Asia,* or the other from *Italy,* after such campaigns as Mr. Howe has gone through?–I leave mankind to judge.–In what manner would *Augustus,* or *Julius* have treated a General, whose account must in effect have been no more than this?–"Sire, I embarked your army at New-York, and providentially your royal navy, under my brother's command, landed safe at Chesapeak Bay, when, with equal ease, they might have been landed from the Delaware; but that is not my business. I brought them, except a small skirmish, the which I could not avoid, safe to *Philadelphia,* their destination, where I cantonned them warmly, and snugly in winter quarters; there I made it my business to countenance, and encourage your Majesty's most inveterate enemies; to your friends, there was no need of encouragement–all rivitted to your cause by duty, and loyalty!–The enemy lay buried under snow in their huts, a few miles from us, ill cloathed, ill paid, and every way so despicably, and miserably appointed as an army, either fit for attack or defence, that it would have disgraced your Majesty's arms, and even shocked humanity to have routed the poor devils from their burrows, and cabins, until stores came to their aid, and some foreign reinforcements, to make them worth the notice of your troops to attack."

"Spring brought them into their camp in troops, and summer produced such legions, that I thought it adviseable to leave them the whole country to themselves, and re–embark your troops to New York and Long Island, as more healthful and excellent summer quarters, where diversions without molestation may be enjoyed. Having in all these things done my duty as a general, I am come home to breathe my native air, and to receive such applause and congratulations from my sovereign and country, as my eminent services for the state *deserve*!"

Poor Mr. Burgoyne has been denied the presence of his sovereign for having saved his army from slaughter and death; but Mr. Howe has been received by his sovereign for his humanity, in not disturbing the poor American army in their winter cantonments, and restoring to the congress their original imperial seat of council, Philadelphia. Had the Duke of Cumberland in April, 1746, so treated the poor starved Highlanders, who for four days before the battle of Culloden, had not one man's proper provisions amongst six of them, the which his Highness well knew, instead of forcing them to a battle, and thereby breaking the neck of the rebellion,— what do you think George King George the second would have said to his favourite son, Mr. Editor? You will say that was a different kind of rebellion perhaps; I own it. The clans were headed by men of honour and gentlemen, although unfortunately addicted to mistaken political principles. The Americans are a set of abandoned ingrates, without the shadow of either virtue or principle, to give colour to their rebellion; and unless it be some renegado from either of these three kingdoms, not a gentleman is there to be found in all their armies, that can tell where his grandfather was born;

besides they are the sworn enemies of monarchy and Kingly government; no doubt in some measure pleasing in their principles to
those who have treated them with such compassion and humanity.

It is time for administration to change their mode of choosing
their Commanders in Chief, either for land or sea, and out of
minority men! else woe will be the fate of poor Old England!

GUSTAVUS VASSA

Hungerford Coffee-house,
July 8, 1778.

SECTION 2
1783

The anonymous letter of 18 March 1783 featured in this section was written to *The Morning Chronicle, and London Advertiser.* It may have been written by Vassa or by both Vassa and Ottobah Cugoano.[12] Just as he had sought Granville Sharp's legal advice in 1774 after William Kirkpatrick orchestrated the kidnapping of Jon Annis, the day after the anonymous letter in question was published, on 19 March 1783, Vassa called on Sharp with an account of the 132 African slaves thrown into the sea while on board the *Zong* in November 1781.[13]

The publication of an account of the *Zong* case by Sharp in the newspapers shocked many "virtuous minds," including the Bishop of Chester, Dr. Porteus, the very same man who the author of the anonymous letter mentions having heard preach.[14] It is conceivable that Vassa, who was acquainted with Granville Sharp and increasingly active in the early stages of the abolitionist movement, would have known the Bishop of Chester, and possibly even have been the "friend" who the Bishop alludes to in his response to Sharp: "I return to you many thanks for the copy of the letter you were so obliging as to send me. . . . The letter in the newspapers I had seen before; and I had heard the shocking fact alluded to in it, from a friend of mine."[15]

1. *The Morning Chronicle, and London Advertiser*, 18 March 1783[16]

I had the pleasure of hearing a sermon preached lately before the Society for Propagating Christian Knowledge, at Bow Church. In that discourse, the learned Prelate[17] recommended to the Society's attention, the present state of Negroe Slaves in our Sugar Colonies, secluded as they are from all the advantages of society, yet subject to all its penalties. And in my opinion, he clearly proved, that interest both public and private, was equally concerned with humanity and piety, to ease their burdens and to instruct and bring them forward as members of our community. As this was delivered before a venerable and respectable assembly, and seemed to meet the wish of every thinking person who heard it, I began to congratulate myself, that the time was at last arrived, when Britain, without being dictated to by an haughty rival, or forced by ungrateful rebel children, meant of her own accord, to break asunder the massy chains of slavery, restore liberty, and communicate all her privileges to the sooty sons of Africa, who have, for near two centuries past, dragged out a miserable, wretched existence in our colonies, far from their families, and native country, in deep bondage and unpitied distress, under hard-hearted unfeeling masters.

But from what a pleasing reverie was I soon afterwards awakened.

On March 6, last, I heard the following trial in Guildhall. An action had been brought against the underwriters, to recover the value of 132 African slaves, lost in the passage from the coast of Guinea to Jamaica, of which these were the circumstances....

The Jury, without going out of Court, gave judgment against the Underwriters; the mate [Kelsal] acknowledged he himself had thrown them overboard by the Captain's order, which he thought was to him a sufficient warrant for doing any possible thing, without considering whether it was criminal or not. *The narrative seemed to make everyone present shudder*; and I waited with some impatience, expecting that the Jury, by their foreman, would have applied to the Court for information [on] how to bring the perpetrator of such a horrid deed to justice. A greater aggravation of the crime is, that it is said, the Captain, who died sometime after, was in a delirium, or fit of lunacy when he gave the orders. That there should be bad men to do bad things in all large communities, must be expected; but a community makes the crime general, and provokes divine wrath, when it suffers any member to commit flagrant acts of villainy with impunity. But the claim of the African Slaves on the public is exceedingly strong. They owe us no service, they never have received any benefit from us; then surely we should take care that humanity be not wounded through their sides. It is hardly possible for a state to thrive, where the perpetrator of such complicated guilt, as the present, is not only suffered to go unpunished, but is allowed to glory in the infamy, and carries off the reward of it. Did Providence pass it over, the very negligence, and carelessness of publick honour and publick justice, that is supposed in it, must sink the most flourishing kingdom in anarchy and ruin.

Note, I wish some man of feeling and genius would give poetical language to one of those brave fellows thoughts, whose indignation made him voluntarily share death with his countrymen, rather than life with such unheard of English barbarians. With what noble disdain would he animate his sentiments, with what resignation would he consider himself, when plunging into the ocean, as escaping from brutes in human shape, to throw himself on the unsearchable mercy of his Creator. What a tender adieu would he bid his family and country! What a parting look would he cast on a glorious world, on the sun and heavens, disgraced by such scene. What dreadful imprecations would he utter against such monsters, and against the barbarous, unfeeling country that sent them out, or wished to profit by their trade. It is certainly worthy of observation that our Legislature can every session find time to enquire into and regulate the matter of killing a partridge, that no abuse should be committed, and that he should be fairly shot; and yet it has never thought proper to enquire into the manner of annually kidnapping above 50,000 poor wretches, who never injured us, by a set of the most cruel monsters, that this country can send out.

Anonymous

SECTION 3

1790s

This final section of possible Vassa attributions includes three documents: the written attack on the slave trade and slavery, signed "Gustavus," which appeared in the *Glasgow Courier* on 15 March 1792; the anti-war statement signed "Othello," which was published in *The Cabinet* in January 1795; and an 11 November 1796 letter from "Gust Vassa" to Thomas Atwood Digges.

While the irrefutable attribution of these letters to Vassa is impossible, the most likely of the letters to have been written by Vassa is the anti-war tract published in March 1795 and signed by "Othello," a personage Vassa was likened to by a reviewer of his autobiography in July 1789.[18] External references within the 11 November 1796 letter, which was discovered by Michale D. Benjamin in the Moorland-Spingarn Research Center at Howard University, suggest that it is a forgery by Thomas Atwood Digges.[19]

---

1. To the Editor of the *Glasgow Courier*, 15 March 1792[20]

SIR,

The adherents of the AFRICAN SLAVE TRADE appear now to be sensible, that they must reason upon the subject, and that mere exclamations and complaints against vain philosophy, and the enthusiasm of humanity, will no longer be regarded by the public. Among a few other attempts of this nature, I lately met, in your Paper, with a letter, under the signature of COLUMBUS, in which the writer boldly defends the practice of Slavery, and maintains that its abolition by Government would be contrary to justice. I shall beg leave to offer a few remarks upon that extraordinary performance; and if it should be found, that I belong to that unhappy race of men, who have been the object of this barbarous traffic, I hope the public will give the more indulgence to any errors or mistakes which I may fall into, or to any impropriety of expression which may escape me.

COLUMBUS begins with complaining, that his adversaries, instead of printing the *whole* evidence taken by the Committee of the Commons, "have garbled and selected such parts of it as suited their own views and purposes." It is submitted to the public, whether this be a candid insinuation. The abstract of the evidence, which has been published and circulated, is avowed to contain an abridgement of the evidence only that was brought by the Petitioners; but that it is an unfair or partial abridgement, no person, it is believed, will venture to allege. It exhibits a simple statement of the cruelties with which we have been treated, and the various enormities arising from the Slave Trade, in all its branches. The evidence brought on the other side, by adducing witnesses who, from their situation and rank, had not seen these enormities, can be of little importance. It is merely of a *negative kind,* which can have no weight in opposition to such a large and solid body of *positive testimony.* But if the supporters of the Slave Trade think otherwise, why have they not produced this negative evidence? Why do they complain of what they themselves might so easily rectify? Or rather, how can it be believed, that if this publication could have been of any service to their cause, it would not have appeared long ago? Would they have taken so much pains in retailing the misrepresentations in the Speech made by the white of St. Domingo, and in spreading groundless reports of the insurrections and disorders committed by the Negroes in the other Islands, if they had been capable of producing any real facts to palliate their conduct, if they could have produced a single rag to cover them from the shame to which they stand exposed in the eyes of the whole world?

After this preface, Columbus opens his defence of Slavery, by observing, that Providence, for wise purposes, has formed mankind of different abilities and ranks, and linked them together in a chain of mutual dependence; from which he appears to conclude, that, in this chain, the Negroes were intended to be Slaves.

I am no stranger to this claim of *natural superiority* over my countrymen, which the white people are so ready to advance. But are not the many disadvantages we lie under, with regard to the cultivation of our minds, sufficient, in a great measure, to account for the inferiority of our endowments?

The superior education enjoyed by the free people of the West Indies, may, on the other hand, go some length in accounting for that superiority of talents, and for that refinement of manners, for which they are so much distinguished.

In how many parts of the world, are even white people plunged in utter darkness and barbarism? In what a miserable state were the Britons, when they admitted the practice of selling their own children? If the Negroes appear to the Europeans in a meaner light than other rude nations, it may be attributed to that very slavery into which they have been reduced, and by which their minds are peculiarly debased. May I not, at the same time, be permitted the vanity of observing, that Egypt, the nursery of science in Europe, was originally inhabited by people of similar colour and features to those unfortunate Africans, who are, at this day, treated with so much contempt?

But admitting that the Negroes are inferior in abilities to every other people upon earth, will it thence be inferred, that it is lawful to injure and oppress them, and to deprive them of those rights which belong to all other men? Is it by such a system of morality, that white men propose to demonstrate their superiority over the Negroes? Is it by a doctrine so absurd, that Columbus means to assert that rank of understanding, by which he supposes himself to be placed at the upper end of what he calls the chain of human dependence? Is wisdom given us by providence, that we may impose upon folly? Are we endowed with strength, that we may be enabled to prey upon the weak. Are we not all children of the same father, possessed of an immortal soul, equally accountable for the deeds done in this life? But it is observed by a great author, that Europeans have been in the right, not to allow us to be men; lest, if we were, a suspicion might arise that they are *no longer Christians.*

To prop a little the foregoing argument, from the natural inequality of ranks, your correspondent is pleased to mention, in justification of slavery that it arose from the operations of war and conquest; "whereby[,"] he says, "captives became the property of the conquerors." Concerning this *right of conquest,* it is not my intention to employ many words. It seems now to be admitted by every person of a liberal mind, that superior force can never bestow upon a conqueror any right which he did not previously possess. To suppose the contrary, is to suppose that mere power is the foundation of right, and that every man is entitled to do whatever he has the opportunity of executing. According to this hypothesis, which, to the scandal of jurisprudence, was formerly too much countenanced, the people detained in slavery, whenever they acquire the power, have a right to cut their masters' throats; and, if on that occasion, instead of putting them to death, should oblige their masters to perpetual service, under the discipline of the *Jumper* [whip] it would be an act of lenity and mercy.

But Columbus has only touched upon these particulars, as he hastens to his main object, which is to prove, that if the Legislature shall abolish the African Slave Trade, it is bound, in justice, to indemnify the West India Traders for the loss which they may sustain upon that account.

The British government, he contends, has introduced and promoted this very slavery, and bestowed upon it the sanction of different acts of parliament. The planters and traders were, in that business, the mere tools of the Legislature, and purchased their estates, or employed their capitals, upon the faith of government;

which, therefore, will be forfeited if, without their consent, that slavery, *how immoral soever and unjust in itself*, should be withdrawn and prohibited.

It may in the first place, be remarked, that this writer is guilty of a little misrepresentation, when he insinuates that government took the lead in the introduction of the African Slave Trade. It is well known, that when domestic slavery had been abolished in Europe, it was revived in America by the obstinacy of the European settlers, and in opposition to the remonstrances and prohibitions of the mother country. The settlers urged the necessity of slavery for procuring labourers; and my unfortunate countrymen, without any colour of justice, were dragged from a distant land, and substituted to the weaker and more effeminate natives of America.

The Spanish government first, and the other European governments afterwards, were obliged to comply with their refractory subjects, and to connive at an evil which they were unable to prevent.

But the times are now altered. The meridian beams of knowledge have now brought to light those enormous abuses, which were hid from the public eye; and the feelings of an enlightened age are shocked by a treatment of our fellow creatures so repugnant to the plain rules of justice. The interested clamours of avarice will no longer be endured; and men conscious of the iniquity of their former conduct, must be willing to atone for it, by hastening to abolish those practices, which they blush to have ever permitted.

With all my heart, says Columbus; let this trade be as wicked and unjust as you please. Let it be abolished whenever you think fit. But, the bond! The bond! Justice requires that we be indemnified.

In answer to this demand, I will beg leave to state a parallel case. In all the European Kingdoms, a few centuries ago, every feudal baron enjoyed the privilege of making private war, that is, of robbing and plundering all his neighbours. This privilege was universally admitted, and sanctioned by public authority. But in more civilized ages, a practice, so inconsistent with justice and good order, came to be entirely prohibited. Might not any one of those plunderers, with equal reason to your correspondent Columbus, have demanded an indemnification for the pecuniary loss which he sustained.

"I laid out my capital in this manner, I became a feudal baron, upon the faith of the law as it stood. I was but the tool of government, which encouraged and assisted me in settling in this part of the country. During a good michaelmas moon, I could have seized many hundred head of Cattle; but of this, and all *similar* gains, I am now totally deprived. If my neighbours had offended me, I might have murdered or carried off their wives and their children. But I must now tamely put up with every affront. By these new-fangled and unjust regulations, there will be an entire stagnation of all the business of society."

What answer would a sovereign be entitled to make to any of his subjects who had the effrontery to talk to him in this manner? "You are mistaken in thinking that you have a right to rob, or steal, or murder. Though the public was obliged to temporize, and to connive at your practices, they could give you no right to commit crimes. But though the law was bad enough of itself, you have rendered it a thousand times worse by your abuse of it. Instead of indemnification you deserve punishment; and were you to meet with a proper retribution for your offences, the least you could expect is, in the language of the old Scottish historian, *that you should be justified.*"

Such is the answer which, I think, might with propriety be given to Colombus, were it proposed instantly to abolish the institution of slavery in the West Indies. But he knows very well that no such thing is intended; and he has taken a poetical license in stating the facts, that he might obtain the shadow of an argument from his own erroneous statement. The known intention of the proposed application to parliament is, not to abolish, but to regulate the servitude of the West India Negroes. When the further importation of Negroes is prohibited, the planters will be under the necessity of rearing from the slaves which they already possess, and of treating them with some degree of humanity. It is the universal belief that all other attempts for protecting this unfortunate class of men, in the European colonies, will be fruitless, and that all proposals of regulation, by the inhabitants themselves, are mere pretences which will have no effect after the present investigation shall be laid aside.

Now I would ask, whether the British government has a right from views of justice and utility to regulate the trade and manufactures of the kingdom? or whether every regulation of the national commerce must be accompanied with an indemnification to all those who pretend to be suffered by the alteration? When a tax is laid on claret, must the wine merchants be paid for the diminution of their trade in that article? When there is a prohibition of whisky, on account of it being prejudiced to the health or the morals of the people, must there be a pecuniary compensation to the distillers of that spirit, or to the growers of barley?

After all, it is time to inquire what reason Columbus has to apprehend any loss whatever from the proposed regulation. It is clearly proved that, with proper management, the stock of slaves already in the Islands will be sufficient to maintain itself. By allowing them some gratuity, as a reward for extraordinary labour, it is evident that their industry, their skill, and their dexterity, may be wonderfully increased. Thus, by a gradual alteration without any hazard of disorder, the condition of the Negroes may be improved; and even the prospect will arise, that their future emancipation, at a distant period perhaps, may be found of general advantage. At the end of the eighteenth century, when the British House of Commons are every day quoting the celebrated author of "the Wealth of Nations"; and when the eyes of the mercantile world are so much opened to perceive the mischievous tendency of monopoly and restraint in every branch of commerce, is it not a curious spectacle, to observe, that in every part of his Majesty's dominions, there still is a class of restrainers upon trade, so destitute of information, and so overrun with prejudice, as to imagine that the emancipation of the labourers, proceeding from the gradual operation of their masters, would not be beneficial change? I agree with Columbus in thinking that, in point of abilities, mankind are composed of different ranks. At the same time when Sir Isaac Newton discovered the true system of the universe, there were persons, of some education, who still believed in judicial astrology, and the influence of the stars. If the inferiority of un[der]standing in my countrymen lays a foundation for supposing them an *inferior race* to the whites, one would almost be tempted to believe, that there is no variety of *races* even among the white people themselves.

GUSTAVUS

2. OTHELLO, 17 January 1795[21]

The Cabinet. By a Society of *Gentlemen,* 3 vols. (Norwich: Printed and Sold by J.March. Sold also by J.S. Jordan, Fleet-street, London, 1795)

Epigraph: "...The country claims our active aid; / That let us roam, and where we find a spark / Of public virtue, blow it into flame." Thomson

Preface addressed "To the Readers of the Cabinet," dated "Norwich, 17th Jan. 1795," opens, "No work in the English language, perhaps, ever appeared to the world, under circumstances more inauspicious and depressing than the CABINET." "But if tyrants did not read at Milan, do they not read in this country? Not indeed to improve their minds, or to learn the ends and purposes of the authority they are abusing, [1] but to mark for persecution and penalty a careless or unguarded stricture, a warm or intemperate remonstrance" [1–2]. [Charles Marsh (1774?-1835?].

Mischievous Effects of War
War is a game, which, were their subjects wise,
Kings would not play at.   Bishop of London

Of all the evils to which weeping humanity is liable, there is no one so much to be dreaded as war, whether we consider it in its most immediate effects, or in its remoter consequences. The truth of this proposition is too palpable to be disputed; nor is there an individual in Europe, whose mind is perfectly free, that does not at this instant deprecate the impending issue which this alarming calamity will produce. But without looking forward to what greater ills may happen, or anticipating sorrows that will too soon arrive– it is sufficient just to dwell for a few moments on the scene already before us, and contemplate the objects it presents.

To a sympathizing mind, what a picture is here! What horrors! What desolation continually opens to view! ... Where are those laughing fields that yesterday waved their golden heads, and bade the husbandman rejoice in an assurance of plenty? Alas! They are destroyed–trodden to the ground, and a de [174]sert remains in their place!–What is become of that noble city, which but a few days ago rose so majestically before us? Where its cloud–capped spires, which appeared to hail the traveller off and its lofty turrets that bade him welcome on his near approach? What is become of those ramparts and fortifications which seemed to defy the destroy-ing–hand of time? Where the sumptuous palaces and costly build-ings which existed, the admiration and wonder of every beholder, on which the embellishments of art and the refinements of science had been so lavishly bestowed?–Where is the stately dome–the tri-umphal through which the hero has oft been conducted, crowned with all the honors of victory? Where the magazines of stores and provisions that supplied a numerous people with the comforts of life? Where the habitations of the artist and mechanic–those schools of industry established for the promotion of universal hap-piness–for the benefit of all mankind? Ah! Where are they? Behold their ruins! Desolating war has almost levelled them with the ground! No habitation remains–no place where a human being can take up his abode! But, where shall we look for the living multitude that every day appeared in its streets, whose hands were continuously employed in the execution of those schemes which their minds had conceived for the diffusion of happiness among themselves and their fellow-creatures? Surely they are safe–they have been preserved from the general wreck–Alas! no–in defence of their rights and liberties, they were forced to take up [175] arms– but were unsuccessful! Behold, on yonder plains, how their mangled bodies strew the ground–there raged the dreadful conflict –incensed at the bold defence they made against numbers far greater than themselves, their unfeeling conquerors pursued their exterminating plan "til slaughter had no more to do!"

Brave unfortunates! let a stranger shed a tear over your hallowed remains. Your valour shall be remembered with respectful admiration, as long as virtue and liberty shall be esteemed among mankind.

This is not a fancied picture, an imaginary thing–the scene is real–for a long time it has been exhibited, and is now exhibiting, to the view of all the world. Numbers of our fellow beings from every town and village in Europe have been victims in this fatal tragedy.–Our kindred and acquaintance still form a part in the dramatis personae, and wait the common chance of war .... In the name of heaven, why and for what are they reduced to this alarming situation? Is it necessary for the happiness of one part of the creation that the other part should be made miserable, or totally annihilated? Can such horrid devastation produce so much good to mankind, that instead of endeavouring to stop its progress, every nerve should be strained to make it more extensive? In the sacred name of humanity, which part of a community is it that benefits from such carnage? Is it the labouring poor? Certainly not–they can only expect fatigues and danger, and death, from it–they must bear every hardship and brave every difficulty;–there is no alter

[176] native for them–"tis their's to bleed and die in quarrels not their own." Nor is it the honest industrious tradesman that is benefitted. What advantage does he obtain from the most successful war? None–the consequence to him is–decay of trade–decrease of fortune and accumulation of taxes. . . . If these two classes then, that form the great bulk of a nation, reap no advantage from wars, but on the contrary suffer considerably by them–which part of the community is it that are the gainers, that find an interest in fomenting broils between nations?–'Tis the pampered minion–the sycophantic courtier–the unprincipled placeman–the worthless pensioner, and an undeserving croud [*sic*], that riot in the distress and ruin of their *country.* It is these, and only these, that find a benefit in war–that feel a pecuniary interest in fomenting national quarrels.–These are the men that can take pleasure in such scenes of blood–that can exultingly laugh at "Victories for which the conquerors mourn, so many fall."

OTHELLO

Vol. 2, 174-7

3. 11 November 1796[22]

Gust Vassa presents his best respects to his kind benefactor & friend Mr. Diggs and sends him pr. Bearer the only *bound* Vol: of his Narrative which he has by him. He has no Edinburgh edition of his book in London. He intreats Mr. Digges to forgive him the freedom of publishing (without leave) the letter in the preface page XII.= It was much Service to him at Carrickfurgus & Belfast after Mr. D. went from thence to Dublin. G.V. intreats Mr. D. to call on him when convenient, as he longs to introduce to his notice & regard Mrs. Vassa, his wife, a virtuous & good woman, to whom I owe the prolongation of life, (as my health & strength daily decreases) for I know I am going *"to that bourne from which no traveller returns"*.= not I hope to An *Eternal Sleep*!, as you once jocosely express'd to myself & McCoy on our quarrel about the *colour of the Devil*. But *I* trust to a happy Resurrection!! And whether *black* or *white* I care not. May your intended voyage to a [Turn Over] peaceful & happy home in maryland be Successful; & when in that rising & flourishing country continue, as I have experienced from you in many instances, & in variety of Companys, the friend of freedom & the Enemy of Slavery in whatever Shape. *Remember the poor black*: Is He not a man and your Brother?

Limington [?] near London Nov. 11. 1796.

CHAPTER

V

Miscellaneous

The twelve documents in this chapter do not fall into a specific category. Together, the example of Vassa's poetry (document 1); the note about his name written by J. Phillips on the verso of Vassa's 6 May 1780 letter to Granville Sharp (document 2); the inscription on a copy of his *Interesting Narrative* (document 11); references to him in a variety of publications (documents 3, 9, 10, and 12); the accusations made against him in two newspapers in April 1792 (documents 4 and 5), which are the topics of two letters in May 1792 (documents 6 and 7); and the entry about him in Katherine Plymley's diary (document 8) provide us with further insights into the complex world and range of situations in which Vassa found himself.

1. *Miscellaneous Verses, or Reflections on the State of my mind during my first Convictions; of the Necessity of believing the Truth, and experiencing the inestimable Benefits of Christianity*, ca. mid 1770s[1]

Well may I say my life has been
One scene of sorrow and of pain;
From early days I griefs have known,
And as I grew my griefs have grown.

Dangers were always in my path,
And fear of wrath and sometimes death;
While pale dejection in me reign'd,
I often wept, by grief constrain'd.

When taken from my native land,
By an unjust and cruel band,
How did uncommon dread prevail!
My sighs no more I could conceal.

To ease my mind I often strove,
And tried my trouble to remove:
I sung, and utter'd sighs between–
Assay'd to stifle guilt with sin.

But O! not all that I could do
Would stop the current of my woe;
Conviction still my vileness shew'd;
How great my guilt–how lost to good.

"Prevented, that I could not die,
Nor could to one sure refuge fly;

An orphan state I had to mourn,–
Forsook by all, and left forlorn."

Those who beheld my downcast mien.
Could not guess at my woes unseen:
They by appearance could not know
The troubles that I waded through.

Lust, anger, blasphemy, and pride,
With legions of such ills beside,
"Troubled my thoughts," while doubts and fears
Clouded and darken'd most my years.

"Sighs now no more would be confin'd–
They breath'd the trouble of my mind:"
I wish'd for death, but check'd the word,
And often pray'd unto the Lord.

Unhappy, more than some on earth,
I thought the place that gave me birth–
Strange thoughts oppress'd–while I replied,
"Why not in Ethiopia died?"

And why thus spar'd, nigh to hell!–
God only knew–I could not tell!–
"A tott'ring fence, a bowing wall,
I thought myself e're since the fall."

Oft times I mus'd, and nigh despair,
While birds melodious fill'd the air.
"Thrice happy songsters, ever free,"
How bless'd were they compar'd to me!'

Thus all things added to my pain;
While grief compell'd me to complain;
When sable clouds began to rise,
My mind grew darker than the skies.

The English nation forc'd to leave,
How did my breast with sorrows heave!
I long'd for rest–cried "Help me, Lord!
Some mitigation, Lord, afford!"

Yet on, dejected, still I went–
Heart-throbbing woes within me pent;
Nor land, nor sea, could comfort give,
Nor aught my anxious mind relieve.

Weary with troubles, yet unknown
To all but God and self alone,
Numerous months for peace I strove,
And numerous foes I had to prove.

Inur'd to dangers, griefs, and woes,
Train'd up 'midst perils, deaths, and foes,
I said "Must it thus ever be?
No quiet is permitted me."

Hard hap, and more than heavy lot!
I pray'd to God "Forget me not–
What thou ordain'st help me to bear;
But O! deliver from despair!"

Strivings and wrestling seem'd in vain;
Nothing I did could ease my pain:
Then gave I up my work and will,
Confess'd and own'd my doom was hell!

Like some poor pris'ner at the bar,
Conscious of guilt, of sin, and fear,
Arraign'd, and self-condemn'd, I stood,
"Lost in the world, and in my blood!"

Yet here, 'midst blackest clouds confin'd,
A beam from Christ, the day-star, shin'd;
Surely, thought I, if Jesus please,
He can at once sign my release.

I, ignorant of his righteousness,
Set up my labours in its place;
"Forgot for why his blood was shed,
And pray'd and fasted in his stead."

He dy'd for sinners–I am one;
Might not his blood for me atone?
Tho' I am nothing else but sin,
Yet surely he can make me clean!

Thus light came in, and I believ'd;
Myself forgot, and help receiv'd!
My Saviour then I know I found,
For, eas'd from guilt, no more I groan'd.

O, happy hour, in which I ceas'd
To mourn, for then I found a rest!
My soul and Christ were now as one–
Thy light, O Jesus, in me shone!

Bless'd be thy name; for now I know
I and my works can nothing do;
"The Lord alone can ransom man–
For this the spotless Lamb was slain!"

When sacrifices, works, and pray'r,
Prov'd vain, and ineffectual were,
"Lo then I come!" the Saviour cry'd
And, bleeding, bow'd his head and dy'd.

He dy'd for all who ever saw
No help in them, nor by the law:
I this have seen and gladly own
"Salvation is by Christ alone!"

---

2. VERSO of Letter to Granville Sharp Esq.r, In Old Jewry Cheapside, 6 May 1780[2]

Sierra Leone Collection, box 4, supplement 1, folder 1. University of Illinois at Chicago Library, Special Collections.

a Black & an African, who
wrote his own life
He fell into fits if any
one pronounced his
real name, which was
Olaudah Equiano
My Father knew
him – J. Philli[p]s[3]
    of MiddleHill

---

3. The Bee, Or Literary Weekly Intelligencer, 1792[4]

TO CORRESPONDENTS.

In answer to *Gustavus Vasa*, the Editor deferred inserting any more of the *Index Indicatorius*, partly from motives of convenience which respected himself only; but chiefly because he was not certain if that device was relished by his readers. Of late he has got several intimations, that it will be agreeable to have it continued; and it shall be so from time to time.

---

4. The Oracle, 25 April 1792[5]

It was well observed by Chubb, that there is no absurdity, however gross, but popular credulity has a throat wide enough to swallow it. It is a fact that the Public may depend on, that *Gustavus Vasa*, who has publicly asserted that he was kidnapped in Africa, never was upon that Continent, but was born and bred in the Danish Island of Santa Cruz, in the West Indies [now Saint Croix in the

U.S. Virgin Islands]. *Ex hoc uno disce omnes* [that one fact tells all]. What, we will ask any man [o]f plain understanding, must that cause be, which can lean for support on falsehoods as audaciously propagated as they are easily detected?

Modern Patriotism, which wantons so much in sentiment, is *really* founded rather in private interested views, than in a regard for the Public Weal. The conduct of the friends to the Abolition is a proof of the justice of this remark. It is a fact, of which, perhaps, the People are not apprized, but which it well becomes them to know, that WILBERFORCE and the THORNTONS are concerned in settling the Island of Bulam in Sugar Plantations; of course their interests clash with those of the present Planters and hence their clamour against the Slave Trade.

"Old Cato is as great a Rogue as You."

5. *The Star*, 27 April 1792[6]

The Negroe, called GUSTAVUS VASA, who has published an history of his life, and gives so admirable an account of the laws, religion, and natural productions of the interior parts of Africa; and in which he relates his having been kidnapped in his infancy; is neither more nor less, than a native of the Danish island of Santa Cruz.

6. Letter, of Alexander Tillock to John Montieth, Esq. Glasgow, 5 May 1792[7]

DEAR SIR,

YOUR note of the 30th ult. I would have answered in course; but wished first to inform you what paper we had taken the article from which respected GUSTAVUS VASSA. By this day's post, [we] have sent you a copy of the Oracle of Wednesday the 25th–in the last column of the 3th page, you will find the article from which we inserted the one in the Star of the 27th ult.–If it be erroneous, you will see it had not its origin with us. As to G.V. I know nothing about him.

After examining the paragraph in the Oracle which immediately follows the one in question, I am inclined to believe that the one respecting G.V. may have been fabricated by some of the advocates for continuing the Slave Trade, for the purpose of weakening the force of the evidence brought against that trade; for, I believe, if they could, they would stifle the evidence altogether.

Having sent you the Oracle, we have sent all that we can say about the business. I am,

> DEAR SIR,
>
> > Your most humble Servant,
>
> ALEX. TILLOC[K].
> *Star Office, 5th May, 1792.*[8]

---

7. Letter from the Rev. Dr. J. Baker, of May Fair Chapel, London, to Mr. Gustavus Vassa, at David Dale's Esq. Glasgow, 14 May 1792[9]

DEAR SIR,
I went after Mr. [Buchanan] Millan (the printer of the Oracle), but he was not at home. I understood that an apology would be made to you, and I desired it might be a proper one, such as would give fair satisfaction, and take off any disadvantageous impressions which the paragraph alluded to may have made. Whether the matter will bear action or not, I do not know, and have not inquired whether you can punish by law; because I think it is not worth

while to go to the expence of a law-suit, especially if a proper apology is made; for, can any man that reads your Narrative believe that you are not a native of Africa? I see therefore no good reason for not printing a fifth edition, on account of a scandalous paragraph in a newspaper.

> I remain,
>> DEAR SIR,
>>> Your sincere friend,
>>>> J. BAKER.

Grosvenor–street, May 14, 1792.[10]

8. Excerpt of Diary Entry of Katherine Plymley, Sister of Joseph Plymley, Archdeacon of Shropshire, 20 June 1793[11]

[M]y Brother had then purchased of him the memoires of his life written by himself; & I believe his business at this time was to get introduced wherever he could, & to dispose of them–my Brother was rather concerned at his going through the country for this purpose, as he feared it would only tend to increase the difficulty of getting subscriptions when wanted, for carrying on the business of the abolition. The luke-warm would be too apt to think if, this be the case, & we are to have Negroes come about in this way, it will be very troublesome; my brother thought there was something not quite right about him or he would have been at Sierra Leone. . . . Be that as it may, had my Brother been at home, he would have done all he could for him, & did endeavour to see him afterwards in Shrewsbury but he was gone.

9. *The Morning Post and Gazetteer* (London), 30 January 1798[12]

THE ANIMATED SKELETON

"_____ I oft have sought,
With friendly tender of some worthier service,
To win him from his temper, but he shuns
All offers_____
_____ Is there cause for this?
For sin without temptation, calm, cool villainy___
Deliberate mischief, unimpassioned lust,
And smiling murder____"

GUSTAVUS VASA.
Printed at the Minerva Press, for William Lane, Leadenhall-street.

10. John Lowe, "The Shipwreck of a Slave Ship," 1803[13]

When "an English Gentleman saved from a former Shipwreck, and Whidah, a Negro Princess" observe the crew of "a Slave Ship driven on the Coast of Africa" abandon the vessel with its "cargo" of enslaved Africans locked in its hold, Whidah turns to her companion and exclaims,

Fly to England!—and tell 'Vassa'
To desist 'Tis all in Vain. (56)

11. Inscription to T. Bennett on copy of 1791 edition of *The Interesting Narrative*, 1829[14]

The Gift of his Aunt at Southhampton. Let he who reads the horrors practiced on West Indian slaves use all his influence to put it down.

12. *Glasgow Herald*, 31 January 1853[15]

Reprints "Smock Marriage in New York" from *Notes & Queries*, which refers to Equiano's biography as "a curious old book."

Appendix 1
Maps of Vassa's Travels

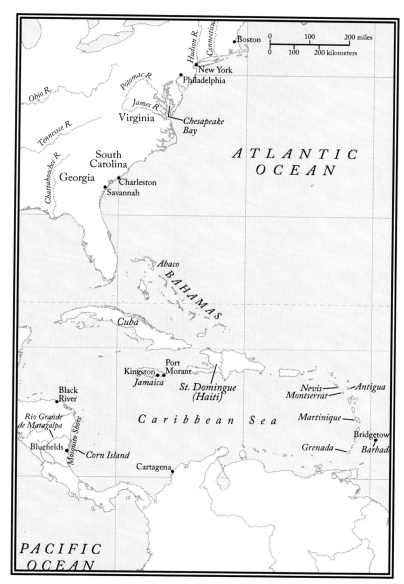

The Circum Caribbean World, Late 18th Century

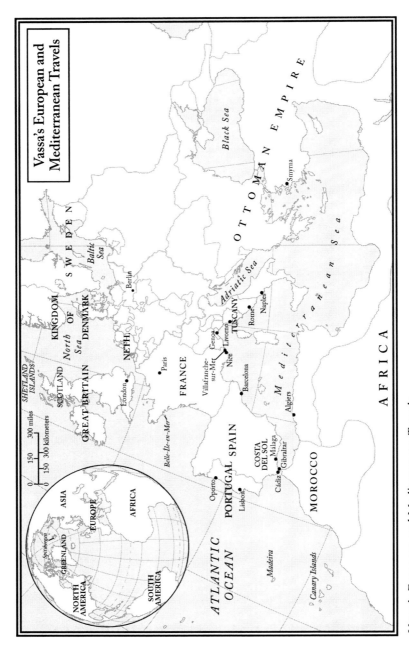

Vassa's European and Mediterranean Travels

United Kingdom, 1790s

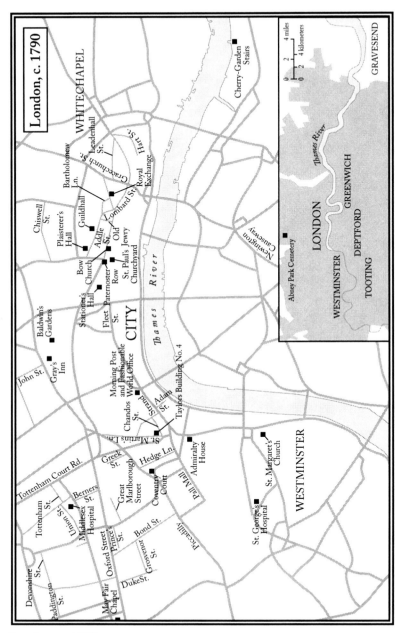

London, c. 1790

Appendix 2
Vassa Chronology

c. 1742 born in Essaka, in what is now southeastern Nigeria

1753 kidnapped, sold to the coast (probably Bonny)

1754 (beginning of March) leaves Africa via Bight of Biafra and endures Middle Passage on the *Ogden*

1754 (9 May) arrives in Barbados

1754 (21 May–13 June) trans-shipped to Virginia on the *Nancy*

1754 (early summer) purchased by planter named Mr. Campbell

1754 (summer) bought by British Naval Officer Michael Henry Pascal for his cousins (of the Maynard family); named Gustavus Vassa and taken to England

1754-1763 slave to Captain Pascal

1754 (September) arrives in Falmouth, England, after 13-week voyage on the *Industrious Bee* commanded by Pascal from Newfoundland, Canada

1754 befriends Pascal's servant, Richard Baker

1755 (August) joins Pascal aboard the *HMS Roebuck*

1756-1762 aboard Royal Navy vessels before and during Seven Years War

1756 (14 December) leaves the *HMS Roebuck*

1757 serves on the *Savage* and the *Preston*

1757 (end of January–beginning of November) hospitalized for chilblains and smallpox at St. George's Hospital

1758 (12 January) works as servant on the *Royal George*

1758 (27 January) transferred to the *Namur*

1758 (2 June) reaches Battle of Louisbourg on the northeast coast of Nova Scotia, Canada

1758-1759 (winter) meets General Wolfe on voyage to English coast

1759 (9 February) baptized at St. Margaret's Church, Westminster, London (at Elizabeth Martha Maynard's request of Pascal); receives his first book from clergyman who baptized him

1759 (spring) returns to sea on the *Namur*, patrolling the Mediterranean

1759 (August) works as one of Pascal's two servants on the *Aetna*

1760-1761 (fall and winter) lives in England

1761 (March) serves on the *Aetna* during attack on Belle-Île-en-Mer

1762 (29 September) promoted by Pascal to rating of able seaman

1762 slave to James Doran, captain of the *Charming Sally*

1762 (30 December) the *Charming Sally* sets sail from England

1763 (13 February) arrives at Montserrat

1763 (mid-May) sold to Robert King in Montserrat

1763-1766 slave to Robert King

1763 (end of) befriends Captain Thomas Farmer

1765 (11 February) allegedly hears founder of Methodism, George Whitfield, preach in Savannah, Georgia

1765 (to beginning of 1766) in Philadelphia; Robert King sets Vassa's emancipation at £40

1766 (beginning) in Savannah, Georgia

1766 (May) reaches Charleston, South Carolina

1766 (11 July) purchases his freedom; works for Robert King

1766 (August) sails aboard the *Nancy*

1767 (29 January) the *Nancy* sails toward Georgia

1767 shipwrecked in the Bahamas

1767 (late spring) books passage to Montserrat from Savannah on the *Speedwell*

1767 (26 July) leaves Montserrat for London on the *Andromache*

1767 (September) the *Andromache* arrives at Cherry-Garden Stairs, south bank of the Thames

1767-1768 (September 1767–February 1768) trains under a hairdresser in Coventry Court, Haymarket; pays neighbor to teach him to play French horn; learns arithmetic

1768 (February) hired as hairdresser for Dr. Charles Irving

1768 (July) works for John Jolly aboard the *Delaware*; travels to Villefranche-sur-Mer and Nice, France; Livorno on the Tuscany coast; and Smyrna [Isna] in the Ottoman Porte

1769 (May) at Oporto, Portugal, during carnival

1769 (September) at Genoa

1769 (December) at Smyrna [Isna] for the second time

1770 (March) returns to England

1771 (April) hired by William Robertson as steward on the *Grenada Planter*, bound for Madeira, Barbados, and Grenada

1772 (early) hired by Captain David Watt as steward on the *Jamaica*, bound for Nevis and Jamaica

1772 (22 June) Lord Mansfield's verdict in the case of James Somerset

1772 (August) in London; works again for Dr. Charles Irving, who is celebrated for his successful experiments making seawater fresh

1773 (17 May) hired as assistant on the *HMS Racehorse* to Dr. Charles Irving on Arctic expedition of Constantine John Phipps (later Lord Mulgrave)

1773 (11 June) Arctic expedition reaches the Shetland Islands; (15 June) passes latitude 60° north and reaches southern coast of Spitsbergen at latitude 78° north

1773 (30 September) the *HMS Racehorse* and *HMS Carcass* sail into Deptford, ending Arctic voyage

1773 (October) in London, working as hairdresser

1774 meets James Ramsay

1774 (early) hired by Captain John Hughes as steward on the *Anglicana* destined for Smyrna [Isna]

1774 (4 April) John Annis affair

1774 (September) hired by Captain Richard Strange on the *Hope* destined for Cádiz

1774 (6 October) undergoes conversion to Methodism of the Huntingdonian persuasion

1774 (December) returns to London

1775 (March) sails onboard the *Hope* to Cádiz, Gibraltar, and Málaga on the Costa del Sol

1775 (late May–June) sails to Cádiz and then to England

1775 (November) hired by Dr. Charles Irving and Alexander Blair on venture to establish a plantation on the Mosquito Shore

1775 (13 November) sets sail at Gravesend, downriver from London, for Jamaica on the *Morning Star* (co-owned by Irving and Blair) under command of David Miller

1776 (mid-January) the *Morning Star* reaches Jamaica

1776 (30 April) the *Morning Star* is seized by the Spanish *guardacostas* at Black River

1776 (mid-June) leaves Mosquito Shore for Jamaica

1776 (10 July) on the *Indian Queen* commanded by John Baker

1776 (14 October) the *Indian Queen* reaches Jamaica

1777 (7 January) reaches Plymouth on board the *Squirrel*

1777 (24 July–10 July 1778) ten letters signed "Gustavus Vassa" appear in the London newspaper *The Morning Post, and Daily Advertiser*

1778 Scottish court declares slavery illegal in Scotland

1779 (early) hired by governor of Senegambia, Mathias Macnamara

1779 (11 March) lives on Hedge Lane, Charing Cross, Westminster

1779 (March) seeks appointment as missionary to Africa from Robert Lowth, Lord Bishop of London; Macnamara and Wallace write letters in support of his application

1779 leaves Macnamara's employ

1780 (6 May) writes letter to Granville Sharp from No. 67 Berners Street, Oxford

1780-1782 works for George Pitt, Baron Rivers

1783 tours eight counties in Wales

1783 (19 March) informs abolitionist Granville Sharp of the *Zong* massacre (1781)

1783 Society of Friends petitions parliament for the abolition of the slave trade

1784 hired as steward on the *London* commanded by Martin Hopkins, destined for New York

1785 (January) returns to England on the *London*

1785 (March) sails with Hopkins to Philadelphia

1785 (August) returns to London

1785 (21 October) Vassa and fellow Africans send Address of Thanks to the Gentlemen Called Friends or Quakers, in Grace-church-Court Lombard-Street

1786 (March) hired as steward on American ship the *Harmony* under Captain John Willett, bound for Philadelphia

1786 (3 August) the *Harmony* reaches Gravesend; Vassa returns to London

1786 (November) appointed Commissary for Sierra Leone expedition by the Committee for Relief of the Black Poor in London

1786 (29 December) *Morning Herald* mentions Vassa in piece about the Black Poor

1787 (16 January) receives letter from Commissioners of the Navy Office

1787 (21 March) Thomas Thompson writes to Navy Board denouncing conduct of Vassa; similar complaint appeared 29 December 1786 in *Morning Herald;* Vassa dismissed as Commissary for the Sierra Leone expedition

1787 (24 March) Vassa letter to Cugoano published in *Public Advertiser* (4 April); debate ensues in *Public Advertiser* (critiques of Vassa 11 April and 14 April; his response 12 May); Reverend Patrick Fraser accusations against Vassa in *London Chronicle* and

Morning Chronicle (2 and 3 July); Vassa responds in *Public Advertiser* (14 July)

1787 (22 May) the Society for Effecting the Abolition of the Slave Trade (SEAST) is formed

1787 (15 December) Vassa and Sons of Africa send Address of Thanks to Granville Sharp

1788 lives in Baldwin's Gardens, Holborn

1788 (28 January) book review by Vassa, in *Public Advertiser*, of James Tobin's *Cursory Remarks & Rejoinder*

1788 (5 February) book review by Vassa, in *Public Advertiser*, of Gordon Turnbull's *Apology for Negro Slavery*

1788 (5 February) yearlong debate, including attacks on Vassa, begins among pseudonymous correspondents in *Morning Chronicle, and London Advertiser*. Pseudonyms of correspondents include "Civis," "Christian," "Benezet, jun.," "Humanitas," "Matth. Goodenough," and "George Fox."

1788 (13 February) signs letter "Aethiopianus" to the Senate of Great Britain, published in *Public Advertiser*; republished 21 February in *Morning Post, and Daily Advertiser* (signed "Gustavus Vasa, for the Ethiopians")

1788 (13 March) letter to Lord Hawkesbury (for British Legislature Board of Trade) (signed Gustavus Vassa, late Commissary for the African Settlement); slightly revised version is published in *London Advertiser* on 31 March

1788 (21 March) presents anti-slave trade petition to Queen Charlotte, wife of King George II

1788 (March) letter to *Gentleman's Magazine* signed "Gustavus"

1788 (28 April) book review by Vassa, in *Public Advertiser*, of Raymond Harris's *Scripture Researches on the Licitness of the Slave Trade*

1788 (19 June) letter of thanks from Vassa to British Senate in *Public Advertiser* after William Dolben's regulation bill is passed in the House of Commons (18 June)

1788 (27 June) book review by Vassa, in *Morning Chronicle, and London Advertiser*, of Samuel Jackson Pratt's *Humanity, or the Rights of Nature, a Poem: in Two Books*

1788 (28 June) letter from Vassa to Lord Sidney in *Public Advertiser*

1788 (1 July) piece on Vassa by "Civis" in *Morning Chronicle, and London Advertiser*

1788 (5 July) pieces on Vassa in *Times* and *Morning Post, and Daily Advertiser*

1788 (15 July) letters signed by Vassa and other "persons of colour" in *Morning Chronicle, and London Advertiser* to William Dolben, William Pitt, and Charles James Fox

1788 (6 September) letter to Vassa from James Ramsay

1788 (November) letter to Josiah Wedgwood written on first printed solicitation for subscriptions to *The Interesting Narrative*

1789 (14 February) letter of thanks in *Public Advertiser* to the Committee for the Abolition of the Slave Trade at Plymouth for sending plate of the slave ship *Brookes* to Thomas Clarkson

1789 (6 March) letter to Ann Berry

1789 (24 March) first edition of *The Interesting Narrative* published in London; Vassa registers it at Stationers' Hall

1789 (24 March) lists his address as Union-Street, Mary-le-bone

1789 (24 March) writes letter to Parliament advertising his *Interesting Narrative*

1789 (24 March) an advertisement for *The Interesting Narrative* appears in *The World*

1789 (25 April) letter from Vassa and eight others of African descent to William Dickson (formerly Private Secretary to Edward Hay, Governor of Barbados) in *The Diary; or Woodfall's Register*

1789 (29 April–1 May) *Morning Star* advertisement for *The Interesting Narrative*

1789 (May) Mary Wollstonecraft's review of *The Interesting Narrative* in *The Analytical Review*

1789 (9 May) *Gazetteer and New Daily Advertiser* announces Vassa's speech at upcoming city debate on the abolition of the slave trade

1789 (June) Richard Gough publishes review of *The Interesting Narrative* in *The Analytical Review*

1789 (June) anonymous review of *The Interesting Narrative* in *Monthly Review*

1789 (July) anonymous review of *The Interesting Narrative* published by printer Thomas Bellamy in the *General Magazine and Impartial Review*

1789 (c. summer) volunteers to go to Africa under the sponsorship of the Association for Promoting the Discovery of the Interior Parts of Africa

1789 (9 July) begins first book tour in Cambridge with a letter of introduction from Thomas Clarkson to Reverend Thomas Jones, Master of Trinity College, Cambridge

1789 (July) likely meets Susannah Cullen while in Cambridge

1789 (1 August) letter of thanks to Francis Hodson, printer of the *Cambridge Chronicle and Journal; and General Advertiser for The Counties of Cambridge, Huntingdon, Lincoln, Rutland, Bedford, Herts, Isle of Ely, &c.*

1789 (12 August) reference to Vassa in *Oracle Bell's New World*

1789 (24 December) second edition of *The Interesting Narrative* published in London

1790 (20 February) advertisement for second edition of *The Interesting Narrative* in *The General Evening Post* (London); essentially the same advertisement had appeared in *The World* (London) on 5 January 1790

1790 (26 May) letter of recommendation from Reverend Peter Peckard

1790 (14 June) advertisement for second edition of *The Interesting Narrative* in *Aris's Birmingham Gazette* (dated 24 December 1789)

1790 (28 June) letter of thanks to printer of the *Birmingham Gazette* in *Aris's Birmingham Gazette*

1790 (20 July) advertisement for second edition of *The Interesting Narrative* in *Manchester Mercury, & Harrop's General Advertiser*

1790 (23 July) letter of recommendation from Thomas Walker

1790 (20 August) advertisement for second edition of *Interesting Narrative* in *The Sheffield Register, Yorkshire, Derbyshire, & Nottinghamshire Universal Advertiser*

1790 (late August) letter of recommendation from "Friends of Humanity" in Sheffield

1790 (27 August) letter about Vassa in *Sheffield Register, Yorkshire, Derbyshire, & Nottinghamshire Universal Advertiser*

1790 (31 August) letter of thanks to printer of *Manchester Mercury, & Harrop's General Advertiser*

1790 (2 September) letter of thanks to Joseph Gales, printer of *Sheffield Register, Yorkshire, Derbyshire, & Nottinghamshire Universal Advertiser*

1790 (fall) resides with Thomas Hardy, secretary of the London Corresponding Society, and Hardy's wife, Lydia, at No. 4 Taylor's Buildings, St. Martin's-Lane

1790 (30 October) third edition of *The Interesting Narrative* published in London; Vassa registers it at Stationers' Hall

1790 (23–25 November) advertisement for third edition of *The Interesting Narrative* in *The St. James's Chronicle; or, British Evening-Post* (London)

1790 (1 December) *Times* advertises third edition of *The Interesting Narrative*; letters of introduction from Reverend Peter Peckard, Cambridge; Thomas Walker, Manchester; and six residents of Sheffield

1790 unauthorized translation of *The Interesting Narrative* is published in Rotterdam

1791 unauthorized reprint of *The Interesting Narrative* is published in New York

1791 (17 January) letter of recommendation from ten gentlemen in Nottingham

1791 (February) in Derby; *Derby Mercury* prints poem and comment referring to Vassa (10 February)

1791 (March) in Nottingham and Halifax

1791 (29 March) letter to Vassa from Susannah Atkinson of Mould Green

1791 (19 April) *Leeds Mercury* prints Vassa's letter addressed to its printer, which calls for subscriptions to the London Abolition Society

1791 (22 April) advertisement for third edition of *The Interesting Narrative* in *York Chronicle*

1791 (20 May) fourth edition of *The Interesting Narrative* published in Dublin

1791 (31 May–2 June) advertisement for fourth edition of *The Interesting Narrative* in *Freeman's Journal* (Dublin)

1791 (December) befriends political radical Samuel Nielson

1791 (20 December) advertisement for fourth edition of *The Interesting Narrative* in *Belfast News-letter*

1791 (25 December) letter of introduction from Thomas Atwood Digges

1792 (end of January) sails from London to Scotland

1792 (February) returns to London; lives again with Thomas and Lydia Hardy at No. 4 Taylor's Buildings

1792 (27 February) letter to Reverend G. Walker and family in Nottingham

1792 (winter) unauthorized translation of *The Interesting Narrative* published in Germany

1792 (15 March) *Glasgow Courier* publishes an antislavery response from "Gustavus" addressed to "Columbus"

1792 (7 April) marries Susannah Cullen of Soham, Cambridgeshire

1792 (10 April) Vassa and Susannah arrive in Scotland; travel to Paisley and Glasgow

1792 (19–21 April) marriage announced in the *General Evening Post*

1792 (25 April) accusations about Vassa's birth appear in the *Oracle*

1792 (27 April) accusations about Vassa's birth appear in the *Star*

1792 (27–30 April) advertisement for fourth edition of *The Interesting Narrative* in *Glasgow Advertiser and Evening Intelligencer*

1792 (early May) Vassa and Susannah in Edinburgh

1792 (5 May) letter of recommendation from Alexander Tillock of the *Star*

1792 (14 May) letter of recommendation from Reverend Dr. John Baker

1792 (21 May) advertisement for fourth edition of *The Interesting Narrative* in *The Caledonian Mercury* (Edinburgh)

1792 (26 May) letter of thanks to the General Assembly of the Church of Scotland in *Edinburgh Evening Courant*

1792 (28 May) letter to Thomas Hardy

1792 (30 May) *Gazetteer and New Daily Advertiser* reports on Vassa's activities

1792 (June) fifth edition of *The Interesting Narrative* published in Edinburgh; includes character references by Alexander Tillock, publisher of the *Star* (dated 5 May 1792) and Reverend Dr. John Baker (dated 14 May 1792)

1792 (June) letter "To the Reader" counterattacking accusations in the *Oracle* and the *Star* (printed in fifth and subsequent editions of *The Interesting Narrative*)

1792 (summer) visits Aberdeen, Dundee and Perth

1792 (20 August) advertisement for fifth edition of *The Interesting Narrative* in *Aberdeen Journal*

1792 (15 September) advertisement for fifth edition of *The Interesting Narrative* in *Newcastle Chronicle or Weekly Advertiser, and Register of News Commerce, and Entertainment*

1792 (6 October) *Newcastle Chronicle* and *Newcastle Courant* print Vassa's letter of thanks

1792 (October) in Durham on his way south

1792 (November) in Hull

1792 (30 December) sixth edition of *The Interesting Narrative* published in London; letters of introduction from (1) William Eddis of Durham (dated 25 October) and (2) Friends of Humanity in Hull (dated 12 November)

1793 (June) Katherine Plymley writes about Vassa's attempt to visit in Longnor

1793 in Tewkesbury; letter of introduction from Stanley Pumphrey to William Bell

1793 (1 July) letter of thanks to Stanley Pumphrey

1793 (15 July) advertisement for sixth edition of *The Interesting Narrative* in *Gloucester Journal*

1793 (August) seventh edition of *The Interesting Narrative* published in London

1793 (21 August) letter to Josiah Wedgwood telling him of his plans to go to Bristol, and reminding him of his offer of protection

1793 (late August–early September) travels to Bristol and stops in the town of Devizes on his way back to London

1793 (19 September) receives reply from Wedgwood after Vassa has already returned to London

1793 (10 October) receives letter of introduction from William Langworthy to William Hughes

1793 (16 October) Anna Maria Vassa is born in Soham

1794 unauthorized translation of *The Interesting Narrative* published in Russia

1794 (February to spring) in Suffolk, Norfolk, and Essex; he spends much of this tour in Norwich

1794 (13 February) attends meeting of Tusculun School (a Norwich debating society)

1794 (22 February) advertisements for eighth edition of *The Interesting Narrative* in *Norfolk Chronicle* and *Norwich Mercury*

1794 (March) eighth edition of *The Interesting Narrative* published in Norwich

1794 (7 March) attends Tusculun School debate for the second time

1794 (15 March) letter of thanks in *Norfolk Chronicle*

1794 in Lynn and Ipswich gathering subscribers for ninth edition of *The Interesting Narrative*

1794 ninth edition of *The Interesting Narrative* published in London

1794 (May) Thomas Hardy arrested for high treason

1794 (19 June) receives letter of introduction from John Mead Ray

1794 (20 June) sends letter to Mr. or Mrs. Liversege, Linen Draper, Ipswich

1794 (October 1794–September 1795) anti-war essay under the pseudonym "Othello" (possibly written by Vassa) published in *The Cabinet. By a Society of Gentlemen*, a bi-weekly periodical published in Norwich

1794 (November) subscribes to Carl Bernhard Wadstrom's *An Essay on Colonization, particularly applied to the West Coast of Africa* (London: Darton and Harvey, Gracechurch Street)

1795 (11 April) Joanna Vassa is born in Soham

1796 (20 February) Susannah dies in Soham

1796 (28 May) writes his will and last testament at Plasters' Hall in London

1796 (summer/early fall) lives on John Street, off Tottenham Court Road in the County of Middlesex, London

1797 (31 March) dies in London

1797 (21 July) Anna Maria Vassa dies, aged four

1798 (30 January) Vassa's name appears in *The Morning Post and Gazetteer*

1803 reference to Vassa in John Lowe's book of poetry

1807 (25 March) abolition of the British slave trade

1829 inscription to T. Bennett on copy of the 1791 edition of *The Interesting Narrative*

1853 (31 January) reference to Vassa in *Glasgow Herald*

1857 (10 March) Joanna Vassa dies, aged sixty-one

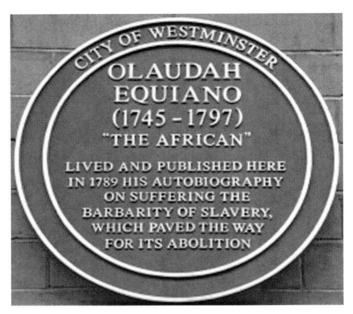

City of Westminster Commemorative Plaque in memory of the place (10 Union Street, London) where Vassa wrote *The Interesting Narrative*, 1789.

The Equiano Society Commemorative Plaque at St. Margaret's Church, Westminster Abbey, 9 February 2009, in honor of Olaudah Equiano.

Appendix 3
The Middle Passage

Gustavus Vassa's description of the Middle Passage constituted the core of what he said on his speaking tours and was central to the campaign to abolish the slave trade. The following excerpt is from the ninth and final edition of his *Interesting Narrative*, as published in Vincent Carretta's *The Interesting Narrative*, 55-60.

The first object which saluted my eyes when I arrived on the coast was the sea, and a slave-ship, which was then riding at anchor, and waiting for its cargo. These filled me with astonishment, which was soon converted into terror, which I am yet at a loss to describe, nor the then feelings of my mind. When I was carried on board I was immediately handled, and tossed up, to see if I were sound, by some of the crew; and I was now persuaded that I had gotten into a world of bad spirits, and that they were going to kill me. Their complexions too differing so much from ours, their long hair, and the language they spoke, which was very different from any I had ever heard, united to confirm me in this belief. Indeed, such were the horrors of my views and fears at the moment, that, if ten thousand worlds had been my own, I would have freely parted with them all to have exchanged my condition with that of the meanest slave in my own country. When I looked round the ship too, and saw a large furnace of copper boiling, and a multitude of black people of every description chained together, every one of their countenances expressing dejection and sorrow, I no longer doubted of my fate, and, quite overpowered with horror and anguish, I fell motionless on the deck and fainted. When I recovered a little, I found some black people about me, who I believed were some of those who brought me on board, and had been receiving their pay; they talked to me in order to cheer me, but all in vain. I asked them if we were not to be eaten by those white men with horrible looks, red faces, and long hair! They told me I was not; and one of the crew brought me a small portion of spirituous liquor in a wine glass; but, being afraid of him, I would not take it out of his hand. One of the blacks therefore took it from him and gave it to me, and I took a little down my palate, which, instead of reviving me, as they thought it would, threw me into the greatest consternation at the strange feeling it produced, having never tasted any such liquor before. Soon after this, the blacks who brought me on board went off, and left me abandoned to despair. I now saw myself deprived of all chance of returning to my native country, or even the least glimpse of hope of gaining the shore, which I now considered as friendly: and I even wished for my former slavery in preference to my present situation, which was filled with horrors of every kind, still heightened by my ignorance of what I was to undergo. I was not long suffered to indulge my grief. I was soon put down under the decks, and there I received such a salutation in my nostrils as I had never experienced in my life; so that with the loathsomeness of the stench, and crying together, I became so sick and low that I was not able to eat, nor had I the least desire to taste any thing. I now wished for the last friend, Death, to relieve me; but soon, to my grief, two of the white men offered me eatables; and, on my refusing to eat, one of them held me fast by the hands, and laid me across, I think, the windlass, and tied my feet, while the other flogged me severely. I had never experienced any thing of this kind before; and although, not being used to the water, I naturally feared that element the first time I saw it; yet, nevertheless, could I have got over the nettings, I would have jumped over the side, but I could not; and, besides, the crew used to watch us very closely who were not chained down to the decks, lest we should leap into the water; and I have seen some of these poor African prisoners most severely cut for attempting to do so, and hourly whipped for not eating. This indeed was often the case with myself. In a little time after, amongst the poor chained men, I found some of my own nation, which in a small degree gave ease to my mind. I inquired of these what was to be done with us? they gave me to understand we were to be carried to these white people's country to work for them. I then was a little revived, and thought, if it were no worse than working, my situation was not so desperate: but still I feared I should be put to death, the white people looked and acted, as I thought, in so savage a manner; for I had never seen among any people such instances of brutal cruelty; and this not only shewn towards us blacks, but also to some of the whites themselves. One white man in particular I saw, when we were permitted to be on deck, flogged so unmercifully with a large rope near the foremast, that he died in consequence of it; and they tossed him over the side as they would have done a brute. This made me fear these people the more; and I expected nothing less than to be treated in the same manner. I could not help expressing my fears and ap-prehensions to some of my countrymen: I asked them if these people had no country, but lived in this hollow place the ship? they told me they did not, but came from a distant one. "Then," said I, "how comes it in all our country we never heard of them?" They told me, because they lived so very far off. I then asked where were their women? had they any like themselves! I was told they had: "And why," said I, "do we not see them?" they answered, because they were left behind. I asked how the vessel could go? they told me they could not tell; but that there were cloths put upon the masts by the help of the ropes I saw, and then the vessel went on; and the white men had some spell or magic they put in the water when they liked in order to stop the vessel. I was exceedingly amazed at this account, and really thought they were spirits. I therefore wished much to be from amongst them, for I expected they would sacrifice me: but my wishes were vain; for we were so quartered that it was impossible for any of us to make our escape. While we staid on the coast I was mostly on deck; and one day, to my great astonishment, I saw one of these vessels coming in with the sails up. As soon as the whites saw it, they gave a great shout, at which we were amazed; and the more so as the vessel appeared larger by approaching nearer. At last she came to an anchor in my sight, and when the anchor was let go, I and my countrymen who saw it were lost in astonishment to observe the vessel stop; and were now convinced it was done by magic. Soon after this the other ship got her boats out, and they came on board of us, and the people of both ships seemed very glad to see each other. Several of the strangers also shook hands with us black people, and made motions with their hands, signifying, I suppose, we were to go to their country; but we did not understand them. At last, when the ship we were in had got in all her cargo, they made ready with many fearful

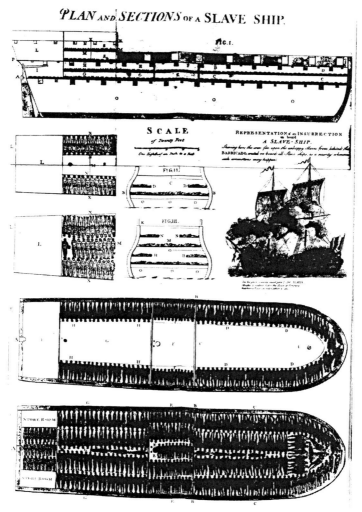

The *Brookes* of Liverpool. On 14 February 1789, a letter of thanks by
Vassa to the Committee for the Abolition of the Slave Trade at Plymouth
was published in the *Public Advertiser*. He thanked the committee for
sending a plate of the slave ship *Brookes* to Thomas Clarkson. The de-
piction of the *Brookes* of Liverpool shocked the public when it appeared
in 1789. It validated the abolitionists' claim that slaves were jam-packed
into ships, many of them dislocating shoulders or hips as a result. It was
said that 482 slaves were regularly packed on board the *Brookes* for the
six-to-eight-week voyage to the West Indies, and it is alleged that on one
voyage the *Brookes* carried 609 slaves.

noises, and we were all put under deck, so that we could not see how they managed the vessel. But this disappointment was the least of my sorrow. The stench of the hold while we were on the coast was so intolerably loathsome, that it was dangerous to remain there for any time, and some of us had been permitted to stay on the deck for the fresh air; but now that the whole ship's cargo were confined together, it became absolutely pestilential. The closeness of the place, and the heat of the climate, added to the number in the ship, which was so crowded that each had scarcely room to turn himself, almost suffocated us. This produced copious perspirations, so that the air soon became unfit for respiration, from a variety of loathsome smells, and brought on a sickness among the slaves, of which many died, thus falling victims to the improvident avarice, as I may call it, of their purchasers. This wretched situation was again aggravated by the galling of the chains, now become insupportable; and the filth of the necessary tubs, into which the children often fell, and were almost suffocated. The shrieks of the women, and the groans of the dying, rendered the whole a scene of horror almost inconceiveable. Happily perhaps for myself I was soon reduced so low here that it was thought necessary to keep me almost always on deck; and from my extreme youth I was not put in fetters. In this situation I expected every hour to share the fate of my companions, some of whom were almost daily brought upon deck at the point-of death, which I began to hope would soon put an end to my miseries. Often did I think many of the inhabitants of the deep much more happy than myself; I envied them the freedom they enjoyed, and as often wished I could change my condition for theirs. Every circumstance I met with served only to render my state more painful, and heighten my apprehensions, and my opinion of the cruelty of the whites. One day they had taken a number of fishes; and when they had killed and satisfied themselves with as many as they thought fit, to our astonishment who were on the deck, rather than give any of them to us to eat, as we expected, they tossed the remaining fish into the sea again, although we begged and prayed for some as well as we could, but in vain; and some of my countrymen, being pressed by hunger, took an opportunity, when they thought no one saw them, of trying to get a little privately; but they were discovered, and the attempt procured them some very severe floggings.

One day, when we had a smooth sea, and moderate wind, two of my wearied countrymen, who were chained together (I was near them at the time), preferring death to such a life of misery, somehow made through the nettings, and jumped into the sea: immediately another quite dejected fellow, who, on account of his illness, was suffered to be out of irons, also followed their example; and I believe many more would very soon have done the same, if they had not been prevented by the ship's crew, who were instantly alarmed. Those of us that were the most active were, in a moment, put down under the deck; and there was such a noise and confusion amongst the people of the ship as I never heard before, to stop her, and get the boat out to go after the slaves. However, two of the wretches were drowned, but they got the other, and afterwards flogged him unmercifully, for thus attempting to prefer death to slavery. In this manner we continued to undergo more hardships than I can now relate; hardships which are inseparable from this accursed trade.–Many a time we were near suffocation, from the want of fresh air, which we were often without for whole days together. This, and the stench of the necessary tubs, carried off many. During our passage I first saw flying fishes, which surprised me very much: they used frequently to fly across the ship, and many of them fell on the deck. I also now first saw the use of the quadrant. I had often with astonishment seen the mariners make observations with it, and I could not think what it meant. They at last took notice of my surprise; and one of them, willing to increase it, as well as to gratify my curiosity, made me one day look through it. The clouds appeared to me to be land, which disappeared as they passed along. This heightened my wonder: and I was now more persuaded than ever that I was in another world, and that every thing about me was magic. At last we came in sight of the island of Barbadoes, at which the whites on board gave a great shout, and made many signs of joy to us. We did not know what to think of this; but as the vessel drew nearer we plainly saw the harbour, and other ships of different kinds and sizes: and we soon anchored amongst them off Bridge Town.

Appendix 4
Places, Individuals, and Groups Associated with Vassa

Places

Abaco
Aberdeen
Abney Park Cemetery, Stoke Newington, Hackney, London
Adam Street, No. 9, Adelphi, London
Addle Street, Aldermanbury, London
Admiralty House, London
Africa
Albany
America
Anderton's Coffee House, Aston-street, Birmingham
Antigua
Arctic
Asia

Bahamas
Baldwin's Gardens
Baldwin's Gardens No. 53, Holborn
Banff, North Britain
Barbados
Barcelona
Bartholomew Lane, London
Bath
Bedford
Belfast
Belle-Île-en-Mer
Benyon-terrace, Beckingham-road, London
Berlin
Berners Street No. 67, Oxford Circus (West End of London)
Bigg Market, Newcastle

Bight of Biafra
Birmingham
Black River
Bluefields, Nicaragua
Bocking, Essex
Bond Street (West End of London)
Bonny
Boston
Bow Church
Bridgestreet, St. George's (Colegate parish), opposite the Turk's Head
Bridgetown, Barbados
Bristol
British House of Commons
British Legislature
Bull-street, Birmingham
Bury Street, Salford
Bury St. Edmund's, Suffolk

Cádiz
Cairo
Caledonia
Cambridge
Cambridgeshire
Canada
Cape Devarde Islands
Capel-Court, Bartholomew-Lane, Opposite the Bank, London
Capel-street 151, Dublin (Vassa's residence)
Carlisle
Carrickfurgus
Cartegena
Castlegate
Chalmers's Close, High Street, Edinburgh
Chamber of Manufactories of Great Britain
Chandos Street, Taylors Building No. 4, Covent Garden (residence of
    Thomas and Lydia Hardy)
Charing Cross
Charleston, South Carolina
Chatham
Chelmsford
Cherry-Garden Stairs, south bank of the Thames
Chesapeake Bay
Chiswell Street, London

Church of Scotland
Cockhill, Ratcliff
Coggeshall, Essex
Colchester
Comer of Green-Street, Cambridge Cape Coast Castle
Confession James Hunt Hall
Corn Island
Cornhill, No. 102
Costa del Sol, Spain
Costa Rica
Coventry Court, Haymarket
Crown and Anchor Tavern, Strand, London (meeting place of London
    Corresponding Society)
Cuba

Dame-street, no.28, Dublin (residence of Mr. William Sleater)
Delaware
Denmark
Deptford
Derby
Derbyshire
Devizes
Devonshire Street, Queen's-square, London
Dover
Dover Cliffs
Dublin
Duke Street, Westminster, London
Dundee
Durham

East Indies
Edinburgh
Egypt
Elland
Ely
England
Essaka (present-day southeastern Nigeria)
Essex
Essex Street
Ethiopia
Europe
Exeter

Hull
Hungerford Coffee-house
Huntingdon

Ipswich
Ireland
Island of Bulam
Isle of Ely
Isna, Turkey (Smyrna)
Italy

Jamaica
John Banks High Street, Colchester
John Street, off Tottenham Court Road, County of Middlesex, London

Kelvedon
King's Arms Inn, Trongate
Kingston, Jamaica

Leadenhall-street, London (Minerva Press, for William Lane)
Leeds
Leicester
Leverian Museum Blackfriars Road, County of Surrey
Limington
Lincoln
Liquor Pond Street, Parish of Saint Andrews Holborn,
    County of Middlesex
Lisbon
Little Pultney-Street, Golden Square
Liverpool
Livorno, Italy (Leghorn)
Lombard Street
London
Long Island
Longnor
Lynn

Macedonia
Madera
Magdalen College, Cambridge
Málaga
Manchester

Margate
Marishal Street
Market Street Lane, Manchester
Martinique
Maryland
May Fair Chapel, London
Mediterranean
Middle Hill
Middle Passage
Middlesex
Middlesex Hospital, No. 10, Union Street
Milan
Montserrat
Morning Post and Fashionable World Office, opposite Somerset-Place,
    Strand, London
Mosquito Shore
Mother Red Caps Hampstead Road, County of Middlesex
Mould Green
Mr. Wilson's Hair-dresser, Anchor Close

Naples
Navy Office
Netherlands
Nevis
New England
New York
Newcastle
Newcastle upon Tyne
Newfoundland, Canada
Newington Causeway, Southwark, London
Nicaragua
Nice
Norfolk
Norfolk Arms, Market-place, Norwich
North Pole
Norwich
Nottingham
Nottinghamshire
Nova Scotia, Canada

Old Jewry Cheapside, London
Oporto, Portugal

Ottoman Empire
Ousegate, York
Oxford
Oxford Street, London

Paddington Road
Paisley
Pall Mall, Plymouth
Paris
Parish of St. Anthony
Parish of St. James, Liberty of Westminster, County of Middlesex
Parliament of Great Britain
Paternoster-row, London
Perth
Philadelphia
Piccadilly, London
Plaisterers' Hall, Addle Street No. 25, London
Plymouth
Plymouth Sound
Port Morant, Jamaica
Portsmouth
Portugal
Prince's Street, Soho, London

Quay (Mr. Mullan's)
Quebec
Queen Street, St. Ann's

Rio Grande de Matagalpa (Nicaragua)
Rochester
Rome, Italy
Royal Exchange, London
Russia
Rutland

Saint-Croix (U.S. Virgin Islands)
Salford
Sandwich
Santa Cruz, Teneriffe
Saratoga
Savannah, Georgia
Scotland

Senegambia
Sheffield
Shetland Islands
Shropshire
Sierra Leone
Soham
South Carolina
Southhampton
Spain
Spitsbergen
Spring Gardens, No. 12 (residence of Mrs. Lord)
St. Andrew's Church, Chesterton, Cambridge
St. Domingue (present-day Haiti)
St. George's Hospital
St. Margaret's Church, Westminster, London
St. Martin's-Lane, No. 4 Taylor's Buildings
St. Paul's Church-yard, London
Star Office
Stationers' Hall, London
Stones Croft, Bristol
Strand, London
Sudbury
Suffolk
Sutton and Mepal, Isle of Ely, County of Cambridge
Sweden

Tewkesbury
Thames River
Thule
Tooting
Tottenham Court Road
Tottenham Street No. 13
Tuscany
Tusculun School

Union Street, Parish of St. James, County of Middlesex
Union Street No. 10, Marylebone

Villefranche-sur-Mer
Virginia

Wales
Waring-street (residence of Samuel Neilson)
West India colonies
West Indian islands
West Indies
Westminster
Westwell, County of Oxford
Whitechapel, London
Wisbech
Woolmer, Exeter

Yorkshire

Individuals and Groups

Adams, John
Aelane, Yahne (also known by the name Joseph Sanders)
Almaze, Joseph
Ammere, Cojoh (also known by the name George Williams)
Anderson, James
Angus, Mr. and Son
Annis, Jon
Arnold, John
Assembly of the Church of Scotland
Atkinson, Susannah
Atkinson, Law and Family
Atkinson, Revd. Mr. L. & Wife
Audley, John, Esq.

Bailey, James
Baker, Reverend Dr. John
Baker, Samuel
Banks, Joseph
Barlow, John
Bass, Rev. Mr.
Bateman
Bayley, the Rev. Dr.
Bedford, James
Bell, William
Bennett, T.
Berry, Ann
Berry, Arthur

Cope, John
Cope, William
Cork, Mr.
Cotterell, Joseph
Cugoano, Ottobah (also known by the name of Mr. John Stewart)
Cullen, Mrs. Ann
Cumberland, Duke of
Currie, Dr.

Dale, David, Esq.
Danvers, Charles
Davis, Lockyer
Delamain, Mr.
Dennison, Robert
Denton, Robert
Dickenson, John
Dickson, William (formerly private secretary to Edward Hay,
    Governor of Barbados)
Digges, Thomas Atwood
Dolben, Sir William
Doran, James
Down, Messrs., Thornton and Company Bankers
Duke of Cumberland
Dunmore, Lord

Eddis, William
Equiano, Olaudah, the African (Gustavus Vassa)

Farmer, Capt. Thomas
Flower, Benjamin
Folkes, Francis and wife
Ford, Mr.
Ford, Samuel
Foulkes, Mr.
Fox, Charles James
Francis, Thomas
Fraser, Patrick Rev.
Freer, John, Jun.
Freeth, Benjamin
Friends of Freedom
Friends of Humanity
Frith, Miss

Hoare, Mr.
Hodgson, Solomon
Hodson, Francis
Hopkins, Martin
Hornby, William, Esq. of Gainsborough House of Lords
Houseman, Mr.
Howe, Sir William (Gen.)
Hughes, Captain John
Hughes, Reverend
Hughes, William, Esq.
Humphreys, G.
Humphreys, Wm.
Hunt, James
Hunt, William

Ind, Edward
Irving, Dr. Charles
Irwin, Joseph

Jackson
Jenkinson, Charles created Baron Hawkesbury in 1786
Jogensmel, Broughwar (also known by the name Jasper Goree)
Johnson, George, Esq.
Johnson, Joseph
Johnson, Mr. Jacob
Johnson, Stephen
Johnstone, Dr. Edward
Jollie, F.
Jolly, John
Jones, Reverend Thomas
Jordan, Mr. J.S.
Jukes, John

Kearsley
Kelsal
Kerrich, John, Esq.
Ketland, Thomas
King, Robert
King, Thomas
King George the Second
Kirkham, Mr. Ralph
Kirkpatrick, William
Knight, Robert, Esq.

Lackington, James
Langworthy, William
Laurence, Thomas
Lawless, J.
Lee, John
Legay, D. Terry
Lewis, Mr.
Leybourn, Mrs. Ann
Liversege, Mr. and Mrs.
Lloyd, Sampson and Charles, Esqrs. of Birmingham (and families)
London Corresponding Society
Lord, Mrs.
Lords Spiritual and Temporal, and the Commons of the Parliament of
    Great Britain
Lowe, John
Lowth, Rev. Robert, Lord Bishop of London

M'Laren's, Mr.
Macnamara, Mathias
Mandeville, George Robert
Mansfield, Lord
March, John
Marlborough
Marsh, Charles
Marsh, George
Marshall, Samuel
Mathews, David
Mathews, Mr. Alexander
Mawley, John
Maynard family (cousins of Captain Michael Henry Pascal)
McCoy
Medley, William
Middleton, Sir Charles
Millan, Mr. Buchanan
Miller, David
Montieth, John, Esq.
Morris, John
Moss, Isaac, Jun., Esq.
Mountains, Mr. John
Mullan, Mr.
Murray, David
Murray, John

Neilson, Samuel
Nelson, Horatio
Newton, Sir Isaac
Nortcoft, Mr. William
North, Lord

Officers and Commissions of His Majesty's Navy
Oran Otang philosophers ("Ourang Outangs, Jackoos, and other
   next of kin to the African Negroes")
Osborn, James
Othello (author of possible attribution)
Oxford, Thomas

Paine, Tom
Palmer, Edward, Esq.
Palmer, W.
Parkes, Thomas
Parkinson, James, Esq. of the Leverian Museum
Parsons, John
Pascal, Captain Michael Henry
Pearce, Rev. Mr.
Pearson, Thomas
Pease, Jos. R., Esq.
Peckard, Rev. Dr. P.
Peckover, Jonathan
Pemberton, Samuel
Perkins, Henry
Peters, Mr. & Mrs.
Phillips, J. (Son)
Phillips, James (Father)
Phipps, Constantine John (later Lord Mulgrave)
Piercy, Edward
Piercy, Mr. J.W.
Pitt, Hon. George
Pitt, William
Plymley, Katherine, sister of Joseph
Porteus, Dr. Beilby, Bishop of Chester
Pratt, Samuel Jackson
Price, Thomas
Priestley, Rev. Dr. Joseph
Privy Council
Pumphrey, Stanley

Walker, Thomas, Esq.
Wallace, George
Wallace, Thomas
Ward, John
Washington, Gen.
Watt, Capt. David
Webb, Edward
Webster, Rowland, Esq. Stockton
Wedgwood, Josiah
Whitbread, Mr.
White, S., M.D.
Whitfield, George
Whitwell, Matthew
Wiggin, Mrs.
Wilberforce, William
Wilkes, Mr.
Wilkins, T.
Wilkinson, Rev. James
Willett, Capt. John
Wilson, Mr.
Wolfe, Gen.
Wollstonecraft, Mary
Wood, T.
Wright, John

Notes

Note on Names:
Gustavus Vassa and/or Olaudah Equiano

1. Paul E. Lovejoy, "Olaudah Equiano or Gustavus Vassa–What's in a Name?" *Atlantic Studies: Literary, Cultural and Historical Perspectives* 9:2 (2012), 177.
2. Carretta, *The Interesting Narrative*, xix.
3. Walvin, *An African's Life: The Life and Times of Olaudah Equiano, 1745-1797* (Washington: Cassell, 1998), xv. In his 2005 biography of Vassa, Carretta similarly states that "Outside of his autobiography, the author of *The Interesting Narrative* almost never called himself Equiano. He retained Gustavus Vassa as his legal name, and it appears on his baptismal, naval, and marriage records as well as in his will. In all his writings other than *The Interesting Narrative* he used Vassa in public and private." See Vincent Carretta, *Equiano, the African: Biography of a Self-Made Man* (Athens: University of Georgia Press, 2005), xvi.
4. See pages 53 and 197.
5. See page 64.
6. Gustavus Vassa to Granville Sharp, 6 May 1780, in anti-slave trade movement Great Britain Correspondence, Sierra Leone Collection, Series VI, box 1, supplement 1, folder 1, University of Illinois at Chicago Library, Special Collections.
7. Lovejoy, "Olaudah Equiano or Gustavus Vassa—What's in a Name?" 166.

Introduction

1. Folarin Shyllon, *Black People in Britain 1555–1833* (London: Oxford University Press, 1977), 154. Scholars disagree over Vassa's date of birth. He may have been born in 1742 or in 1747 rather than in 1745 as he claims in *The Interesting Narrative*. See Paul Lovejoy, "Construction of Identity: Olaudah Equiano or Gustavus Vassa?" *Historically Speaking* 7:3 (2006), 8-9.

2. Quoted in James Walvin, *An African's Life*, 189. Vassa's eloquent text served to show the British public that "an African could aspire to all that was good and worthwhile, all that was refined and sensitive" (ibid., 162).
3. Vincent Carretta, *Equiano, the African*, xii.
4. See, in particular, the responses by Vincent Carretta, Trevor Burnard, Paul Lovejoy, and Jon Sensbach in "Olaudah Equiano, the South Carolinian? A Forum," *Historically Speaking* 7:3 (2006): 2-16. As Carretta has noted, interest in Vassa has not been restricted to academia. He has been the subject of films, newspaper articles, television shows, comic books, and children's books. Moreover, he is an integral part of African, African-American, Anglo-American, African-British, and Afro-Caribbean popular culture.
5. For Vassa's subscribers, see Vincent Carretta's description in *The Interesting Narrative*, xvi-xviii.
6. See the comprehensive bibliography at the end of this collection; it includes a list of helpful primary sources as well as a list of the editions of *The Interesting Narrative*.
7. See Nini Rodgers's piece, "Equiano in Belfast: A Study of the Anti-Slavery Ethos in a Northern Town," *Slavery and Abolition* 18:2 (1997), 73-89. For a description of Vassa's participation in the London Corresponding Society and his friendship with Thomas Hardy, see Peter Linebaugh and Marcus Rediker, *The Many-Headed Hydra: Sailors, Slaves, Commoners, and the Hidden History of the Revolutionary Atlantic* (Boston: Beacon Press, 2000), 334-341.
8. See Shyllon, *Black People in Britain*, 245-272.
9. Ibid., 274.

Chapter I

1. See Carretta, *Equiano, the African,* 80-81.
2. Ibid., 146. A young Horatio Nelson also participated in the expedition. He was on board Lutwidge's accompanying ship, the *HMS Carcass*.
3. By 1792, Vassa was well established in England. He may have first met his wife during his book tour in Cambridge in July 1789. Paul Edwards determined that "He may have met her through Dr. Peter Peckard, Master of Magdalen College, Cambridge, and Dean of Peterborough, with whom he appears to have been on good terms." See Edwards, ed., *Equiano's Travels. His Autobiography: The Interesting Narrative of the Life of Olaudah Equiano, or, Gustavus Vassa,*

the African, Written by Himself (London: Heinemann Educational Books Ltd, 1967; 2d ed., 1969), xii. Edwards also presented the following quotation from the notice of Vassa's marriage in *The Gentleman's Magazine*: "At Soham, co. Cambridge, Gustavus Vassa the African, well know as the champion and advocate for procuring the suppression of the slave trade, to Miss Cullen, daughter of Mr C. Of Ely, in the same county." Ibid. In his letter dated 1 August 1789, and addressed to the *Cambridge Chronicle*, Vassa promoted his exoticism. John Bugg has pointed out that Vassa printed versions of this notice after several of his appearances, but that this is the only one that includes the statement "Nor have even the fair-sex refused to countenance the sooty African." See "The Other Interesting Narrative: Olaudah Equiano's Public Book Tour," *The Modern Language Association of America* PMLA 121.5 (2006), 1436. As Bugg explains, "With its playful puns, this may be Equiano's private nod to Susannah Cullen, the white Cambridgeshire woman he would marry three years later." Ibid. Vassa announces his marriage in his letter to Thomas Hardy of 28 May 1792. See page 40. As early as January 1788, four years before his marriage, Vassa wrote a book review of James Tobin's publication, which makes a forceful case for intermarriages at home and in the colonies. See pages 96-97.

4. On 20 February 1796, the *Cambridge Chronicle and Journal* reported that "On Tuesday died at Soham, after a long illness, which she supported with Christian fortitude, Mrs. Susannah Vassa, the wife of Gustavus Vassa the African." Carretta, *Equiano, the African*, 363.

5. According to Carretta, this is the equivalent of approximately $160,000 today.

6. This is the version in Carretta, *The Interesting Narrative*, 137.

7. Ibid., *The Interesting Narrative*, 373-375.

8. James Walvin acknowledges the late Paul Edwards for having brought this to his attention. See Walvin, *An African's Life*, 188.

9. This is the version in Vincent Carretta, "New Equiana," *Early American Literature* 44, 1 (2009), 160.

Chapter II

1. David Killingray, ed., *Africans in Britain* (Portland: Frank Cass, 1994), 48. See *Report of the Lords of the Committee of the Privy Council . . . concerning the present State of the Trade of Africa, and particularly the Trade in Slaves* (1789), Part 1, No.14. Vassa's letter to Lord Hawkesbury is dated 13 March 1788. The text of this letter

was published in Paul Edwards's *Equiano's Travels. His Autobiography: The Interesting Narrative of Olaudah Equiano, or, Gustavus Vassa, the African. Written by Himself* (London: Heinemann Educational Books Ltd, 1967; 2d ed., 1969, lix-lxi, and in Appendix One of Shyllon's *Black People in Britain*).

2. On 25 April 1792, charges appeared in *The Oracle* that Vassa was not a native African but born on the Danish island of Santa Cruz in the West Indies. This story was reproduced in *The Star*. The editor of *The Star* later apologized, and J. Baker, a friend of Vassa's, requested that the editor of *The Oracle* do the same. Edwards, *Equiano's Travels*, 1969, ix and xiii. See documents 4, 5, 6, and 7 in Chapter V: Miscellaneous.

3. Vassa's letter of 20 June 1794, which Bugg published in the August 2008 *Times Literary Supplement* "reveals that in the harrowing spring of 1794 he was as occupied by the Pitt Ministry's sweeping arrests as he was by his book tour." See Bugg, "The Sons of Belial," 15.

4. This is the version in Carretta, *The Interesting Narrative*, 221-223. Vassa attached letters in support of his application from Mathias Macnamara and Thomas Wallace.

5. This is my transcription of Vassa's letter to Granville Sharp, 6 May 1780, in Sierra Leone Collection, box 4, supplement 1, folder 1. University of Illinois at Chicago Library, Special Collections. I am grateful to Neil Marshall, who identified this letter in November 2011, and to Paul Lovejoy for drawing it to my attention.

6. This is the version in Shyllon, *Black People in Britain*, 247-248.

7. The note attached here to the bottom of this letter is also the version in Shyllon. The Memorial reached the Treasury on 25 May 1787. The backsheet to the Memorial dated 6 July 1787 reads: "Write to Comm. Navy to pay him £50 in full of expenses and wages." This letter was printed by Vassa in the 9th edition of the *Narrative*. Ibid., 248.

8. Ibid., 254-255. Charles Jenkinson (1729-1808), created Baron Hawkesbury in 1786, was President of the Board of Trade, 1786-1804. Vassa published a slightly revised version of this letter in *The Public Advertiser*, 31 March 1788. See Carretta, *The Interesting Narrative*, note 6, 368.

9. This is the version in Carretta, *The Interesting Narrative*, 231-232.

10. It appears that this note was written on Vassa's printed solicitation "TO THE NOBILITY, GENTRY AND OTHERS." Ibid., 345.

11. This is the version in Carretta, "New Equiana," 148-149.

12. This is the version in Shyllon, *Black People in Britain*, 261.

13. The date for this letter differs according to the various editions of

Vassa's autobiography. March 24 is the date listed in the first edition published by Shyllon. March 1789 is the date listed in the 9th edition published by Carretta. As Carretta notes, "the March 1789 ed. 1 reads, 'Union-Street, Mary-le-bone, March 24, 1789'; ed. 2 reads, 'No. 10, Union-Street, Mary-le-bone, Dec. 24, 1789'; eds. 3 and 4 read, 'No. 4, Taylor's Buildings, St. Martin's-Lane, October 30, 1790'; ed. 5 reads, 'June 1792'; ed. 6 reads, 'December 1792'; eds. 7 and 8 read, 'March 1789.'" See *The Interesting Narrative*, 239.

14. Reverend Walker was one of Vassa's original subscribers. This is my transcription based on the original primary source version. It differs slightly from the version published in Carretta, *The Interesting Narrative*, 358-359.

15. This is my transcription based on the primary sources and the version published in Carretta, *The Interesting Narrative*, 361-362. Carretta notes that "This letter was one of the documents seized when the authorities arrested its addressee, on 12 May 1794. Hardy was tried and acquitted on 5 November 1794 on a charge of high treason for his role in the London Corresponding Society." Ibid., note 28, 371.

16. Carretta explains that "Karks" is related to "kirks, the Scottish word for churches." *Interesting Narrative*, note 31, 371.

17. This is the version in Carretta, *The Interesting Narrative*, 5. Vassa responded to these charges on the first page of the 9th edition of his autobiography in 1794. The date and page number differ in other editions of the *Narrative*. See, for example, Shyllon, *Black People in Britain*, 263.

18. This is my transcription of the primary source document from the Worcestershire Record Office, BA8720/1(ii) 8. See the image of this manuscript letter by Vassa to Pumphrey in John Bugg, "The Other Interesting Narrative," 1432. Also see Carretta, *Equiano, the African*, 355-356. Carretta does not provide the reference or a transcription but alludes to a letter of introduction written by Stanley Pumphrey on behalf of Vassa to abolitionist William Bell Crafton in the period prior to this letter of thanks written to Pumphrey from Vassa.

19. This is the version in Carretta, *The Interesting Narrative*, 364. He cites the Trustees of the Wedgwood Museum, Barlaston, Staffordshire, England.

20. This is my transcription based on the primary source version. John Bugg first published a transcription of this letter in August 2008. Carretta has also published a transcription in "New Equiana," 155-156. As Bugg explains, this letter was posted in Colchester, and from the towns Vassa mentions, he seems to have been travelling south from Ipswich and Colchester to Kelvedon and Chelmsford. Both Suffolk

and Essex were active in the abolition movement, and the Quaker banker and abolitionist Jonathan Peckover, mentioned by Vassa, was from nearby Ipswich. However, Bugg erroneously states that Thomas Clarkson was from Ipswich. The latter was from Wisbech, approximately seventy miles northwest of Ipswich. See "The Sons of Belial," 15.

21. This is the version in Carretta, *The Interesting Narrative*, 366-367. He cites Ferrar Papers, Magdalene College, Cambridge.

22. This is my transcription based on the original in MS Box W2/5/14 © Religious Society of Friends in Britain.

23. This is the version in *The Interesting Narrative*, 328-329. Carretta cites Prince Hoare, *Memoirs of Granville Sharp* (London, 1820), 367. Sharp was one of the founders of the Society for Effecting the Abolition of the Slave Trade (SEAST), formally organized on 22 May 1787. See Carretta, *Equiano, the African*, 256-257.

24. This is the version in Carretta, *The Interesting Narrative*, 227.

25. Ibid., 354-355. Susannah Atkinson was the wife of Law Atkinson, and Mould Green is near Huddersfield, which is approximately thirty miles northwest of Sheffield.

26. This is the version in Carretta, *The Interesting Narrative*, 365. He cites the Trustees of the Wedgwood Museum, Barlaston, Staffordshire, England.

27. Vassa was aware of Thomas Clarkson's negative reception at Bristol. As Carretta notes, Clarkson required a bodyguard when he gathered evidence in Bristol a few years prior. Vassa also knew that he was liable to being pressed into service in the Royal Navy. See *Equiano, the African*, 357.

28. According to Bugg, "The primary record of Equiano's book tour derives from the letters of reference he carried as he promoted his autobiography, which he included as marketing matter in the third and subsequent editions" of his autobiography. After each stop on his tour, Vassa extended *The Interesting Narrative*'s subscription index by publishing the names of his supporters in local newspapers. While his encouragement to his supporters to take part in the sugar boycott campaign goes unmentioned in his autobiography, Vassa advocated for this during his book tour. See Bugg, "The Other Interesting Narrative, 1430-1431.

29. This is the version in Carretta, *The Interesting Narrative*, 163.

30. Ibid., 210.

31. Ibid., 222.

32. Ibid., 222-223.

33. This is the version in Carretta, *Equiano, the African*, 335.

34. This is the version in Carretta, *The Interesting Narrative*, 8. Carretta suggests that this letter of recommendation was typical of those Vassa carried with him. *Equiano, the African*, 340.
35. This is the version in Carretta, *The Interesting Narrative*, 8-9.
36. Ibid., 9.
37. Ibid.
38. Ibid., 10. See the possible impersonation of Vassa by Thomas Atwood Digges in the letter dated 11 November 1796 on pages 186–187.
39. This is the version in Carretta, *The Interesting Narrative*, 10-11. Vassa included this letter in the 6th edition of his autobiography.
40. Ibid., 11. Vassa also included this letter in the 6th edition of his autobiography.
41. Ibid., 11-12.
42. This is my direct transcription from the primary source document in the Cambridgeshire Archives: 132/B3.

Chapter III

1. See Carretta, *Equiano, the African*, 234-235.
2. This is the version in Shyllon, *Black People in Britain*, 151.
3. This is my transcription based on the primary source version from the National Archives, Kew, England: T 1/643, no. 681, f. 87.
4. This letter from Vassa to Cugoano was written on 24 March 1787 and published in *The Public Advertiser* on 4 April 1787. It is the version in Shyllon, *Black People in Britain*, 246-247. As Carretta notes, "*The Public Advertiser*, *The Morning Chronicle*, and *London Advertiser*, and *The Diary* were pro-Pitt London newspapers subsidized at the time by the Treasury, under the direction of George Rose (1744-1818), one of the original subscribers to *The Interesting Narrative*." *The Interesting Narrative*, note 1, 367.
5. Although this letter was reproduced without attribution, Carretta believes that its content, tone, diction, and style suggest that Ottobah Cugoano was its author. See *Equiano, the African*, 230-231.
6. This is the version in Shyllon, *Black People in Britain*, 154.
7. Ibid., 154-155.
8. As Shyllon explains, "It was after George Harvey took over from Vassa as Commissary that some of the blacks made their way into the centre of Plymouth after bolting from the ships." *Black People in Britain*, note 10, 158.
9. According to Shyllon, "One of these was John Mawley whose dismissal Joseph Irwin procured, because, as he wrote in *The Morning*

Herald on 13 January 1787, Mawley 'laboured at different times to create prejudices against me, to sow dissensions amongst the blacks, and retard or frustrate the execution of the plan.' Apparently everyone was to blame except Irwin himself." *Black People in Britain*, note 11, 158.

10. This was in fact an undertaking of the Society for the Propagation of the Gospel. Shyllon, *Black People in Britain*, note 12, 158.

11. This is the version in Carretta, *Equiano, the African*, 234.

12. This is the version in Shyllon, *Black People in Britain*, 248. It is Vassa's reply to the letter written by Patrick Fraser and published on 2 July 1787 in *The Public Advertiser*. It also appeared in *The London Chronicle* and *The Morning Chronicle, and London Advertiser*.

13. This is the version in Shyllon, *Black People in Britain*, 253.

14. The term "pathetic" here means emotionally moving. As Carretta explains, "Dr. Beilby Porteus (1731-1808), bishop of London 1787-1808, delivered the first abolitionist speech by a prominent Anglican." *The Interesting Narrative*, note 5, 367-368. Also see Shyllon, *Black People in Britain*, note 7, 264.

15. As Carretta explains, "although the letter is signed 'Aethiopianus,'" Vassa was the author, and "the same letter appeared on 21 February in the *Morning Post, and Daily Advertiser*, signed 'Gustavus Vasa, for the Ethiopians.'" *Equiano, the African*, 264.

16. This is the version in Shyllon, *Black People in Britain*, 256-257. As Carretta notes, this letter was also published in the 20 June 1788 issue of *The Morning Chronicle, and London Advertiser*. See *The Interesting Narrative*, note 8, 368.

17. Both Shyllon and Carretta suggest that these are probably references to James Ramsay and Thomas Clarkson.

18. This is the version in Shyllon, *Black People in Britain*, 258-260.

19. Thomas Townsend (1733-1800) was made Baron Sydney in 1783, Home Secretary of State from 1784-1789, and President of the Board of Control from 1784-1790. Carretta, *The Interesting Narrative*, note 12, 369.

20. This is the version in Shyllon, *Black People in Britain*, 260-261.

21. The plate Vassa is referring to here is the one of the *Brookes* of Liverpool, reproduced in Thomas Clarkson's *History of the Rise, Progress, and Accomplishment of the Abolition of the Slave Trade by the British Parliament* (London, 1808), facing 2: 111. See illustration in Appendix 3.

22. This is the version in Carretta, *The Interesting Narrative*, 361. Edwards first published this letter in his article "Afro-British Authors of the late Georgian Period," published six years later in David

Killingray's *Africans in Britain*, 1994.

23. Shyllon, *Black People in Britain*, 269-270.
24. As Carretta explains, "Dolben (1727-1814) led the successful legislative fight in 1788 for a law regulating overcrowding of slave ships." *The Interesting Narrative*, note 13, 369.
25. This is the version in Shyllon, *Black People in Britain*, 270-271.
26. Ibid.
27. Ibid., 271-272.
28. William Dickson was a subscriber to Vassa's *Interesting Narrative* and wrote *Letters on Slavery. . . . To Which Are Added, Addresses to the Whites, and to the Free Negroes of Barbadoes: and Accounts of Some Negroes Eminent for their Virtues and Abilities* (London, 1789). Carretta, *The Interesting Narrative*, note 16, 369.
29. Shyllon, *Black People in Britain*, 249-251.
30. Lex Talionis refers to the law of retribution of an eye for an eye. Carretta, *The Interesting Narrative*, note 4, 367.
31. Shyllon, *Black People in Britain*, 251-253.
32. See Cugoano, *Thoughts and Sentiments*, 14, where the same phrases occur. Shyllon, *Black People in Britain*, note 6, 264.
33. This is the first indication of Vassa's desire to write and publish his testimony.
34. This is the version in Carretta, *The Interesting Narrative*, 337-339.
35. As Carretta explains, "Harris, whose real name was Hormassa, was a Spanish-born Jesuit. For his efforts on behalf of the slave trade and slavery, he received an award of £100 from the city of Liverpool. Among the responses to Harris were the Reverend Hughes (d. 1798), *An Answer to the Rev. Mr. Harris's 'Scriptural Researches on the Licitness of the Slave-Trade'* (London, 1788) and the Reverend James Ramsay, *An Examination of the Rev. Mr. Harris's 'Scriptural Researches on the Licitness of the Slave Trade'* (London, 1788)." *The Interesting Narrative*, note 7, 368.
36. This is the version in Shyllon, *Black People in Britain*, 257-258.
37. The author in question is Samuel Jackson Pratt, and the full reference to his book is *Humanity, or the Rights of Nature, a Poem: in Two Books. By the Author of Sympathy* (London, 1788). Carretta, *The Interesting Narrative*, note 11, 369.
38. This is the version in Carretta, *The Interesting Narrative*, 345-347. The source cited by Carretta is Mark Jones, Keele University Library Special Collections, Reference 74 / 12632.
39. This is the version in Carretta, "New Equiana," 149.
40. Erin Sadlack brought this document to Carretta's attention. See *The Interesting Narrative*, 349-350. Also note that according to Carretta,

essentially the same advertisement was printed on 21 May 1789 in *The Star* (London), and on 18 June 1789 in *The World*. See "New Equiana," 150.

41. This advertisement appeared in London. Essentially the same advertisement had appeared in *The World* (London) on 5 January 1790. See Caretta, "New Equiana," 150-151.

42. This is the version in Carretta, *The Interesting Narrative*, 350-351.

43. As Carretta explains, William Bliss was one of Vassa's subscribers. Ibid., note 18, 369.

44. This is the version in Carretta, *The Interesting Narrative*, 352-353.

45. As Carretta explains, "Edmund Holme's 1788 *A Directory of the Towns of Manchester and Salford, for the Year 1788* (Manchester: Printed for the Author), includes 'Harrop, Joseph, gent. Bury street, Salford,' 'Harrop, James, printer and stationer, Marketplace,' and 'Thomson, John, writing stationer, at Mers. Lighthasle's milliner, Queen street, St. Ann's.' Both James and Joseph Harrop were members of the Society for Effecting the Abolition of the Slave Trade." Ibid., note 19, 369.

46. This is the version in Carretta, *The Interesting Narrative*, 353-354.

47. As Carretta explains, "Bryant was a member of the Society for Effecting the Abolition of the Slave Trade. During his book promotion tours in the provinces, Equiano apparently recruited, or at least identified, potential members for the London Corresponding Society, a radical working-class organization begun on 25 January 1792 by Thomas Hardy." Ibid., note 20, 369-370.

48. This is the version in Carretta, "New Equiana," 154-155.

49. This is the version in Carretta, *The Interesting Narrative*, 356. The source listed by Carretta is the York Reference Library, England.

50. Carretta explains that "Tuke, a Quaker and member of the Society for Effecting the Abolition of the Slave Trade, was a tea-dealer; Spence (buried 9 August 1824, aged 75), was a bookseller. The same page prints the transcript of part of the slave-trade debate in the House of Commons, including William Wilberforce's statements." Ibid., note 22, 370.

51. This advertisement appeared in Dublin. This version is from Carretta, *The Interesting Narrative*, 357. An image of the primary source can be seen in John Bugg's "The Other Interesting Narrative," 1437.

52. Carretta explains that "Sleater, one of Equiano's Dublin subscribers, was printer for the Anglo-Irish parliament; Byrne, on the other hand, was a successful Roman Catholic bookseller and printer supporting the Irish national opposition, Catholic emancipation, and parliamentary reform. He published the *Universal Magazine*, which sympa-

thetically covered the progress of the French Revolution. He also later published the political pamphlets of Wolfe Tone, the Irish radical, and became printer to the Catholic Committee and to the United Irishmen." *The Interesting Narrative*, note 23, 370.

53. This is the version in Carretta, *The Interesting Narrative*, 357-358.

54. Nini Rodgers, "Equiano in Belfast: A Study of the Anti-slavery Ethos in a Northern Town" (1997), draws attention to the *Belfast News-Letter* of 20 December 1791 and reminds us that "Vassa's most supportive patrons were unusual, if prominent, members of Belfast society" (77). Additional documents she has located confirm the influence Vassa had in Belfast and the radical atmosphere there, as well as the fact that supporters of his came from the most radical political grouping in Ireland. These supporters included the infamous Samuel Neilson. Rodgers cites J. Lawless's nineteenth-century collection, *The Belfast Politics Enlarged; being a compendium of the political history of Ireland for the last forty years* (1816), suggesting that Vassa may have prolonged his stay in Belfast in order to attend a 29 January 1792 meeting whose participants discussed a gradualist approach to abolition (82).

55. This is the version in Carretta, *The Interesting Narrative*, 359-360.

56. Carretta notes that "Andrew Dunbar was the inn-keeper at the sign of the King's Arms, Trongate." Ibid., note 26, 371.

57. This is the version in Carretta, *The Interesting Narrative*, 360.

58. Ibid., 362-363.

59. Ibid., 363-364.

60. Ibid., 365-366. Carretta notes that this advertisement as well as the one following "appeared on the same two days in Yarrington & Bacon's *Norwich Mercury*" (365).

61. Johann Friedrich Blumenbach would later publish a German review of the first edition in the *Goettingische Anzeigen von Gelehrten Sachen*. According to my research, the German review was translated into English in January 2011 by Christoph Freydorf. I was not able to locate this review or the 6 April 1797 review of the ninth edition of the *Narrative* published on page 356 in edition 67 of *The Gentleman's Magazine*.

62. This is the version in Carretta, *Equiano, the African*, 331-332.

63. This is the version in Carretta, *The Interesting Narrative*, xxvii. It appeared on page 539 of volume 59 of *The Gentleman's Magazine*.

64. This is the version in Carretta, *The Interesting Narrative*, 12-13. It appeared on pages 551-552 of the *Monthly Review*. See Gates and Davis, eds., *The Slave's Narrative*, 1985, 5, and Carretta, *Equiano, the African*, 333.

65. This is the version in Carretta, *The Interesting Narrative*, 13-14. *The General Magazine and Impartial Review* was published by Thomas Bellamy.
66. Vassa is adopting this phrase from *Othello*.
67. Bugg published an excerpt of this letter in "The Other Interesting Narrative," 1435. I am grateful to Arthur Torrington, who drew my attention to this letter and sent me a transcription in 2008. Carretta published the full version in 2009 in "New Equiana," 151-152.
68. This is the version in Shyllon, *Black People in Britain*, 262.
69. Paul Edwards was the first to locate this letter; he cited it in his 1967 edition of *The Interesting Narrative*.
70. Bugg has published an excerpt of this letter in "The Other Interesting Narrative," 1430. I am grateful to Arthur Torrington, who drew my attention to this letter and sent me a transcription in 2008. Carretta published the full version in 2009 in "New Equiana," 153.
71. I am grateful to Arthur Torrington, who drew my attention to this letter and sent me a transcription in 2008. Carretta published the full version in 2009 in "New Equiana," 154. The inscription to T. Bennett, dated 1829, on the copy of the 1791 edition of *The Interesting Narrative*, reads as follows: "The Gift of his Aunt at Southhampton. Let he who reads the horrors practiced on West Indian slaves use all his influence to put it down." Bodleian Lib., University of Oxford, Vet. AS e. 6629.
72. This is the version in Carretta, *The Interesting Narrative*, 355-356.
73. This is the version in Carretta, "New Equiana," 155.
74. This is the version in Carretta, *The Interesting Narrative*, 366.
75. This is the version in Carretta, *Equiano, the African*, 263.
76. This is the version in Carretta, "New Equiana," 147.
77. Ibid., 149-150.
78. Ibid., 152.
79. Bugg has published an excerpt of this letter in "The Other Interesting Narrative," 1436-1437. I am grateful to Arthur Torrington, who sent me a transcription in 2008. Carretta published the full version in 2009 in "New Equiana," 152-153.
80. See Carretta, *Equiano, the African*, 340-341. I have not been able to locate the poem.
81. This is the version in Carretta, *The Interesting Narrative*, note 27, 371.
82. This is the version in Carretta, "New Equiana," 156-157.
83. Ibid., 157-158.

Chapter IV

1. This is the transcription published by Carretta in "Possible Gustavus Vassa/Olaudah Equiano Attributions," in *The Faces of Anonymity: Anonymous and Pseudonymous Publication from the Sixteenth to the Twentieth Century*, edited by Robert J. Griffin, 103-139 (New York: Palgrave Macmillan, 2003), 110-111.

2. Ibid., 112-114.

3. Ibid., 114-116.

4. Ibid., 116-119.

5. Ibid., 119-120.

6. Ibid., 120-121.

7. The English translation of this sentence is: "old British manuscript, from which Tacitus took the famous speech of Galgacus."

8. This is the transcription by Carretta in Griffin, ed., *Faces of Anonymity*, 122-123.

9. Ibid., 124-126.

10. Ibid., 126-128.

11. Ibid., 129-131.

12. Based on their textual analysis, Gates and Davis posited in *The Slave's Narrative: Texts and Contexts* (New York: Oxford University Press, 1985) that Ottobah Cugoano's *Thoughts and Sentiments on the Evil of Slavery* (1787) was written by both Cugoano and Vassa. It is also possible that Cugoano and Vassa collaborated to write this letter.

13. In reference to a March 1783 diary entry by Granville Sharp regarding the *Zong* tragedy, James Walvin states that "Curiously though, Equiano makes no mention whatsoever of this, the most chilling of all maritime slave outrages in his lifetime, in his autobiography written only six years later. It was an event which provided some of the most graphic and damning evidence about the Atlantic slave trade, yet Equiano chose not to use it in a book which was specifically designed as a contribution to the abolition debate." Walvin, *An African's Life*, 153. This was also noted by Shyllon in the 1970s. See James Walvin, *The Zong* (New Haven, CT: Yale University Press, 2011).

14. Shyllon, *Black People in Britain*, 197-198.

15. Cited in ibid., 198.

16. This is the transcription in Shyllon's *Black Slaves in Britain* (London: Oxford University Press, 1974) 187-188. As mentioned above, the anonymous letter may have been written by Vassa or by Vassa and Cugoano together.

17. Dr. Beilby Porteus was the Bishop of Chester and London. The ser-

mon referred to was preached on 21 February 1783. Ibid., 187.
18. Carretta in Griffin, ed., *Faces of Anonymity*, 108-109.
19. See Vincent Carretta, "A New Letter by Gustavus Vassa/Olaudah Equiano?" *Early American Literature* 39, no. 2 (2004), 355-361. This is the same Thomas Atwood Digges who wrote Vassa a letter of introduction on 25 December 1791.
20. This is the transcription by Carretta in Griffin, *The Faces of Anonymity*, 131-136.
21. Ibid., 136-139. See Carretta's analysis of this document in *Equiano, the African*, 360-361.
22. Carretta, "A New Letter by Gustavus Vassa/Olaudah Equiano?" 360.

Chapter V

1. This is the version Vassa printed in the first edition of his autobiography in 1789. Subsequent versions contain slight changes. See Carretta, *The Interesting Narrative*, 194-197.
2. This is my transcription of the primary source version in Sierra Leone Collection, box 4, supplement 1, folder 1, University of Illinois at Chicago Library, Special Collections.
3. This may be the J. Phillips of George-Yard, Lombard Street, who published W.B.C.'s *A Short Sketch of the Evidence for the Abolition of the Slave Trade, Delivered before a Committee of the House of Commons, to which is added, a Recommendation of the Subject to the Serious Attention of People in General* (London, 1792).
4. This is the version in Carretta, "New Equiana," 158-159. The full reference reads *The Bee, Or Literary Weekly Intelligencer, Consisting of Original Pieces, and Selections from Performances of Merit, Foreign and Domestic. A Work Calculated to Disseminate Useful Knowledge Among All Ranks of People at a Small* Expence. By James Anderson. (Edinburgh: Printed by Mundell & Son, Parliament Stairs), Vol. 4, #7 (1792), 34.
5. This is the version in Carretta, *The Interesting Narrative*, note 2, 237-238.
6. Ibid., note 3, 238.
7. This is the version in Shyllon, *Black People in Britain*, 265-266. Tillock was the printer of the *Star*. He appears in the fifth edition of *The Interesting Narrative* onwards.
8. As Carretta notes, the date is different according to the edition of *The Interesting Narrative*. See *The Interesting Narrative*, 5-6.
9. This is the version in Shyllon, *Black People in Britain*, 266. Baker's

reference appears in the fifth edition of the *Narrative* onwards.

10. Here again, the date is different depending on the edition of *The Interesting Narrative*.

11. This is the version in Carretta, *Equiano, the African*, 355-356. Bugg has printed most of the diary entry in "The Other Interesting Narrative," 1435. As Carretta notes, Joseph Plymley was an active member of the Society for Effecting the Abolition of the Slave Trade for Shropshire.

12. This is the version in Carretta, "New Equiana," 158. This was published after Vassa's death on 31 March, 1797.

13. This is the version in Carretta, "New Equiana," 159. The full reference reads "John Lowe, Jun., 'The Shipwreck of a Slave Ship, in Poems' (Manchester: R. and W. Dean, 1803), 52–57." John Bugg brought this citation to Carretta's attention. Lowe was a subscriber to *The Interesting Narrative*.

14. Ibid. Carretta cites the Bodleian Lib., University of Oxford, Vet. A5 e. 6629.

15. This is the version in Carretta, "New Equiana," 160.

Bibliography and Further Reading

Editions of *The Interesting Narrative*

1st edition. 2 vols. London, 1789.

2nd edition. 2 vols. London, 1789.

3rd edition. London, 1790.

4th edition. Dublin, 1791.

5th edition. Edinburgh, 1792.

6th edition. London, 1793.

7th edition. London, 1793.

8th edition. Norwich, 1794.

9th edition. London, 1794.

The Interesting Narrative of the life of Olaudah Equiano, or Gustavus Vassa, the African. Written by himself. Belper: S. Mason, 1809.

The Interesting Narrative of the life of Olaudah Equiano, or Gustavus Vassa, the African. Written by himself. Halifax: J. Nicholson & Co, 1814.

The Interesting Narrative of the life of Olaudah Equiano, or Gustavus Vassa, the African. Written by himself. Leeds: James Nichols, 1814.

The Interesting Narrative of the life of Olaudah Equiano, or Gustavus Vassa, the African. Written by himself. Penryn: W. Cock, 1816.

The Life of Olaudah Equiano. Boston: I. Knapp, 1837.

Equiano's Travels. His Autobiography. The Interesting Narrative of Olaudah Equiano, or, Gustavus Vassa, the African. Abridged and edited by Paul Edwards, African Writers Series 10. London and Ibadan: Heinemann Educational Books, 1967; and New York: Praeger, 1967.

The Life of Olaudah Equiano, or, Gustavus Vassa the African. Reprinted with an introduction by Paul Edwards, Colonial History Series. London: Dawson, 1969.

The Life of Olaudah Equiano, or Gustavus Vassa, the African, Written by Himself. New York: Negro Universities Press, 1969.

"The Interesting Narrative of the Life of Olaudah Equiano." In *The Classic Slave Narratives*, edited with an introduction by Henry Louis

Gates, Jr. New York: Mentor, 1987.

The Interesting Narrative of the Life of Olaudah Equiano, or Gustavus Vassa, the African. Written by Himself. Edited with an introduction by Wilfred D. Samuels. Miami, FL: Mnemosyne Pub. Co., 1988.

The Interesting Narrative of the Life of Olaudah Equiano, or Gustavus Vassa, the African. Written by Himself. Edited with an introduction by Paul Edwards. Harlow and White Plains, NY: Longman, 1989.

The Interesting Narrative of the Life of Olaudah Equiano, or Gustavus Vassa, the African. Written by Himself. Edited with an introduction by Robert J. Allison. Boston: Bedford Books of St. Martin's Press, 1995.

Equiano's Travels. His Autobiography. The Interesting Narrative of Olaudah Equiano, or, Gustavus Vassa, the African. Abridged and edited by Paul Edwards. New edition. Oxford: Heinemann, 1996.

The African: The Interesting Narrative of the Life of Olaudah Equiano. London: Black Classics, 1998.

The Interesting Narrative of the Life of Olaudah Equiano, or Gustavus Vassa, the African. Edited by Joslyn T. Pine. New York: Dover Publications, 1999.

The Interesting Narrative of the life of Olaudah Equiano, or Gustavus Vassa, the African, written by himself. Edited by Werner Sollors. New York: Norton Critical Editions, 2001.

The Interesting Narrative of the life of Olaudah Equiano. Edited by Angelo Costanzo. New York: Broadview Literary Texts, 2001.

The Interesting Narrative and Other Writings. Edited with an introduction and notes by Vincent Carretta. London and New York: Penguin Books, 1995; 2d ed., 2003.

Primary Sources

Clarkson, Thomas. *The History of the Rise, Progress, and Accomplishment of the Abolition of the Slave Trade by the British Parliament.* 2 vols. London, 1808.

Cugoano, Ottobah. *Thoughts and Sentiments on the Evil of Slavery.* London, 1787.

Dickson, William. *Letters on Slavery. . . . To Which Are Added, Addresses to the Whites, and to the Free Negroes of Barbadoes: and Accounts of Some Negroes Eminent for their Virtues and Abilities.* London: J. Phillips, 1789.

George, David. "An Account of the Life of Mr. David George, from Sierra Leone in Africa, Given by Himself in a Conversation with Brother Rippon of London, and Brother Pearce of Birmingham." *The Baptist Annual Register* (1790-1793): 473-484.

Gøbel, Erik. "The Danish Edict of 16th March 1792 to Abolish the Slave Trade." In *Orbis in Orbem Liber Amicorum John Everaer*, ed. Jan Parmentier and Sander Spanoghe. Ghent: Academia Press, 2001, 251-263.

Grégoire, Henri Babtiste (Abbé Grégoire). *De La Littérature Des Nègres, ou, Recherches sur leur facultés intellectuelles, leur qualitiés Morales et leur littérature; Suivies de Notices sur la vie et les ouvrages des Nègres qui se sont distingués dans les Sciences, les Lettres et les Arts.* Paris: Maradan, 1808. [English translation: *An Enquiry concerning the intellectual and moral faculties, and literature of Negroes; followed with an account of the life and works of fifteen Negroes and Mulattoes distinguished in Science, Literature and the Arts.* Brooklyn: Thomas Kirk, 1810.]

Hardy, Thomas. *Memoir of Thomas Hardy.* London: J. Ridgway, 1832.

Hoare, Prince. *Memoirs of Granville Sharp, Esq. Composed from his own Manuscripts and Other Authentic Documents in the Possession of his Family and of the African Institution.* London, 1820.

King, Boston. "Memoirs of the Life of Boston King, a Black Preacher." *The Methodist Magazine* 21 (1798): 105-110.

Phipps, Constantine John. *A Voyage to the North Pole undertaken by His Majesty's Command, 1773.* London, 1774.

Postlewayt, Malachy. *The Universal Dictionary of Trade and Commerce.* London, 1757.

Ramsay, James. *An Inquiry into the Effects of Putting a Stop to the African Slave Trade and of Granting Liberty to the Slaves in the British Sugar Colonies.* London: James Phillips, 1784.

Sharp, Granville. "An Account of the Murder of 132 Negro Slaves on Board the Ship *Zong*, or Zung, with Some Remarks on the Argument of an Eminent Lawyer in Defence of that Inhuman Transaction." British Library, Ms. 1783.

Smeathman, Henry. *Plan of a Settlement to be made near Sierra Leone on the Grain Coast of Africa.* London, 1786.

Wesley, John. *The Journal of the Rev. John Wesley.* 8 vols. London, 1916.

Wilberforce, R.T., and S. Wilberforce. *The Life of William Wilberforce.* 5 vols. London, 1838.

Secondary Sources

Abrams, M.H. et al. *The Norton Anthology of English Literature*, 7th ed. London and New York: W.W. Norton, 2000, vol. 1, pp. 2812-2821.

Acholonu, Catherine Obianuju. "The Home of Olaudah Equiano—A Linguistic and Anthropological Survey." *The Journal of Commonwealth Literature* 22 (1987): 5-16.

———. *The Igbo Roots of Olaudah Equiano*. Owerri: AFA Publications, 1989.

Adams, Francis D., and Barry Sanders, eds. *Three Black Writers in Eighteenth-Century England*. Belmont: Wadsworth Publishing, 1971.

Afigbo, Adiele E. "Through a Glass Darkly: Eighteenth-Century Igbo Society through Equiano's Narrative." In Afigbo, *Ropes of Sand*. Oxford: Oxford University Press, 1981, 145-186.

Andrews, William. *To Tell a Free Story: The First Century of Afro-American Autobiography*. Bloomington: University of Illinois Press, 1986.

Apap, Christopher. "Caught between Two Opinions: Africans, Europeans and Indians in Olaudah Equiano's *Interesting Narrative*." *Comparative American Studies* 4, 1 (2006): 5-24.

Aravamudan, Srinivas. "Equiano Lite." *Eighteenth-Century Studies* 34, no. 4 (2001): 615-619.

Blackett, R.J.M. *Building an Antislavery Wall: Black Americans in the Atlantic Abolitionist Movement, 1830-1860*. Baton Rouge: Louisiana State University Press, 1983.

Bolster, W. Jeffrey. *Black Jacks: African American Seamen in the Age of Sail*. Cambridge: Harvard University Press, 1997.

Boulukos, George E. "Olaudah Equiano and the Eighteenth-Century Debate on Africa." *Eighteenth-Century Studies* 40, 2 (2007): 241-255.

Bown, Lalage. *Two Centuries of African English: A Survey and Anthology of Non-Fictional English Prose by African Writers Since 1769*. London: Heinemann, 1973.

Bozeman, Terry S. "Interstices, Hybridity, and Identity: Olaudah Equiano and the Discourse of the African Slave Trade." *Studies in the Literary Imagination* 36, 2 (2003): 61-70.

Braidwood, Stephen J. "Initiatives and Organisation of the Black Poor, 1786-1787." *Slavery and Abolition* 3, 3 (1982): 211-227.

———. *Black Poor and White Philanthropists: London's Blacks and the Foundation of the Sierra Leone Settlement, 1786-1791*. Liverpool: Liverpool University Press, 1994.

Brown, Carolyn, Paul E. Lovejoy, and Renée Soulodre-La France, eds. *Repercussions of the Atlantic Slave Trade: The Interior of the Bight of Biafra and the African Diaspora*. Trenton, NJ: Africa World Press, 2004.

Brown, Christopher Leslie. *Moral Capital: Foundations of British Abolitionism*. Chapel Hill: University of North Carolina Press, 2006.

Bugg, John. "The Other Interesting Narrative: Olaudah Equiano's Public Book Tour." *The Modern Language Association of America* PMLA 121.5 (2006): 1424-1442.

———. "Deciphering the Equiano Archives." *The Modern Language Association of America* PMLA 122.2 (2006): 572-573.

———. "The Sons of Belial: Olaudah Equiano in 1794." *Times Literary Supplement* August (2008): 15.

Burnard, Trevor. "Goodbye, Equiano, the African." *Historically Speaking: The Bulletin of the Historical Society* 7, 3 (2006): 10-11.

Byrd, Alexander X. "Captives & Voyages: Black Migrants across the Eighteenth-Century World of Olaudah Equiano." Ph.D. thesis, Duke University, 2001.

Caldwell, Tanya. "'Talking Too Much English': Languages of Economy and Politics in Equiano's 'The Interesting Narrative.'" *Early American Literature* 34, no. 3 (1999): 263-282.

Cameron, Ann. *The Kidnapped Prince: The Life of Olaudah Equiano*. New York: Random House, 2000.

Carey, Brycchan. "Olaudah Equiano: An African Slave in Guernsey." *The Review of the Guernsey Society* 59, 2 (Summer 2003): 47-50.

———. "Olaudah Equiano: African or American?" In *1650-1850: Ideas, Aesthetics, and Inquiries in the Early Modern Era* 17 (2010): 229-248.

Carretta, Vincent. *Unchained Voices: An Anthology of Black Authors in the English-Speaking World of the Eighteenth Century*. Lexington: University Press of Kentucky, 1996.

——— . "Three West Indian Writers of the 1780s Revisited and Revised." *Research in African Literature* 29, 4 (Winter 1998): 73-86.

———. "Olaudah Equiano or Gustavus Vassa? New Light on an Eighteenth-Century Question of Identity." *Slavery and Abolition* 20, no. 3 (1999): 96-105.

———. "Defining a Gentleman: The Status of Olaudah Equiano or Gustavus Vassa." *Language Sciences* 22 (2000): 385-399.

———. "'Property of Author': Olaudah Equiano's Place in the History of the Book." In *Genius in Bondage: Literature of the Early Black*

Atlantic, edited by Vincent Carretta and Philip Gould. Lexington: University Press of Kentucky, 2001, 130-150.

———. "More New Light on the Identity of Olaudah Equiano or Gustavus Vassa." In *The Global Eighteenth Century*, edited by Felicity Nussbaum. Baltimore, MD: Johns Hopkins University Press, 2003.

———. "Possible Gustavus Vassa/Olaudah Equiano Attributions." In *The Faces of Anonymity: Anonymous and Pseudonymous Publication from the Sixteenth to the Twentieth Century*, edited by Robert J. Griffin, 103-139. New York: Palgrave Macmillan, 2003.

———. "A New Letter by Gustavus Vassa/Olaudah Equiano?" *Early American Literature* 39, no. 2 (2004): 355-361.

———. *Equiano, the African: Biography of a Self-Made Man*. Athens: University of Georgia Press, 2005.

———. "Deciphering the Equiano Archives." *The Modern Language Association of America* PMLA 122.2 (2006): 571-573.

———. "Olaudah Equiano, the South Carolinian? A Forum." *Historically Speaking: The Bulletin of the Historical Society* 7, 3 (2006): 2-7.

———. "Response to Paul Lovejoy's 'Autobiography and Memory: Gustavus Vassa, alias Olaudah Equiano, the African.'" *Slavery and Abolition* 28, 1 (2007): 115-119.

———. "New Equiana." *Early American Literature* 44, 1 (2009): 147-160.

Casmier-Paz, Lynn A. "Slave Narratives and the Rhetoric of Author Portraiture." *New Literary History* 34, no. 1 (2003): 91-116.

Chambers, Douglas, "'My Own Nation': Igbo Exiles in the Diaspora." *Slavery and Abolition* 18, 1 (1997): 72-97.

———. "Tracing Igbo into the African Diaspora." In Paul E. Lovejoy, ed., *Identity in the Shadow of Slavery*. London: Continuum, 2000, 55-71.

Coleman, Deirdre. *Romantic Colonization and British Anti-Slavery*. Cambridge: Cambridge University Press, 2005.

Corley, Ide. "The Subject of Abolitionist Rhetoric: Freedom and Trauma in 'The Life of Olaudah Equiano.'" *Modern Language Studies* 32, no. 2 (2002): 139-156.

Costanzo, Angelo. *Surprizing Narrative: Olaudah Equiano and the Beginnings of Black Autobiography*. New York: Greenwood Press, 1987.

Curtin, Philip D. *Africa Remembered: Narratives of West Africans from the Era of the Slave Trade*. Madison: University of Wisconsin Press, 1967.

Dabydeen, David, ed. *The Black Presence in English Literature.* Manchester: Manchester University Press, 1985.

Doherty, Thomas. "Olaudah Equiano's Journeys: The Geography of a Slave Narrative." *Partisan Review* 4 (1997).

Earley, Samantha Manchester. "Writing from the Center or the Margins? Olaudah Equiano's Writing Life Reassessed." *African Studies Review* 46, 2 (2003): 1-16.

Edwards, Paul. "Embrenche and Ndichie." *Journal of the Historical Society of Nigeria* 2, 3 (1962): 401-402.

———. *Equiano's Travels. His Autobiography: The Interesting Narrative of Olaudah Equiano, or, Gustavus Vassa, the African. Written by Himself.* London: Heinemann Educational Books Ltd, 1967; 2d ed., 1969.

———. "'. . . Written by Himself . . .' A Manuscript Letter of Olaudah Equiano." *Notes and Queries* (1968): 222-225.

———. *The Life of Olaudah Equiano, or, Gustavus Vassa the African.* London: Dawson, 1969.

———. "Equiano and His Captains." In Anna Rutherford, ed., *Commonwealth.* London: Edward Arnold, 1971.

———. "Equiano's Lost Family: 'Master' and 'Father' in 'The Interesting Narrative.'" *Slavery and Abolition* 11, no. 2 (1990): 216-226.

———. *Unreconciled Strivings and Ironic Strategies: Three Afro-British Authors of the Georgian Era: Ignatius Sancho, Olaudah Equiano, Robert Wedderburn.* Edinburgh: Edinburgh University Press, 1992.

———. "Afro-British Authors of the Late Georgian Period." In David Killingray, ed., *Africans in Britain.* Portland, OR: Frank Cass, 1994.

———, ed. *The Life of Olaudah Equiano.* Essex: Longman Group UK, 1988.

———, ed. "A Descriptive List of Manuscripts in the Cambridgeshire Record Office Relating to the Will of Gustavus Vassa (Olaudah Equiano)." *Research in African Literature* 20 (1989).

Edwards, Paul, and James Walvin. *Black Personalities in the Era of the Slave Trade.* London: Macmillan, 1983.

Edwards, Paul, and Rosiland Shaw. "The Invisible Chi in Equiano's Interesting Narrative." *Journal of Religion in Africa* 19 (1989): 146-156.

Edwards, Paul, and David Dabydeen, eds. *Black Writers in Britain, 1760-1890.* Edinburgh: Edinburgh University Press, 1991.

Eke, Maureen N. "(Re)Imagining Community: Olaudah Equiano and the (Re)construction of Igbo (African) Identity." In *Olaudah Equiano & the Igbo World*, edited by Chima J. Korieh. Trenton, NJ: Africa World

Press, 2009, 23-48.

Elrod, Eileen Razzari. "Moses and the Egyptian: Religious Authority in Olaudah Equiano's Interesting Narrative." *African American Review* 35, no. 3 (NA): 409-425.

Fichtelberg, Joseph. "Word between Worlds: The Economy of Equiano's Narrative." *American Literary History* 5, no. 3 (1993): 459-480.

Figueroa, Peter. "The Autobiographical Account of the Education of an African Slave in Eighteenth-Century England." In Michael Erben, ed., *Biography and Education: A Reader.* London: Falmer Press, 1998, 149-163.

Finseth, Ian. "In Essaka Once: Time and History in Olaudah Equiano's Autobiography." *Arizona Quarterly* 58, no. 1 (2002): 1-35.

Fryer, Peter. *Staying Power: The History of Black People in Britain.* London: Pluto Press, 1984. Gates, Henry L., Jr., ed. *Black Literature and Literary Theory.* London, 1984.

———, ed. "The Interesting Narrative of the Life of Olaudah Equiano." In *The Classic Slave Narratives.* New York: Mentor, 1987; 2d ed., 2002.

———, ed. *The Signifying Monkey: Theory of Afro-American Literary Criticism.* Oxford: Oxford University Press, 1989.

Gates, Henry Louis, Jr., and Charles T. Davis, eds. *The Slave's Narrative: Texts and Contexts.* New York: Oxford University Press, 1985.

Gates, Henry L., Jr., and Nellie Y. McKay, eds. *The Norton Anthology of African American Literature.* New York: W. W. Norton, 1997.

Gerzina, Gretchen. *Black England: Life before Emancipation.* London: John Murray, 1995.

Gilroy, Paul. *'There Ain't No Black in the Union Jack': The Cultural Politics of Race and Nation.* London: University of Chicago Press, 1991.

———. *The Black Atlantic: Modernity and Double Consciousness.* Cambridge, MA: Harvard University Press, 1993.

Gomez, Michael A. *Exchanging Our Country Marks: The Transformation of African Identities in the Colonial and Antebellum South.* Chapel Hill: University of North Carolina Press, 1998.

———. "African Identity and Slavery in the Americas." *Radical History Review* 75 (1999): 111-120.

———. "A Quality of Anguish: The Igbo Response to Enslavement in the Americas." In Paul E. Lovejoy and David V. Trotman, eds., *Trans-Atlantic Dimensions of the African Diaspora.* London: Continuum, 2003, 82-95.

Green, James. "The Publishing History of Olaudah Equiano's *Interesting Narrative*." *Slavery and Abolition* 16, 3 (1995): 362-375.

Gunn, Jeffrey. "Literacy and the Humanizing Project in Olaudah Equiano's *The Interesting Narrative* and Ottobah Cugoano's *Thoughts and Sentiments*." *eSharp* 10 (2007): 1-19.

Hinds, Elizabeth Jane Wall. "The Spirit of Trade: Olaudah Equiano's Conversion, Legalism and the Merchant's Life." *African American Review* 32, no. 4 (1998): 635-647.

Hochschild, Adam. *Bury the Chains: The British Struggle to Abolish Slavery*. New York: Houghton Mifflin, 2005.

Hogg, Peter C. *The African Slave Trade and Its Suppression: A Classified and Annotated Bibliography of Books, Pamphlets and Periodical Articles*. London: Frank Cass, 1973.

Ito, Akiyo. "Olaudah Equiano and the New York Artisans: The First American Edition of the Interesting Narrative of the Life of Olaudah Equiano, or Gustavus Vassa." *Early American Literature* 32, 1 (1997): 82.

Jennings, Judith. *The Business of Abolishing the British Slave Trade, 1783-1807*. London: Frank Cass, 1997.

Jones, G.I. "Olaudah Equiano of the Niger Ibo." In Philip D. Curtin, ed., *Africa Remembered: Narratives by West Africans from the Era of the Slave Trade*. Madison and London: University of Wisconsin Press, 1967, 60-98.

Kelleter, Frank. "Ethnic Self-Dramatization and Technologies in Equiano's Travel in The Interesting Narrative of the Life of Olaudah Equiano, or Gustavus Vassa, the African, Written by Himself (1789)." *Early American Literature* 39, no. 1 (2004): 67-84.

Killingray, David, ed. *Africans in Britain*. Portland, OR: Frank Cass, 1994.

Korieh, Chima J. *Olaudah Equiano & the Igbo World*. Trenton, NJ: Africa World Press, 2009.

Langley, April. "Equiano's Landscapes: Viewpoints and Vistas from the Looking Glass, the Lens and the Kaleidoscope." *The Western Journal of Black Studies* 25, no. 1 (2001): 46-60.

Latimer, Douglas A. "Black Resistance to Slavery and Racism in Eighteenth-Century England." In Jagdish S. and Ian Duffield, eds., *Essays on the History of Blacks in Britain*. Aldershot: Avebury, 1992, 58-80.

Levecq, Christine. "Sentiment and Cosmopolitanism in Olaudah Equiano's Narrative." *African and Black Diaspora: An International Jour-*

nal 1, no. 1 (2008): 13-30.

Linebaugh, Peter, and Marcus Rediker. *The Many-Headed Hydra: Sailors, Slaves, Commoners, and the Hidden History of the Revolutionary Atlantic.* Boston: Beacon Press, 2000.

Little, Kenneth. *Negroes in Britain: A Study of Racial Relations in English Society.* London: Kegan Paul, Trench, Trubner & Co., 1947.

Lovejoy, Paul E. *Transformations in Slavery. History of Slavery in Africa.* Cambridge: Cambridge University Press, c. 1987; 2d and revised edition, 2000; 3d edition, 2011.

———. "Letters of the Old Calabar Slave Trade, 1760-89." In *Genius in Bondage: Literature of the Early Black Atlantic,* edited by Vincent Carretta and Philip Gould. Lexington: University Press of Kentucky, 2001, 89-115.

———. "'This Horrid Hole': Royal Authority, Commerce and Credit at Bonny, 1690-1840." *Journal of African History* 45 (2004): 363-392.

———. "Construction of Identity: Olaudah Equiano or Gustavus Vassa?" *Historically Speaking* 7, 3 (January/February 2006): 8-9.

———. "Autobiography and Memory: Gustavus Vassa, alias Olaudah Equiano, the African." *Slavery and Abolition* 27, no. 3 (2006): 317-347.

———. "Issues of Motivation—Vassa/Equiano and Carretta's Critique of the Evidence." *Slavery and Abolition* 28, no. 1 (2007): 121-125.

———. "Las ambiciones imperiales británicas en la Costa de la Mosquitia y la abolición de la esclavitud indígena, 1773-1781." In Rina Cáceres and Paul E. Lovejoy, eds., *Haití—Revolución y emancipación.* San José: Editorial Universidad de Costa Rica, 2008, 98-118.

———. "Gustavus Vassa, Africano quien trató de humanizar la esclavización en la Costa de Mosquitos, 1775-1780." In Jaime Arocha, ed., *Nina S. de Friedemann, cronista de disidencias y resistencias.* Bogota: Universidad Nacional de Colombia, Facultad de Ciencias Humanas, 2009, 205-231.

———. "Personal Memory and the Collective Experience of the Slave Trade in the Autobiography of Gustavus Vassa, alias Olaudah Equiano." In Ana Lucia Araujo, Mariana Pinho Cândido, and Paul E. Lovejoy, eds., *Crossing Memories: Slavery and the African Diaspora.* Trenton, NJ: Africa World Press, 2009.

———. "Gustavus Vassa and the Scottish Enlightenment." Paper presented at the American Historical Association, Annual Meeting, New York, January 2, 2009.

————. "Olaudah Equiano or Gustavus Vassa—What's in a Name?" *Atlantic Studies: Literary, Cultural and Historical Perspectives* 9, 2 (June 2012): 165-184.

Lovejoy Paul E., and David Richardson. "Trust, Pawnship and Atlantic History: The Institutional Foundations of the Old Calabar Slave Trade." *American Historical Review* 104, no. 2 (1999): 332-355.

Marren, Susan. "Between Slavery and Freedom: The Transgressive Self in Olaudah Equiano's Autobiography." *Publications of the Modern Language Association* 108 (1993).

Molesworth, Jesse M. "Equiano's 'Loud Voice': Witnessing the Performance of The Interesting Narrative." *Texas Studies in Literature and Language* 48, no. 2 (2006): 123-144.

Mtubani, Victor C.D. "The black voice in eighteenth-century Britain: African writers against slavery and the slave trade." *Phylon* 45, 2 (1984): 85-97.

Murphy, Geraldine. "Olaudah Equiano: Accidental Tourist." *Eighteenth-Century Studies* 27, 4 (1994).

Northrup, David. "Igbo and Myth Igbo: Culture and Ethnicity in the Atlantic World, 1600-1850." *Slavery and Abolition* 21 (2000).

Nussbaum, Felicity. "Being a Man: Olaudah Equiano and Ignatius Sancho." In *"Genius in Bondage": A Critical Anthology of the Literature of the Early Black Atlantic,* edited by Vincent Carretta and Philip Gould. Lexington: University Press of Kentucky, 2011.

Nwokeji, G. Ugo. *The Slave Trade and Culture in the Bight of Biafra: An African Society in the Atlantic World.* Cambridge: Cambridge University Press, 2010.

Ogude, S.E. "Facts into Fiction: Equiano's Narrative Reconsidered." *Research in African Literatures* 13 (Spring 1982): 31-43.

————. *Genius in Bondage: A Study of the Origins of African Literature in English.* Ile-Ife, Nigeria: University of Ife Press, 1983.

————. "No Roots Here: On the Igbo Roots of Olaudah Equiano." *Review of English and Literary Studies* 5 (1989): 1-16.

Oldfield, J.R. *Popular Politics and British Anti-Slavery: The Mobilisation of Public Opinion against the Slave Trade.* Manchester: Manchester University Press, 1995.

Onogwu, Elizabeth Odachi. "Between Literature, Facts, and Fiction: Perspectives on Olaudah Equiano's *The Interesting Narrative.*" In *Olaudah Equiano & the Igbo World*, edited by Chima J. Korieh. Trenton, NJ: Africa World Press, 2009, 141-156.

Orban, Katalin. "Dominant and Submerged Discourses in The Life of Olaudah Equiano (or Gustavus Vassa?)." *African American Review* 27, 4 (n.d.): 655-664.

Osborne, Angelina. *Equiano's Daughter: The Life of & Times of Joanna Vassa*. London: KrikKrak, 2007.

Ould-Okojie, Jakie. *Olaudah Equiano: Son of Africa*. Manchester: Ahmed Iqbal Ullah Race Relations Resource Centre, 2006.

Pederson, Carl. "Middle Passages: Representations of the Slave Trade in Caribbean and African-American Literature." *The Massachusetts Review* 34, no. 2 (n.d.): 225-238.

Potkay, Adam. "Olaudah Equiano and the Art of Spiritual Autobiography." *Eighteenth-Century Studies* 27, 4 (1994): 677-692.

———. "History, Oratory, and God in Equiano's Interesting Narrative." *Eighteenth-Century Studies* 34, 4 (2001): 601-614.

Potkay, Adam, and Sandra Burr. *Black Atlantic Writers of the Eighteenth Century: Living the New Exodus in England and the Americas*. London: Palgrave, 1995.

Pudaloff, Ross J. "No Change without Purchase: Olaudah Equiano and the Economics of Self and Market." *Early American Literature* 40, 3 (2005): 499-527.

Rice, Allan. "'Who's Eating Whom': The Discourse of Cannibalism in the Literature of the Black Atlantic from Equiano's 'Travels' to Toni Morrison's 'Beloved.'" *Research in African Literatures* 29, 4 (1998): 107-121.

Rodgers, Nini. "Equiano in Belfast: A Study of the Anti-Slavery Ethos in a Northern Town." *Slavery and Abolition* 18, 2 (1997).

———. *Equiano and Anti-slavery in Eighteenth-century Belfast*. Belfast: Belfast Society in Association with the Ulster Historical Foundation, 2000.

Rogers, Nicholas. "Caribbean Borderland: Empire, Ethnicity, and the Exotic on the Mosquito Coast." *Eighteenth-Century Life* 26, no. 3 (2002): 117-138.

Rolingher, Louise. "A Metaphor of Freedom: Olaudah Equiano and Slavery in Africa." *Canadian Journal of African Studies* 38, no. 1 (2004): 88-122.

Rust, Marion. "The Subaltern as Imperialist: Speaking of Olaudah Equiano." In *Passing and the Fictions of Identity*, edited by Elaine K. Ginsbert. Durham, NC: Duke University Press, 1996, pp. 21–36.

Sabino, Robin, and Jennifer Hall. "The Path Not Taken: Cultural Identity in the Interesting Life of Olaudah Equiano." *Melus* 24, no. 1 (2000): 5-19.

Samuels, Wilfred D. "The Disguised Voice in *The Interesting Narrative of Olaudah Equiano.*" *Black American Literature Forum* 19 (1985): 64-69.

Sandiford, Keith. *Measuring the Moment: Strategies of Protest in Eighteenth-Century Afro-English Writing.* London: Associated University Presses, 1988.

Savours, Ann. "'A Very Interesting Point of Geography'—The 1773 Phipps Expedition towards the North Pole." In *Louis Rey Unveiling the Arctic*, ed. Louis Rey. Calgary: The Arctic Institute of North America, 1984, 402-428.

Sheehan, Laurie. *The Slave Boy. The Life of Olaudah Equiano.* Kinloss: Librario, 2002.

Shlensky, Lincoln. "'To Rivet and Record': Conversion and Collective Memory in Equiano's Interesting Narrative." In *Slavery and the Cultures of Abolition: Essays Marking the Bicentennial of the British Abolition Act of 1807*, edited by Brycchan Carey and Peter Kitson, 110-129. Woodbridge: Boydell and Brewer, 2007.

Shyllon, Folarin. *Black Slaves in Britain.* London: Oxford University Press, 1974.

———. *Black People in Britain 1555-1833.* London: Oxford University Press, 1977.

———. "Olaudah Equiano: Nigerian Abolitionist and First National Leader of Africans in Britain." *Journal of African Studies* 4, no. 4 (1977): 433-451.

Sidbury, James. *Becoming African in America: Race and Nation in the Early Black Atlantic.* New York: Oxford University Press, 2007.

Stein, Mark. "'Olaudah Equiano: Representation and Reality': An International One-Day Conference." *Early American Literature* 38, no. 3 (2003): 543-546.

———. "Who's Afraid of Cannibals: Some Uses of the Cannibalism Trope in Olaudah Equiano's *Interesting Narrative.*" In *Discourses of Slavery and Abolition: Britain and Its Colonies, 1760-1838*, edited by Brycchan Carey, Ellis Markman, and Salih Sara. Basingstoke: Palgrave Macmillan, 2004, 96-107.

Sweet, James H. "Mistaken Identities? Olaudah Equiano, Domingos Alvares, and the Methodological Challenges of Studying the African Diaspora." *American Historical Review* 114 (2009): 279-306.

Sypher, Wylie. *Guinea's Captive Kings: British Anti-slavery Literature of the XVIIIth Century*. Chapel Hill: University of North Carolina, 1942.

Thomas, Helen. *Romanticism and Slave Narratives: Transatlantic Testimonies*. Cambridge: Cambridge University Press, 2000.

Torrington, Arthur. "Biography and History: The Debate over Olaudah Equiano's Interesting Narrative." Paper presented at the American Historical Association, Annual Meeting, New York, January 2, 2009.

Walvin, James. *The Black Presence: A Documentary History of the Negro in England, 1555-1860*. New York: Schocken, 1972.

―――. *Black and White: The Negro and English Society, 1555-1945*. London: Allen Lane, the Penguin Press, 1973.

―――. *England, Slaves and Freedom, 1776-1838*. Basingstoke: Macmillan, 1986.

―――. "In Black and White: Recent Publications on British Black Writings." *Slavery and Abolition* 16 (1995): 376-382.

―――. *An African's Life: The Life and Times of Olaudah Equiano, 1745-1797*. Washington: Cassell, 1998.

―――. *Making the Black Atlantic: Britain and the African Diaspora*. Washington: Cassell, 2000.

―――. *Black Ivory: Slavery in the British Empire*. 2d ed. Oxford: Blackwell, 2001.

―――. *The Zong: A Massacre, the Law & the End of Slavery*. New Haven, CT: Yale University Press, 2011.

Wheeler, Roxanne. "Domesticating Equiano's Interesting Narrative." *Eighteenth-Century Studies* 34, no. 4 (2001): 620-624.

Whyte, Iain. *Scotland and the Abolition of Black Slavery, 1756-1838*. Edinburgh: Edinburgh University Press, 2006.

Wiley, Michael. "Consuming Africa: Geography and Identity in Olaudah Equiano's Interesting Narrative." *Studies in Romanticism* 44, no. 2 (2005): 151-164.

Woodard, Helena. *African British Writings in the Eighteenth Century: The Politics of Race and Reason*. Westport, CT: Greenwood Press, 1999.

Youngquist, Paul. "The Afro Futurism of DJ Vassa." *European Romantic Review* 16, no. 2 (2005): 181-192.

CPSIA information can be obtained at www.ICGtesting.com
Printed in the USA
BVOW071952300113

312014BV00001B/5/P